ECOCRITICAL PERCEPTION AND ROBERT FROST

ECOCRITICAL PERCEPTION AND ROBERT FROST

Dr. Subas Chandra Rout

AUTHORSPRESS

Worldwide Circulation through Authorspress Global Network
First Published in 2022
by
Authorspress
Q-2A Hauz Khas Enclave, New Delhi-110 016 (India)
Phone: (0) 9818049852
E-mail: authorspressgroup@gmail.com
Website: www.authorspressbooks.com

Ecocritical Perception and Robert Frost
ISBN 978-93-5529-248-3

Printed in India at Kensington press

For Mami Apa

Preface

Frost's poetry is impregnated with capsule of thoughts. His deep insight into the facts of life portrays him as an architecture recognising the conflict between nature and culture. As an artist, he penetrates into life's complexities from natural process to artificial way. That's why two layers of meanings run through his poetry; the surface layer is related to body, the nature, and the inner is mind, the culture. In the body-mind dualism, Frost constructs the barrier between nature and man. He presents, sometimes, nature as an enemy and man as a stranger to this world. It is obvious that man's step-motherly attitude towards nature makes him a stranger as he exploits and damages the value and dignity of nature. In some of his poems, readers find him as a profoundly countryman in search of harmonies in nature. His powerful vision depicts the seasonal cycle of nature starting from the autumnal settings to the deeds and images of winter, spring and summer. Besides, the effects of climate-change make the contradictions and nature seems to be indifferent and hostile towards man. As an ecologist, he experiences nature, at one side, as malevolent and cruel, but it is also, at the other, benevolently divine and life-sustaining. The upper level of his poems basically studies the rustic backgrounds with local environment that struggles against the American glorification of big business, commercialism, capitalism and advanced industrialism. The ecological threats operate from the exploitations of these networks of materialism and consumerism. The book is an initiative to promulgate the importance of nature in the creative outputs of Frost and to formulate awareness on environmental issues.

Dr. Subas Chandra Rout

Acknowledgement

First and foremost, I am indebted to Prof. Shrinibas Tripathy, Dr. Md. Akhtar Jamal Khan, Prof. Jatin Kumar Nayak, Prof. Guru Charan Behera, Dr. Sulekha Samantaray, Mr. Deba Prasad Dhal, Dr. Udaya N. Majhi, Dr. Suvash Chandra Pradhan, Mrs. Snigdha Samantaray and all the members of Samantaray family for their inspiration, cooperation, advice and guidance to complete this book. I would like to thank Mr. Priti Chandra Rout, Mr. Pramit Chandra Rout and Mr. Sourav Subhasnata for their uninterrupted support and help throughout the various stages of this work. I earnestly convey my heartfelt profound gratitude to Mr. Sudarshan Kcherry and all the members of Authorspress for their sincere cooperation to make my dream come true.

Dr. Subas Chandra Rout

Contents

The Discussed Poems

A Boy's Will

Ghost House
My November Guest
A Late Walk
Stars
Storm Fear
To the Thawing Wind
A Prayer in Spring
Flower- Gathering
Rose Pogonias
Waiting
In a Vale
The Vantage Point
Mowing
Going for Water
The Trial by Existence
The Tuft of Flowers
Pan with Us
In Hardwood Groves
A Line-Storm Song
October
My Butterfly

❖❖❖

North of Boston

Mending Wall
The Death of the Hired Man
The Mountain
Home Burial
A Servant to Servants
The Black Cottage

Blueberries
After Apple-Picking
The Generations of Men
The Fear
The Self-Seeker
The Wood-Pile

❖❖❖

Mountain Interval

The Road Not Taken
Christmas Trees
An Old Man's Winter Night
The Exposed Nest
A Patch of Old Snow
Hyla Brook
The Oven Bird
Birches
Putting in the Seed
Range-Finding
The Bonfire
A Girl's Garden
The Last Word of a Bluebird
'Out, Out – '
The Gum-Gatherer
The Line-Gang
The Vanishing Red
The Sound of Trees

❖❖❖

New Hampshire

New Hampshire
The Census-Taker
The Star-splitter
Maple
The Ax-Helve
Wild Grapes
Two Witches

Fragmentary Blue
Fire and Ice
Dust of Snow
To E. T.
Nothing Gold Can Stay
The Runaway
Stopping by Woods on a Snowy Evening
For Once, Then, Something
Blue- Butterfly Day
The Onset
To Earthward
Good-by and Keep Cold
Two Look at Two
Not to Keep
A Brook in the City
Looking for a Sunset Bird in Winter
A Boundless Moment
Gathering Leaves
Misgiving
A Hillside Thaw
On a Tree Fallen Across the Road
Our Singing Strength
The Need of Being Versed in Country Things

❖❖❖

West – Running Brook

Spring Pools
The Freedom of the Moon
The Rose Family
Fireflies in the Garden
Devotion
The Cocoon
A Passing Glimpse
A Peck of Gold
Acceptance
Once by the Pacific
Lodged
A Monir Bird
Bereft

Tree at My Window
The Peaceful Shepherd
The Thatch
A Winter Eden
The Flood
Acquainted with the Night
The Lovely Shall Be Choosers
West-Running Brook
Sand Dunes
The Times Table
The Investment
The Last Mowing
The Birthplace
Sitting by a Bush in Broad Sunlight
The Armful
Riders
On Looking Up by Chance at the Constellations
The Bear
The Egg and the Machine

❖❖❖

A Further Range

A Lone Striker
Two Tramps in Mud Time
The White-Tailed Hornet
A Drumlin Woodchuck
The Gold Hesperidee
In Time of Cloudburst
A Roadside Stand
The Old Barn at the Bottom of the Fogs
At Woodward's Gardens
Lost in Heaven
Desert Places
Leaves Compared with Flowers
A Leaf Treader
On Taking from the Top to Broaden the Base
Moon Compasses
Design
On a Bird Singing in its Sleep

Afterflakes
Unharvested
There Are Roughly Zones
A Trial Run
Not Quite Social
Evil Tendencies Cancel
One Guess
The Hardship of Accounting
Not All There
In Dives' Dive

❖❖❖

A Witness Tree

Beech
Sycamore
The Silken Tent
Happiness Makes Up in Height for What It Lacks in Length
Come In
The Most of It
Never Again Would Birds' Song Be the Same
Willful Homing
The Quest of the Purple-Fringed
The Gift Outright
Triple Bronze
Our Hold on the Planet
To a Young Wretch (Boethian)
The Lesson for Today
Time Out
To a Moth Seen in Winter
A Considerable Speck (Microscopic)
November
The Rabbit Hunter
A Loose Mountain (Telescopic)
It Is Almost the Year Two Thousand
Trespass
A Nature Note

❖❖❖

Steeple Bush

A Young Birch
Something for Hope
One Step Backward Taken
Directive
Too Anxious for Rivers
An Unstamped Letter in Our Rural Letter Box
Skeptic
A Cliff Dwelling
Lucretius versus the Lake Poets
Why Wait for Science
Any Size We Please
An Importer
The Planners
No Holy Wars for Them
Bursting Rapture
U.S.1946 King's X
The Broken Drought

❖❖❖

Introduction

The current worldwide problems on climate-change and environmental crisis need to pose debates and discussions in a given framework of critical assessment and inventive perception. As environmental ruination becomes more severe and extensive, green activists, ecologist, environmentalists and academicians give stress on the urgency of actions to create awareness for environmental protection. Each one should be guided and controlled by a sense of actions on what is good for the ecosystem as a whole. But most of human beings do not yet understand the reality of the issue as extremely grave and dreadful. Their love for progress and super-power corrodes nature terribly. To commemorate the puffed-up ego and to consign self-interest for political mileage, countries make rat-race in the growth of science and technology that inversely contaminate the life-sustaining air and reduce the landscape into 'toxic riskscape'[1]. Living in the atomic age, man shows his potentiality for turning the earth into a dumping yard of radioactive wastes. The rapid degradation and deterioration of biological diversity and an alarming extinction of countless species of plants, insects, birds and animals seem to be the basic cause for climate change and global warming. Presently, air-borne viruses rewrite the fate of the universe.

It is obvious that environmental damage is for man's apathetic and callous attitude towards nature. Basically, he assumes nature as a platform for his paramount economic success. 'The material and cultural groomed modern society' proportionate the profit-oriented-strategies for quick economic return that stands as 'an inbuilt institution of injustice' to ecosystem. This mindset leads to something sinister for the environment. Greed economy oxidizes the relationship between man and nature. Such culture is violent and ruins the ecosystem. The capitalistic culture chokes off ecological conscience and consciousness. Imposing mastery over nature, man does not comprehend that ecocide is more terrible and horrific than the life-taking nuclear devastation. Environmental imbalance can spell potential disaster to the succeeding generations. It is in the sense that 'life is patchy'[2] and ecosystem shapes linking chains or webs to survive.

The concurrent increasing disruption of ecosphere is the product of a startling advancement of science and technology. The heavy progress of industrialism, commercialism and capitalism despoils the serenity of nature. These propensities provoke man to make excess extraction that causes widespread environmental stress. But the earth is not a tradable commodity. Modern man's progression breeds ecological regression. In consequence, the whole communities of organisms are affected by environmental degradations. The breathless competition for harnessing natural resources to impose superpower is the by-product of human culture that becomes the source of all conflicts, oppressions and environmental holocausts. Hunger for imposing supremacy and madness for capitalism are the vested interest in man that reduces him to a butcher of Earth.

Man should comprehend that any threat to the ecosystem will correspondingly have the result on him. He should not turn the earth into 'a carbon sink'. He should preserve the integrity, stability, sustainability and beauty of the biotic community. His actions should not damage the planet's basic life-support systems. In the current state of the world, the pure and simple element in nature that makes life possible, gets polluted and contaminated on account of unrestraint capitalism and greedy mannerism. The contemporary man lives in the universe that is lost to the cataclysm of global warming, climate-change, hole in the ozone layer, increasing toxicity, industry-discharged biocide, nuclear hazards, famine, tsunami, cyclone, landslides, extinction of species and exhaustion of natural spaces. Besides, the threats like depletion of green cover, vehicular emission, oil-spill, agro-chemicals and pesticide applications etc. are the multifarious agents of ecological crisis. Man should feel ashamed of his culture which is defined by its quantum of pollution and contamination.

The prioritisation of anthropocentric values exploits the earth. It is excessive and, hence, the situation is rapidly aggravating. The outcome of man's exploiting activities gives rise to ecological crisis that will make the planet inhospitable for life of any kind. Today, the appalling climate change stands as a grave issue causing health hazards, crop damages and many other pitfalls like melting of glaciers and rising of sea levels. Man feels threatened in an ecologically degraded world. In such context, the opinion of Timothy W. Luke may be mentioned:

> Nature is turning to 'Denature'. Much of the earth is a 'built environment', a 'planned habitat', or 'managed range' as pollution modifies atmospheric chemistry, urbanisation restructures weather events, architecture encloses whole biomes in sprawling megacities, and biotechnology reengineers the base codes of existing biomass.[3]

Pollution-free ecosystem is the greatest challenge in the contemporary world. The identification of such problem is largely of man's own product that violates the laws of nature. His flaw is his anthropocentric mindset that does not try to understand the concept that 'human beings are alive because the earth is alive'. Thus, man should understand that he lives in nature, and 'nature is his body'. From such angle, he has to maintain a proper relationship with the earth, otherwise it would lead to a catastrophic destruction. Now, it is the proper time to make an introspection and redefinition of individual's role under such trying moments and vulnerable conditions. To realise the importance of nature, man has to cultivate a wide and elaborate mentality that would be capable of judging the concept that he is not alone at the center of creation, rather welfare thoughts should be devoted towards all the plants, birds, animals, and land of the natural environment. Survival and sustenance of oneself not only depend upon harmony and cooperation among human beings but also among all things-both biotic and abiotic.

Ecocritical Conception and Robert Frost

It is usually acknowledged that art and literature have been devoted to expose the interaction between man and nature. Up to the seventeenth century, there was a certain reaction to industrialisation in literature, where as in the eighteenth and nineteenth century, civilisation became complex being occupied with colonialism and capitalism. These two movements started exploiting and looting nature. In colonialism, the colonisers' greed took everything as a resource to be exploited; such as woods, mines, forest products, people, just everyone and everything without giving any thought to environmental hazards. Their will was indomitable but the resource of the earth is limited. Besides, a steady progress of modernity towards capital intensive mindset made the environment highly apocalyptic. In such context, the text-oriented theory became relevant to recognise environmental disorder.

Exploring and examining the relationship between literature and the physical environment, green activists, academicians, environmentalists and ecologists propound literary ecology as the study that reflects and influences human interactions with the natural world. Academicians generally take art and literature as the road map to articulate such vital issues in participatory efforts. That's why beliefs and ideologies are the paradigms for introspection and speculation. Judging upon the gravity of ecological crisis, the study on environment purposively becomes a cumulative thrust into the contemporary man's mindset. The emergence of ecocriticism has been slow to widespread in literary studies. In his article, "Environmentalism and Ecocriticism", Richard Kerridge writes:

> Of the radical movements that came to prominence in the 1960s and 1970s, environmentalism has been the slowest to develop a school of criticism in the academic humanities. The first use of the term 'ecocriticism' seems to have been by US critic William Rueckert in 1978...but it was not until the beginning of the 1990s that ecocriticism became a recognised movement.[4]

It seems proper to point out that ecocriticism has taken a rapid growth in the United States. The Association for the Study of Literature and Environment (ASLE) was established in 1992 in America. Later on, it expanded to countries like Korea, Canada, India, Japan, Taiwan, Australia, New Zealand, Europe and British Isles etc. Corollary to this, critics, scholars and environmentalists delve into the environmental perspectives in contemporary literary studies. They provide the basic definition of ecocriticism as the study of the relationship between literature and environment, between man and nature. Ecocriticism, on the other hand, expands the notion of "the world" to include the entire ecosphere. Today, humans have reached the age of environmental limits. In this troubling time, they have to change the style of their living in order to protect the earth, otherwise they will face ecocatastrophe. If they are not the part of the solution to save the planet, they should not be the part of the problem for destroying the ecosystem. Each one should contribute to environmental restoration.

Many but not the most, have tried to define ecocriticism. William Howarth, a Professor of English at Princeton University, in his article "Some Principles of Ecocriticism" defines:

> *Eco* and *critic* both derive from Greek, *oikos* and *kritis*, and in tandem they mean "house judge", which may surprise many lovers of green, outdoor writing. A long-winded gloss on *ecocritic* might run as follows: "a person

> who judges the merits and faults of writings that depict the effects of culture upon nature, with a view toward celebrating nature, berating its despoilers, and reversing their harm through political action." So the *oikos* is nature, a place Edward Hoagland calls "our widest home", and the *kritos* is an arbiter of taste who wants the house kept in good order, no boots or dishes strewn about to ruin the original décor.[5]

As the world warms and heatwaves make harshest impacts, climate resilient solutions are prioritised. Universities, institutions and organisations hold symposia on environmental education and activism to meet such disasters that cripple life and livelihoods. Academia also has been organised into relatively autonomous bodies to work upon environmental crisis and to create awareness against the climate change and global warming. Eco-consciousness is necessary for life-threatening variables like dangers of the plastic wrapper, electromagnetic radiation, automobile exhausts, combustion of fossil fuels, geological deposits of sewage and garbage, cutting down of trees, population explosion, loss of topsoil and groundwater, and poisoning of the oceans. The paradigm of the troubling awareness arising out of human activities that damage the earth's basic life-supporting systems is the focus of ecocriticism. The vulnerability of climate-impacted humans and non-humans that are under threat is the main drive of this study. The evaluation of texts and ideas pertaining to ecological crisis not only contributes to the awareness programs but also looks into the politics of conservation and preservation of nature. The theoretically well-versed cultural texts are acknowledged as the inspirational movements of ecocriticism. In relation to such cultural texts, Greg Garrard mentions:

> It is generally agreed that modern environmentalism begins with 'A Fable for Tomorrow', in Rachel Carson's *Silent Spring* (1962). Carson's fairy tale opens with the words, 'There was once a town in the heart of America where all life seemed to live in harmony with its surroundings' and, invoking the ancient tradition of the pastoral, goes on to paint a picture of 'prosperous farms', 'green fields', foxes barking in the hills, silent deer, ferns and wild- flowers, 'countless birds' and trout lying in clear, cold streams, all delighted in by those who pass through the town (Carson 1999:21). Concentrating on images of natural beauty and emphasising the 'harmony' of humanity and nature that 'once' existed, the fable at first presents us with a picture of essential changelessness, which human activity scarcely disturbs, and which the annual round of seasons only reinforces. However, pastoral peace rapidly gives way to catastrophic destruction.[6]

Carson's achievements in writing about ecology shine with a certain quality even today. Many ecologists try to restrain the human community from destroying the natural community. They think of the feasibility to find the platforms upon which the two communities-the humans, the natural- can coexist, cooperate, and flourish in the ecosphere. But humans, in the changes of their lifestyle accompanied with unrestricted capitalism, have affected and damaged the non-human world notably. In relation to this, in his article, Lynn White, Jr. writes: "It has been noted, for example, that the advent of the automobile eliminated huge flocks of sparrows that once fed on the horse manure littering every street"[7]. Hence, it is necessary to remind Commoner's first law of Ecology: "Everything is connected to everything else"[8]. Obviously, there is a reciprocal interdependence and mutual interconnectedness of one life process upon another. It seems problematic on the part of humans to survive happily unless all other species survive. Besides, man is such a species of animals whose welfare and subsistence depend upon a successful integration with the plants, animals and land that consist of his environment.

Ecocriticism discusses the interconnections between nature and culture. As 'a critical compass', 'it keeps one foot in literature and the other on land. As a theoretical one, it arbitrates between human and non-human"[9]. Looking at the terrible environmental crisis, man begins to realise that he has grossly underestimated nature and violated the laws of the planet. He is definitely a part of nature; hence, he should not misuse or ill-treat nature. Regarding this, Timothy Clark writes: "At its broadest *nature* is the sum total of the structures, substances and causal powers that are the universe"[10]. He claims that nature is "considered as an object of human contemplation, exploitation, wonder or terror"[11]. However, ecology studies the symbiosis between species and habitats and ecocriticism delves into the intrinsic values. Scholars usually trace the connections among environmental conditions, economic modes of production, and cultural ideas through the passing of time. Regarding the issue, Ross Murfin and Supryia M. Ray define: "Ecocriticism, which is grounded in ecology, natural history and environmental studies, examines how people interact with nature and how these interactions inform and are forged by symbolic representations of nature"[12].

The present aggravating deterioration of the global environment is the product of a dynamic development of supersonic technology.

But before the seventeenth century, life was in harmony with nature. From the eighteenth century onwards, the capitalistic mindset of resource-consuming nations exploited the non-human world. Even today, the non-human world fulfils and meets the demands and needs of the humans. In the dualism of human and non-human, Lawrence Buell opines: "The nonhuman environment is present not merely as a framing device but as a presence that begins to suggest that human history is implicated in natural history"[13]. Ecocritics think of the harmful and life-threatening pollutants in the natural environment. The poisonous chemicals contaminate air, water and food. It happens only for the emphasis on human-centered values. Regarding this, Pramod K. Nayar states: "Ecocriticism originates in bio-social context of unrestrained capitalism, excessive exploitation of nature, worrying definitions and shapes of development and environmental hazard"[14]. Humans have to realise that ecological order does not exist for the sake of their delight. Presently, they have made the bountiful blue-green planet into a toxic place. In such context, Todd A. Borlik writes: "The stark reality is that people have been degrading and exploiting the environment for centuries…"[15]. It is in man's mindset that survival depends upon extracting everything from nature. This tendency is ecocide.

Ecocriticism also exposes fundamental concepts that divide men from women, culture from nature, and mind from body. Besides, the two margins of the binary bring about gendered values. Nature is feminine and culture masculine. Nature is pictured as a woman whose fundamental tasks include reproduction and nurture. Women are like mature because of their biological attributes. From this ground, ecofeminist thought emerges claiming that both women and nature are equally exploited by male ways of thinking and action. In his article, "Ecocritical Theory: Romantic Roots and Impulses from Twentieth-Century European Thinkers", Axel Goodbody writes: "Eco-theorists are sometimes also concerned with theory and practice in the natural sciences, anthropology, social theory, and other branches of knowledge, which relate to the nature/ culture and human/nonhuman relationships"[16]. On the other hand, men exploit the production and labour processes of both women and nature. Critics argue that the destruction of the environment and the historical oppression of women are deeply interconnected. In such context, Timothy Clark states:

> Women were endorsed as somehow 'closer to nature' than men, usually through their connection with motherhood and nurturing. The association of women and the domestic sphere could be reaffirmed as their greater sense of respect for nature as a sort of home ('ecology' being from the Greek 'science of the household'). Few ecofeminists would now agree with such simple assertions.[17]

It can be asserted that ecocriticism is an approach to examine the representation of nature in literary texts. It discusses the interface of man with the earth. It creates an attentiveness in which plants, animals and humans are related to each other. They are so much interdependent on each other that any disturbance in one inevitably disturbs the others.

Apart from this discourse, the book incorporates ecofeminism, ecoracism and Eco-Marxism as these are the analogous work in ecocriticism. It seems necessary as some works of Robert Frost discusses these issues. The American environmental philosopher Dean Curtin defines ecoracism as "the connection, in theory and practice, of race and the environment so that the oppression of one is connected to, and supported by, the oppression of the other"[18]. The readers would meet the binaries between the whites and the non-whites in some poems of Frost. Eco-Marxism approves the Marxist devising that production must be geared to meet the real needs of the people rather than for wealth accumulation. But labour and production are always thought to be multiplied into profit generation which has no limit. Hence, nature is abused.

Ecocritical Perception and Robert Frost

Frost's proclivity to country occupations makes him a countryman and his poetry talks of the landscape, climate and rural activities. He knows the birds and botany, the woods and firms, and also broaches ecological significance of the surroundings through rain, mist, smoke, fog, and snow. Studying the poet, Lawrance Thompson states: "It is the poet's virtue to develop that insight and wisdom which enable him to recognise and represent the apparent conflict between the constructive and destructive elements, the good and the bad, in nature and in human experience"[19]. It is obvious that the scholars will experience, in some of his poems, the concept of man versus nature. The confrontation between man and nature unfolds Frost's ecological perceptions in his poetry.

Frost's first volume, *A Boy's Will,* was published in 1913 when there was no awareness of global warming, climate change, nor environmental consciousness. But the importance of nature became realised through the arrival of a new voice in poetry by Frost. The reader discovers himself in the midst of the wooded valleys and the wooded hills, flora and fauna that response to the seasonal cycles of nature starting from the autumn through the winter, the spring to the summer. The relationship between man and nature, sometimes, becomes benevolent and sometimes turns into malevolent, hostile and indifferent.

North of Boston, the second volume, was published in 1914, presents life in rural New England that proves Frost's genius for portraying "local color". The book is 'a salutary rebellion against a way of life and a mature adjustment to an environment'. In his artistic talent, Frost paints the background of social and economic disturbance in this volume. Agriculture was shrinking down in New England and emphasis was upon urbanisation and industrialisation. Village culture was decreasing and cities were expanding. Something in the countryside and the way of life seem to be an outcome of diseased minds. Environmental conditions and psychological health both are corelated.

The third book is *Mountain Interval* which was published in 1916. The volume tries to maintain the equilibrium between nature and culture, between body and mind; that may be in "The Road Not Taken" or in "Birches". The poems in this volume combine the inner vision of human world with the outer contemplation on natural world. Contrasted with this, is his fourth volume *New Hampshire* which was published in 1923. The book discusses the American success of big business, commercialism, capitalism and consumerism that hamper the environment. Besides, the conflict arises between anthropocentrism and biocentrism.

Published in 1928, the fifth volume West-Running Brook is important because of its ecological significance as the title signifies a lot that gets discussed more in later part of this book. Corollary to this, the next volume *A Further Range*, that was published in 1936, studies the relationship between man and nature. In *A Witness Tree*, the seventh volume, published in 1942, discusses the rural retreat. It also provides satirical drives at the American scene when people call the 'land sterile, bleak and hostile' as they are in nostalgia of traditional beauty of the countryside. The eighth volume is *Steeple*

Bush, which was published in 1947, sums up of Frost's attitude towards New England and towards existence in general as the whole world has undergone two world wars. War is ever destructive and ruins the life-sustaining air in the planet. The sustainable living remains in jeopardy.

As a farmer, in many of his poems, Frost shows his reactions against the life-destroying pesticides and chemical fertilisers. He uses organic manure in his farming. He seems to recognise the interactive connection between humans and nature. He does not approve of scientific method as it violates the organic interactive relationships between man and nature. Besides, Frost's ecological vision asserts that the growth of civilisation is one of the causes for environmental destruction. All these points get justified analysis in this book.

Notes

1. In her article, "The Postnatural Novel: Toxic Consciousness in Fiction of the 1980s", Cynthia Deitering mentions how pollutants make the earth as toxic riskscape, in the book *The Ecocriticism Reader*, edited by Cheryll Glotfelty & Harold Fromm, The Georgia University Press. 1996. p.200. she teaches writing and literature at Indian University-Purdue University at Fort Wayne.
2. In his article, "Some Principles of Ecocriticism", William Howarth writes that life is patchy, ecosystems build linking chains, published in *The Ecocriticism Reader,*1996. p.75. He is a professor of English at Princeton University, where he teaches courses in environmental literature and history.
3. Timothy W. Luke, *Ecocritique: Contesting the Politics of Nature, Economy, and Culture*, Minneapolis: University of Minnesota Press, 1997, p.195.
4. In his article, "Environmentalism and Ecocriticism", Richard Kerridge writes on the prominence of environmental movement in between 1960s and 1970s that became experienced in the whole array of cultural and daily life. The article was published in *Literary Theory and Criticism* by Patricia Waugh, Oxford University Press, 2006. p.530
5. William Howarth, *Ecocriticism Reader,* 1996. p.69
6. Greg Garrard unfolds the present need of ecological consciousness in his book, *Ecocriticism,* Routledge publication,2012, p.1. He is a senior lecturer in English literature at Bath Spa University, UK.
7. In his article, "The Historical Roots of Our Ecologic Crisis", Lynn White, Jr. has stated how the changes in human ways of living often affect nonhuman nature, published in *The Ecocriticism Reader by* Glotfelty & Fromm, The University of Georgia Press, 1996.p. 4. Lynn White Jr. (1907-87), began his teaching career in 1933 at Princeton as an instructor in history. He later taught at Stanford (1937-43), served as President of Mills College (1943-58), directed

the UCLA Center for Medieval and Renaissance Studies (1964-70), finally ending his teaching career as a professor at UCLA in 1974.

8. William Rueckert in his article, "Literature and Ecology" quotes Berry Commoner's first Law of Ecology, published in *The Ecocriticism Reader*, by Glotfelty & Fromm,1996, p.112. He has taught English and American Literature at Russell Sage College, Oberlin College, the University of Illinois at Champaign-Urbana, the University of Rochester, and the State University of New York at Geneseo, from which he retired in 1988.
9. In "Definition of Ecocriticism", Cheryll Glotfelty mentions in *The Ecocriticism Reader,* The University of Georgia Press, 1996. p. xix.
10. Timothy Clark in his book, *The Cambridge Introduction* to *Literature and the Environment,* Cambridge University Press, 2014, explains the natures of nature, p.6. He is a specialist in Romantic, Heideggerian and post-Heideggerian poetics and in environmental criticism.
11. Timothy Clark, p.7
12. Ross Murfin and Supryia M. Ray. The Bedford Glossary of Critical and Literary Terms, Boston, New York. 2013. p.125
13. Lawrence Buell, *The Environmental Imagination*, The Belknap Press of Harvard University Press, 1995, p.7
14. Pramod K. Nayar, *Contemporary Literary and Cultural Theory,* Pearson Education, 2015.p. 241. Pramod K. Nayar teaches at the Department of English, University of Hyderabad, India.
15. Todd A. Borlik, *Ecocriticism and Early Modern English Literature, Routledge*: Taylor & Francis. 2011. p.206.
16. Axel Goodbody, in his article "Ecocritical Theory: Romantic Roots and Impulses from Twentieth-Century European Thinkers", writes about ecocritical theory, published in *The Cambridge Companion to Literature and the Environment*, edited by Louise Westling, Cambridge University Press, 2014, p.61. Alex Goodbody is Professor of Germanic Literature at the University of Bath.
17. Timothy Clark, p118
18. Deane Curtin, *Environmental Ethics for a Postcolonial World*, Lanham, MD; Rowman & Littlefield. 2005. p.145
19. Lawrance Thompson, "Robert Frost's Theory of Poetry" published in *Robert Frost: A Collection of Critical Essays,* edited by James M. Cox, Prentice-Hall, Inc., Englewood Cliffs, N.J. 1962. pp.31-32.

CHAPTER 1

A Boy's Will (1913)

Immensely rich in insight, Frost's poem broaches ecological consciousness. He shows the beauty and complexity of nature that endorses the perception of living. The elementary spectacles in his poetry are obviously the landscapes with its sombre grays and browns, the birds-their sounds and silence, the brightness of rose pogonias and wild orchids, rainfall, mist, fog and snow, thatched house, pasture, fields, woodlands, orchard, brook, birches, apple trees, mowing, snow covered trees and hills, star-lit skies, fallen leaves, butterflies, flora and fauna, and also the fresh salt breeze blowing in from the sea. Besides, the readers meet him as a lone striker, one acquainted with the night, a watcher of the void, and also a slave to a springtime passion for the earth. These local colours fit into the ecological purpose of addressing "poetry in nature, nature in poetry". The pastoral mode discerns the images and concepts to comprehend the reconciliation of the hardships and indifferences in between the two realms-natural and human. The view of Greg Garrard seems appropriate as he asserts:

> It may be that one contemporary pastoral refuge lies within the discourse of ecology itself. At the root of pastoral is the idea of nature as a stable, enduring counterpoint to the disruptive energy and change of human societies.[1]

Frost's ecological understanding posits a natural world that presumably sustains life and life-supporting variables. The study of his work proclaims that neither physically nor psychologically can humans live without nature. That's why his environmental conscience in "Birches" sings: "Earth's the right place for love: / I don't know where it's likely to go better" (CPRF, 153). But his ecological consciousness in "Lucretius Versus the Lake Poets" is understood when he reacts: "Nature meant the Whole Goddam Machinery" (CPRF, 558). It implicates the poet's heightened attentiveness to the existential surroundings. Suggestive is the opinion that "to write about nature is to write about how the mind sees nature, and sometimes about how the mind sees itself"[2]. Life is patchy and ecosystem builds the connective chains or webs to survive.

Frost's poems work so much with nature that focus upon his passionate craving for the existence of harmonies between man and nature. The ecological perspective of his artistry is noticed from his regional kinship with nature. Such regional green orientation of the poet marks a beginning of global awareness in environmental crisis, although he had created poetic abundance before the advent of ecocritical theory. His poetic talent changes the landscape into naturescape which later on becomes a riskscape for rapacious industrialism and consumerism. In regard to this, Lawrence Buell writes:

> Nonfiction writers such as Thoreau, Austin, Berry, Dillard, and Janovy – and poets like Wordsworth, Frost, and Snyder – seem to have begun adulthood as youths with relatively modest degrees of eco-precociousness who became caught up in the quest for environmental literacy.[3]

Understanding of nature and verbalising into poetry contribute to Frost's awareness of self and ecosystem. He writes what he sees. Sometimes he feels the sense of harmony, sometimes he tries to identify with the surroundings. There are also situations when he thinks differently in the apparent identity of his own fluctuating moods in passing seasons. Nature changes dramatically in between seasons and Frost grasps the larger meaning of the harsh and chilling features of the landscapes. The bulk of his poetry attributes to the poet's awareness of the self and non-self, himself and nature. His creation argues for a rereading from an ecocritical perspective. Whenever he speaks of or to nature, it is found that nature is a large component of his creation. In such context, Marion Montgomery reveals:

> The casual reader of Frost's poetry is likely to think of Frost as a nature poet in the tradition of Wordsworth. In a sense, nature is his subject, but to Frost it is never an impulse from a vernal wood. His best poetry is concerned with the drama of man in nature, whereas Wordsworth is generally best when emotionally displaying the panorama of the natural world.[4]

The artist's biocentric mind derives pleasure from realising the significance of hills and snow, meadows and woods. Like *Walden*, his poems enact an agenda of ecological action. It is an example of nature writing at its purest with natural background. Focus upon the first volume, *A Boy's Will* (1913) may be drawn on his creativity and distinctive quality of presenting local habitation and the soil of New England. Sensitively he responds to the uniqueness of a rural landscape. He gives the place a special value with native details. The poems carry on a complete mastery of the pastoral form. It acknowledges the poet's concern for preservation and love for the natural environment. But pastoral disruption in the present era disturbs the nature lovers. The first poem of the volume, "Ghost House" portrays various plants and species of birds such as "the purple-stemmed wild raspberries, grapevines, mowing field, orchard tree, woodpecker, bats and whippoorwill" (CPoRF, 6). The noninterference of man makes ambiance ecotopia. In the ensuing situation, Thoreau also writes in *Walden*:

> I found myself suddenly neighbor to the birds; not by having imprisoned one, but having caged myself near them. I was not only nearer to some of those which commonly frequent the garden and the orchard, but to those wider and more thrilling songsters of the forest…the wood-thrush, the veery, the scarlet tanager, the field-sparrow, the whipp-oorwill, and many others.[5]

The natural beauties of the place signify the influence of nature in human life. Nature is saved if man's consumerist outlook does not prevail upon it. Frost fabricates humanity's relationship with nature that appears to be a common thread in his creation. The last line of the second stanza in "Ghost House", when the persona explains, - "The footpath down to the well is healed", - it underpins nature free from man's exploitation. In other words, the footpath to the well is man-made and akin to an abrasion or a disfigurement upon the nature process. The absence of humanity and its non-interference provides a healing touch to nature for reviving into originality against the tyranny of that beaten path.

Possibly, the significant part of this fascinating phenomenon is the speaker's biocentric revelation. Frost's ruralist vision defends the environment from toxic waste. But in the current state of the world, 'nature undergoes a startling alternation' and the contemporary man puts 'nature in a cage'. In "My November Guest", the persona labels "Sorrow" as his guest: "My Sorrow, when she's here with me, / Thinks these dark days of autumn rain" (CPoRF, 8). The personification of "Sorrow" is a woman who seems to be either physically or mentally present in the poem. There is the reversal of emotion at the declining natural order. That guest feeds on the lifelessness of her surroundings. Hence, Richard Nelson says, "What makes a place special is the way it buries itself inside the heart, not whether it's flat or rugged, rich or austere, wet or arid, gentle or harsh, warm or cold, wild or tame".[6]

Anchoring the natural background in his poems, Frost compels the readers to contemplate upon the puzzle of human emotions and situations. That's why his poetry is a capsule of thoughts. Many layers of meanings emerge from the settings. Like "My November Guest", his next poem "A Late Walk" presents the autumnal atmosphere. The speaker expresses the sights and sounds of autumn day as he walks out into a newly mown field. His ecological vision grieves for the newly mowed flowers and a wilted garden before the approach of winter. On his short walk through the countryside, the speaker observes: "When I go up through the mowing field, / The headless aftermath, / Smooth-laid like thatch with heavy dew, / Half closes the garden path" (CPoRF, 11). The word "headless" indicates the flowers being cut down by man and the word "aftermath" relates to the context of a terrible incident. In tandem of these two words, it seems to the act of "beheading" and the field is reeling from a tragedy. Perhaps, it is the speaker's genuine love for nature meddled with a conscientious fear for its destruction.

The poem "Stars" puts forward indifference in scientific fact to the needs of the humans. The upshot of science and technology ruptures and shatters the prevalence of harmony in nature.

> And yet with neither love nor hate,
> Those stars like some snow-white
> Minerva's snow-white marble eyes
> Without the gift of sight. (CPoRF, 12)

The poet mentions how the distant stars "neither love nor hate" man but they shine "as if with keenness for our fate" (L-5). The Stars appear bright in the cold winter sky and the blanket of crystalline white creates a wonderful beauty for any nature lover. The expression, "with keenness of our fate, / ...neither love nor hate" refers to nature's autonomy and cosmic power. Hence, man has to realise that he is not a supreme creature, but simply a microscopic part of nature, a very small being. In such context, Lynn White, Jr. states, "Human ecology is deeply conditioned by beliefs about our nature and destiny – that is, by religion"[7]. We should rethink our nature and destiny.

The poem, "Storm Fear" discusses human and environmental dimension. Human action becomes limited or even threatened in front of the weather or any challenging situation in atmosphere. At the opening of the poem, the artist expounds:

When the wind works against us in the dark,
And pelts with snow
The lower chamber window on the east,
And whispers with a sort of stifled bark,

Whether 'tis in us to arise with day
And save ourselves unaided. (CPoRF, 13)

It articulates that life is in troubled condition, surrounded by an antagonistic environment. Life is dangerous and risky to live in a hostile ecosystem. The question of safety and security is needed to face the fury of nature.

In the poem, "To the Thawing Wind", the poet asks the Southwest wind to come in order to feed dreams among flowers. By bringing spring and melting the snow, the southwest wind represents the vignettes of life: "Come with rain, O loud Southwester! / Bring the singer, bring the nester, / Give the buried flower a dream" (CPoRF, 16). The birds will sing and build the nest thereby forging inspiration in him; he will come out of the winter cabin. The snow-covered earth seems lifeless. The readers should pay attention to the speaker's vision that recognises the integration of human with natural cycles of life. "Human theory ...entails an understanding of the body and temperament as conditioned by its environment"[8]. The bionetwork defines man-nature symbiosis.

The discussion of "A Prayer in Spring" exposes the artist's longing for peace in the façade of a hectic, endlessly stressful world. For the consummation of desires, the human world remains ever busy and hence is set against 'the overarching background of nature'. The natural world is blissful. The artist looks for "pleasure", "love" and peace for himself and those around him: "Oh, give us pleasure in the flowers today; / And give us not to think so far away / As the uncertain harvest; keep us here / All simply in the springing of the year" (CRoPF, 17). Frost's eco-aesthetic vision promulgates the relevance of locating human's peace in relationships with nature's flora and fauna. It needs to judge the persona's psyche when he repeatedly uses the words ("give us") thrice and ("make us") twice. His expression of getting "pleasure in the flowers" and "in the orchard white" and making him "happy in the happy bees" as well as "in the darting birds" embodies the speaker's feelings and emotions.

Such emotions are expressive of harmony and balance that can be expected from humans' affiliation with nature. Besides, these repetitions seem to implicate that the speaker is unhappy in the devouring world. In the ensuing situation, he states: "For this is love and nothing else is love, / The which it is reserved for God above" (ibid). Man has to understand that he is not master of all, rather he is a puppet in the hand of God. Therefore, in his article, "Historical Roots of Our Ecologic Crisis", Lynn White, Jr. writes: "Human ecology is deeply conditioned by beliefs about our nature and destiny-that is, by religion"[9]. Readers should understand something about the purpose of Frost's psyche. In such context, James M. Cox argues:

> Frost is not completely...adrift; he is actually only half-disengaged from the world, for he maintains an intimate relationship with natural process, and he even tries to establish communication with society. The shrewd aspect of Frost's poetic voice is a reflection of the attention he gives to keeping open an avenue of the retreat to the natural process from his interrupted dialogue with society.[10]

The poem, "Flower-Gathering" propounds the sense that human values and nature's systems are in participatory action. Flower is the medium in which human life transpires and its purpose finds the meaning. In this poem, the persona wishes to communicate his inner feelings to his lover and becomes successful, not through his language but through the gift of flowers: "They are yours, be the measure / Of their worth for you to treasure, / The measure of the little while / That I've been long away" (CPoRF, 18). The flowers convey and embody the feelings and emotions of the persona. Hence, no language is necessary when the language of nature is understood. Nature alone can transcend the language what man is not able to express. In order to have a comprehensive understanding of ecosystem, the symbiosis between man and nature is must.

Nature has the power to transport us into ecstasy. The acknowledgement of our place within the natural world needs a redefinition and revaluation in the contemporary human centred toxic world. In the poem "Rose Pogonias", the air is "stifling sweet / With the breath of many flowers" (CPoRF, 19). But in the current state of the world, it is difficult to get life-sustaining clean air. It is obvious that "the human mind is "exquisitely fitted" to external nature, enabling the possibility of an imaginative sustainability in that relationship..."[11].

The poet's constant process of construing nature heightens his concern for the environment. He brings about pastoral longing in "Waiting-A Field at Dusk". The incorporation of his inner consciousness and external nature is woven into the natural dreamscape that embraces the readers to participate in the crepuscular transitions. His simplified rural world results in an ultimate reduction of anthropocentrism in the poetry. The human mind settles in nature to seek clarifications of its complex thoughts. A mind familiar with nature cannot avoid "things for dream" (CPoRF, 20). Regarding this, John F. Lynen advocates: "Frost's treatment of nature tells us much about the origins of the pastorals themselves".[13]

The Frostian man comparatively prefers to remain in a solitary and simple environment for formulating an alternative vision of existence. This vision will seek for right relations with the earth. The reciprocal relationship between man and nature is necessary to remain away from social and psychological ills. There is the correlation between environmental conditions and mental health. That's why Frost does not encourage to competitive commerce or industrialism. He knows, "In a Vale" why the blooms and birds intimate him with his loneliness. Perhaps, they exist for the persona's entertainment. Hence, he searches for a larger meaning of dwelling in the vale: "And thus it is I know so well / Why the flower has odor, the bird has song / You have only to ask me, and I can tell. / No, not vainly there did I dwell, / Nor vainly listen all the night long" (CPoRF, 21). As a countryman, Frost knows his birds and botany, flora and fauna in the vale.

It acknowledges the divine beauty of nature. The concept of aesthetics wraps the readers. Besides, it seems Frost's interest in environmental aesthetics. The purpose of his expression affirms his lovely concern for nature. His attachment to the vale is his interest in landscape aesthetics. In such context, Neil Evernden writes:

> The aesthetic experience, in Dewey's terminology, lies in the relationship between the individual and the environment, not simply in the object viewed, nor in the mind of the viewer. Rather than a subject-object relationship in which the observer parades before the supposedly beautiful view, we have instead a process, an interaction between the viewer and the viewed, and it is in that joint association that the aesthetic experience lies. Instead of a detachment from the environment, we have a subtle diffusion into it.[14]

The discussion of nature in abundant pastoral scenes demonstrates the artist's concentration on environmental aesthetics. Human life without the role of nature is incomplete. The artist's awareness focuses on the importance of values and meaning of nature. In such context, Todd A. Borlik states: "This yearning for a life in harmony with nature, which finds expression in pastoral, may have political and psychological motivations, but this does not prevent the mode from voicing a real empathetic engagement with the biophysical world"[15]. The natural beauties of flora and fauna of the place presume the magnanimity of aesthetic qualities which need to understand the influence of nature in human life.

The persona in "The Vantage Point" keeps his back to human world and returns again to nature. In the first stanza, he seems to be tired of looking at nature: "If tired of trees I seek again mankind" and hence, wishes to see something of human world. But in the second stanza, he reverses his initial thought and prefers to return again to nature after being tired of mankind. "I have but to turn on my arm"-is a very nice vantage point. He realises the presence of nature through sun, earth and plants. Thus, at the end of the poem, he expresses: "I smell the earth, I smell the bruised plant, / I look into the crater of the ant" (Williams & Honig, 251). Such view propounds that the persona is conscious of the distinction between the two realms-human and nature. He tries to restore harmony with the pastoral ecology that he loses in mankind. Such paradigm needs to be at the forefront of public concern. Indirectly it communicates respect and reverence for the integrity of nature.

Frost's ecological view of nature is reviewed when we face hydro-climatic conditions in the next poem, "Going for Water". Life is dangerous for any creature if there is the depletion of water. "Water shortages mean stress on the environment"[16]. It is such a potential threat that calls for a worldwide recognition and concentrated action. At the dawn of ecocriticism, Frost is conscious of the significance of the sources of water. He knows that water helps to sustain the biological systems. That's why he thinks of the necessity for preserving rivers and brooks: "The well was dry beside the door, / And so we went with pail and can / Across the fields behind the house / To seek the brook if still it ran" (CPoRF, 26)

Apart from global warming and climate change, the present world witnesses water crisis and also the fatal pandemics. Biological evolution itself shows that the plants and animals are in need of water. The poet voices for nature at the beginning of the movement of environmentalism. In such context, Lawrence Buell writes: "…a hegemonic practice of environmental representation can present itself to another subculture…with the likes of Mark Twain, Robert Frost, and Sherwood Anderson"[17].

If the readers think of the title of the next poem "The Trial by Existence", they usually may prefer to take a U-turn to Charles Darwin. The proper study of mankind is to survive as environmental pollution rewrites the fate of the universe. Robert Faggen argues that the title of this poem "is an alternation of the Darwin phrase 'struggle for existence'"[18] and the final stanza underpins that life is a form of dying and pain. The poem seems to have the similar tone with Wordsworth's "Intimations Odes". He conveys that the souls in Heaven wish to come to earth. Man strives for existence and presses upon environment. The Frostian man states: "Heroic in its nakedness, / Against the uttermost of earth" (CPoRF, 29). He wages war against nature but nature is undefeatable and nonnegotiable. His unnatural and unwise treatment of nature causes sad results. The true source of spiritual strength lies in nature. It may be realised in the context of the consciousness of the creation. This realisation is a by – product of existence itself.

A reader may face tricky to comprehend Frost's rural scene. As a self-conscious farmer of environmentalist attitude, he pays attention to flora and fauna as well human's place in the natural world. Man gets flourished by the help of nature. Each part of nature is a viable for man's exposure. In this regard, snow, woods, stones, birds, flowers, butterflies and leaves have been used and fused with Frost's emotions. They are inseparable from his creations. His interest in pastoral gives emphasis on human relationship with nature through husbandry. Line 32 of the poem "The Tuft of Flowers" echoes: "And hear his long scythe whispering to the ground" with line 02 of "Mowing": "And that was my long scythe whispering to the ground". Both "Mowing" and "The Tuft of Flowers" published in *A Boy's Will* present the labour of haymaking. The often-quoted line by the readers from "Mowing" – "The fact is the sweetest dream that labor knows" – strikes the sense of retreat to agrarian life.

It reflects the poet's biocentric vision against the conditions of life in the industrialised urban world. The artist feels a sense of kinship and friendship with his unseen coworker. One becomes mesmerised by his labour; another feels a sense of pervasive loneliness. The readers feel that Frost ties with the belief of William Wordsworth as is seen in "The Solitary Reaper". In such context, John T. Napier writes, "Wordsworth set out as his object in *Lyrical Ballads* "to choose incidents and situations from common life …and, at the same time, to throw over them a certain coloring of imagination, whereby ordinary things should be presented to the mind in an unusual aspect…"[19]. Against this view, we may put Frost's line, "The fact is the sweetest dream that labour knows". But Buell is of opinion:

> The prominence of stolid agriculturalists among the establishment in Thoreau's district provoked him into a mode of pastoralism condescending to actual farmers. This attitude eventually dominated the American literary naturist mainstream, with such partial exceptions as Robert Frost (in poems like "Tuft of Flowers" but less to in the satirical "Mending Wall" and not at all in the dreamy "After Apple – Picking") and with such few clear exceptions as Wendell Berry.[20]

On the other hand, Frost's ecological approach unfolds how the mower participates lightly with "fact" and his imagination of hearing of voices: "Perhaps it was something about the heat of the sun, / Something, perhaps, about the lack of sound – / And that was why it whispered and did not speak" (Oliver, 385). A solitary reaper like Wordsworth's "highland lass", the mower has his song, "scythe whispering to the ground". The mower's activity like the "highland lass" echoes in the landscape. Besides, that echo creates sensations in the woods and pasture and lulls one toward dreamlike intimations. The tactile, visual and audile images shape the mood in which the action of the mower bounds the readers to contemplate. It needs to examine the work of scythe as whispers of the sun and silence; in the same way, labor and love attract and appreciate every detail of effort and landscape. The scythe and labor know the sweetness of dream in the silence of the pasture. This pastoral mode relates to the human lives and their activities which it encompasses. It gives an account of the relationship between self and nature. Now time has come to redefine and revalue of nature.

Many readers would agree that Frost is a nature lover. If any doubt arises, each one will admit that he is a poet of country life. He has tried to keep his countryside free from toxic waste and carbon sink. Trees, flowers and plants, animals, birds and insects, hills and vales, rivers and forests, seasons and seasonal changes etc. make the bountiful green for survival purpose. Hence, Frederick Turner states:

"Our bodies and brains are a result of evolution, which is a natural process so paradigmatic that it could almost be said to be synonymous with nature itself"[21]. The welfare and survival of mankind depends upon what sort of relationship man makes with his surroundings.

Urban life diminishes the scope of nature. The urbanite turns nature into 'denature'. The spirit of nature stands as an outcast. The poem, "Pan with Us" discusses man's entrenchment in the modern world causing marginalisation of nature. The landscape scenario changes as everything becomes urbanised and modernised. Instead of magical tune in nature, there is barrenness, dull and drab reality. Pan, the classical God of the wilds, fertility and music finds Himself estranged from the changing world. His pagan pipes no longer create enchanting melody: "Times were changed from what they were: / Such pipes kept less of power to stir" (CPoRF, 33). In the second stanza of the second line, "naked pasture" refers to the depletion of wilderness. That's why at the beginning of the third stanza, Frost writes: "His heart knew peace, for none came here". Peace lies in nature, not in man-made environment. The implication of "the sun-burned earth" is accurate as the present world is lost to the cataclysm of global warming. In such context, Timothy W. Luke's opinion assumes significance:

> Nature is turning to 'Denature'. Much of the earth is a 'built environment', a 'planned habitat', or 'managed range' as pollution modifies atmospheric chemistry, urbanisation restructures weather events, architecture encloses whole biomes in sprawling megacities, and biotechnology reengineers the base codes of existing biomass.[21]

Besides, in materialistic engulfed world, there is harsh sentiment towards nature. Less peace, more tension. The distinction between the natural and the artificial manipulates human biology. In addition to this, Harold H. Watts views, "This insight is put to one side when Frost suggests that the beliefs that societies have lived by are not "natural" but "artificial". It is as though one should say, "God made nature and man-made the town" –carries only the imprints fumblingly imposed by man"[22]. Simple life with idealised images of groves, meadows and brooks, changes into sophisticated urban living.

Frost's poem "In Hardwood Groves" presents the continuity of life in nature that does not believe in apocalypticism. The idea of nature as a stable and enduring is justified through the life-cycle of a tree. The leaves of the tree obviously fall to the ground and lay around the base: "The same leaves over and over again! / They fall from giving shade above… / They must go down past things coming up. / They must go down into the dark decayed" (CPoRF, 37). After being turned into "dark decayed", these leaves become nutrients for the roots. The tree uses such nutrients to produce new leaves again in spring. This process of making tree strong and healthy attests the poet's knowledge on using organic manure. The repetition of "they must go down" suggests that the root of survival lies in nature. The subtle relationship between man and nature is the subject of inter-relatedness and coevolution. Frost's work shows a reciprocal interdependence of one life process upon another. His mind seems to agree with this thought: 'human beings are alive because the earth is alive'.

The speaker in "A Line-Storm Song" experiences the instability of the weather-beaten world. The impact of the storm is subject to understand as it concurrently converses the influences on the human body. It can be admitted that any disturbance or commotion in nature, simultaneously disturbs the humans. On the other hand, his love for nature gets reflected in the next poem, "October". In this poem, he urges nature: "O hushed October morning mild, / Begin the hours of this day slow. / Hearts not averse to being beguiled, / Beguile us in the way you know" (CPoRF, 40). The leaves fall and the chilly weather begins. Moreover, Catherine Boeckmann gives opinion, "Frost moved to his farm in 1900 at a time when thousands of people were abandoning farms due to industrialisation. Towns in the area started "Old Home Days" celebrations (a tradition practiced today), inviting former residents to spend a week of summer back "home" to experience the best of rural life" (https: //www.almanac.com>blog-poem-october). He yearns for the loss of old-time values of country life. Industrialisation and urbanisation encouraged the influx from country to town. Presently rapacious industrialism turns nature into a dustbin of garbages.

A close look at the poem like "My Butterfly" needs to be revalued in so far as ecological threat is concerned. In "My Butterfly" the speaker expresses that nature bestows beauty and life and also shows its fury in the form of death and destruction. In "Reluctance", the last poem of the volume, the persona travels throughout the world, across mountains and rivers but on his way back home, he observes the signs of the dead season all around him: "crusted snow", "dead leaves", and withered flowers. The emphasis is on qualities that provokes the emotional connection between human mind and perseverance of nature. It signifies Frost's inward possession of the theme of exile and return. The persona faces contradictory necessities:

> Out through the fields and the woods
> And over the walls I have wended;
> I have climbed the hills of view
> And looked at the world, and descended,
> ....
> The heart is still aching to seek,
> But the feet question 'Whither?'
> ....
> Ah, when to the heart of man
> Was it ever less than a treason
> To go with the drift of things,
> To yield with a grace to reason,
> And bow and accept the end
> Of a love or a season? (Oliver, 386)

The poem is an act of body – mind battle. "Body is nature, mind is culture. Emotional is nature, rational is culture"[23]. "And looked at the world"-is human-centred values, similarly "and descended" – is nature-centred systems. The persona hovers between necessity in nature and necessity in mankind. The lines – "The heart is still aching to seek, / But the feet question 'Whither?'" – show 'the expression of the will to believe' and 'the expression of the will to resist'. The last lines "To yield with a grace to reason, / Of a love or a season?" indicate the speaker's dilemma into either biocentric or anthropocentric vision of life.

Notes

1. Greg Garrard, in his book *Ecocriticism,* Routledge, 2012, p.63. discusses on pastoral ecology.
2. Sharon Cameron, *Writing Nature: Henry Thoreau's Journal,* Oxford and New York: Oxford University Press, 1995. P.44
3. Lawrence Buell in his book, *The Environmental Imagination: Thoreau, Nature Writing, and the Formation of American Culture,* The Belknap Press of Harvard university Press, 1995. P.108. discusses on 'Representing Nature'. Buell is a Professor of English at Harvard university.
4. Marion Montgomery in his article, "Robert Frost and His Use of Barriers: Man vs Nature Toward God" highlights on Frost's conception on the natural world, being placed in *Robert Frost: A Collection of Critical Essays,* edited by James M. Cox, Prentice-Hall, Inc. 1962, p.138.

5. Henry David Thoreau, "Where I Lived, and What I Lived For", *The Norton Anthology of American Literature,* W. W. Norton & Company. New York. London. 1979. P.832.
6. Glen A. Love, in his article "Revaluing Nature" quotes anthropologist-writer Richard Nelson's opinion, published in *The Ecocriticism Reader* edited by Cheryll Glotfelty & Harold Fromm, The University of Georgia Press, 1996. Pp.233-234. Glen A. Love is a Professor of English at the university of Oregon. He keeps a long-standing interest in the pastoral and the relationship between literature and the environment.
7. Lynn White, Jr. in his article "The Historical Roots of Our Ecologic Crisis" mentions the activities of humans in their ecology, published in *The Ecocriticism Reader* by Glotfelty & Fromm, 1996, p.9.
8. Todd A. Borlik, *Ecocriticism and Early Modern English Literature,* Routledge, Indian Reprint 2015, p.206.
9. Lynn White, Jr. in his article "The Historical Roots of Our Ecologic Crisis" mentions the activities of humans in their ecology, published in *The Ecocriticism Reader* by Glotfelty & Fromm, 1996, p.9.
10. James M. Cox, *Robert Frost: A Collection of Critical Essays*, , Prentice-Hall, Inc. 1962, p.7.
11. Terry Gifford in his article, "Pastoral, Anti-Pastoral, and Post-Pastoral" states the critical history of pastoral before ecocriticism, published in *The Cambridge Companion to Literature and the Environment*, edited by Louise Westling, Cambridge University Press, 2014. P.21. Terry Gifford is a Visiting Scholar at Bath spa University and Professor Honorifico at the Universidad de Alicante.
12. John F. Lynen, "Frost as Modern Poet" in *Robert Frost: A Collection of Critical Essays*, edited by James M. Cox, Prentice-Hall, Inc. 1962. P.184.
13. Neil Evernden, "Beyond Ecology: Self, Place, and The Pathetic Fallacy" published in *The Ecocriticism Reader* edited by Cheryll Glotfelty & Harold Fromm, The University of Georgia Press, 1996. P.97. Neil Evernden is the Faculty of Environmental Studies at York University.
14. Todd A. Borlik, *Ecocriticism and Early Modern English Literature,* Routledge, Indian Reprint, 2015, p.209.
15. Bonnie Roos and Alex Hunt argue that the environmental issues the world over are interlinked with one another. Their view is exposed in *The Cambridge Companion to Literature and the Environment*, edited by Louise Westling, Cambridge University Press, 2014. P.189.
16. Lawrence Buell, *The Environmental Imagination: Thoreau, Nature Writing, and the Formation of American Culture,* The Belknap Press of Harvard university Press, 1995. Pp. 18-19. Buell is a Professor of English at Harvard university.
17. Faggen, Robert. *Robert Frost and the Challenge of Darwin,* Michigan: The University of Michigan. 1997. P.255.

18. John T. Napier, "A Momentary Stay Against Confusion" in *Robert Frost: A Collection of Critical Essays*, edited by James M. Cox, Prentice-Hall, Inc. 1962. P.129.
19. Lawrence Buell, *The Environmental Imagination: Thoreau, Nature Writing, and the Formation of American Culture,* The Belknap Press of Harvard university Press, 1995.p.128
20. Frederick Turner, "Cultivating the American Garden" in *The Ecocriticism Reader* edited by Cheryll Glotfelty & Harold Fromm, The University of Georgia Press, 1996. P.42.
21. Luke, Timothy W. *Ecocritique: Contesting the Politics of Nature, Economy, and Culture* Minneapolis: University of Minnesota Press, 1997.p.195.
22. Harold H. Watts, "Robert Frost and the Interrupted Dialogue" in *Robert Frost: A Collection of Critical Essays*, edited by James M. Cox, Prentice-Hall, Inc. 1962, p.111.
23. Pramod K. Nayar, *Contemporary Literary and Cultural Theory,*

CHAPTER 2

North of Boston (1914)

North of Boston incorporates with abnormal and alienated people. It is "a book of people" rather of poems. In 1914, when the book was published, "the nineteenth-century political order was collapsing into the violence of the twentieth century"[1]. Such was the impact on the poems of this volume. Man's anthropocentric vision makes the poet alone as he puts his back towards nature. This mindset tends to be self-centered. The anthropocentric standpoint creates the barrier between man and nature, between man and man also.

Besides, when the reader compares *North of Boston* with *A Boy's Will*, he finds matured Frost presenting nature through local habitation of New England. The harmony of humanity and nature that exists in *A Boy's Will* encounters some essential changes in *North of Boston*. It is necessary to acknowledge the statement of John F. Lynen who affirms:

> The pastoralism of the New England poems represents Frost's most fully realised development of the way of thinking implicit in such early nature sketches. When *North of Boston* is compared with *A Boy's Will*, it becomes apparent that the poet found his true medium when he discovered New England. The earlier volume gives glimpses of what is to come, but it is not until his second book that he begins to portray regional life in earnest, and it is just at this point that he first shows complete mastery of the pastoral form. The sudden maturing of his pastoralism in *North of Boston* is paralleled by a simultaneous maturing of his treatment of nature.[2]

Though Frost finds out great natural beauty in New England, he keeps doubts about the people themselves. The ingredients of bleakness, ugliness and dinginess of humanity get contrast with the charm and scenic beauty of nature. The volume unfolds upheaval against way of life and focuses on mature adjustment to the environment. "Mending Wall", the first poem of *North of Boston* discusses the dominance of culture over nature. There is nature-culture opposition in the poem:

> Something there is that doesn't love a wall,
> That sends the frozen-ground-swell under it,
> And spills the upper boulders in the sun;
> And makes gaps even two can pass abreast.
> ....
> He only says, 'Good fences make good neighbors.'
> Spring is the mischief in me, and I wonder
> If I could put a notion in his head:
> 'Why do they make good neighbors? Isn't it
> Where there are cows? But here there are no cows
> Before I built a wall I'd ask to know
> What I was walling in or walling out,
> And to whom I was like to give offense.
> Something there is that doesn't love a wall,
> That wants it down'. I could say 'Elves' to him,
> But it's not elves exactly, and I'd rather
> He said it for himself. (Norton, 1764-1765)

"Fence" or "wall" is human-construct that is not eco-friendly. The beginning line of the poem, – "Something there is that doesn't love a wall" – is the voice of nature. Nature counteracts to human supremacy: "That sends the frozen-ground-swell under it, / And spills the upper boulders in the sun". Mankind exploits nature and for the cause of defending, nature shows its fury to humans. The lines- "Something there is that doesn't love a wall" and "Good fences make good neighbors" – repeatedly written unfurl the debate between eco-consciousness and ego-consciousness. However, "ground-swell" and "the yelping dogs" communicate nature's reaction over man's action. Here, Frost demonstrates man's potential power to erect the barrier between himself and nature, between himself and his fellowmen. Such barrier vested in self-centred ego creates chaotic situation. In order to think of survival behavior, nature should be free from all sorts of control and exploitation. Man should be sober and submissive in order to lead on a harmonious life.

In "The Death of the Hired Man", the persona discovers the meaning of home. Everyone needs at least a place of refuge, a home what the speaker realises. Home is a 'spirit of charity' and nature is our 'widest home'. Man lives in nature. Nature is his body. The poem presents the discussion between the young husband and wife about the staying of an absentee old field hand in their house. Being sick and apparently unable to work again, that truant decides to return and remain with them. The matter is whether he should be allowed or not. In this juncture, nature plays an inevitable role that one has to feel. 'Feeling is behind everything that counts in a man's life'. One has to feel:

> Part of a moon was falling down the west,
> Dragging the whole sky with it to the hills.
> Its light poured softly in her lap. She saw it
> And spread her apron to it. She put out her hand
> Among the harp-like morning-glory strings,
> Taut with the dew from garden bed to eaves,
> As if she played unheard some tenderness
> That wrought on him beside her in the night.
> 'Warren', she said, 'he has come home to die:
> You needn't be afraid he'll leave you this time'
> 'Home', he mocked gently.
> 'Yes, what else but home?
> It all depends on what you mean by home.
> ....
> 'Home is the place where, when you have to go there,
> They have to take you in'. (Norton, 1767-1768)

The tone of tenderness springs from nature and Mary, the wife of Warren. The soft light of the moon and the kind heart of Mary show sympathy towards the poor, old, sick Silas. Mention may be made of the view of Timothy Clark: "Thus women were endorsed as somehow 'closer to nature' than men, usually through their connection with motherhood and nurturing. The association of women and the domestic sphere could be reaffirmed as their greater sense of respect for nature as a sort of home ('ecology' being from the Greek 'science of the household')"[3]. The lunar sweep of the first two lines of such extract is put into a human and household focal point in the third line, when the light of the moon "poured softly in her lap". The sharpness of this clause – "She saw it" – advocates that the wife, Mary is aware of the support she is obtaining from remote influences. Such awareness of the support, drawing from the countryside influences, helps her to feed a benign mood into her husband towards the old Silas. Mary's 'feminine essence'[4] shows sympathy as same with nature's nourishment to human race. Thanks to female biology as they serve like nature to mankind.

The importance of nature in human life through certain agencies cannot be avoided. The beautiful reality of these agencies boosts divinity in human mind. It is in this sense that Mary's gestures embrace these influences while they put forth to play upon domestic artifacts. The expression "morning-glory strings" stretches from the "garden bed" to the eaves under which, most likely, is their marital "bed". The compassion that "wrought on him beside her in the night" seems to stem not from her alone but from nature. Biological circumstances of life shape the psychological mood of a person. Such mood expects to create the commonplace conditions friendly to life. Hence, both environment and human are in participatory action. It is this shared action which is "home".

Frost's craftsmanship is unique. In his work, the process of nature reveals the system of life which it nourishes. His rural characters try to delve into the secrets of nature as is observed in "The Mountain". The speaker's ecological perspective is understood when he says: "When I walked forth at dawn to see new things, / Were fields, a river, and beyond, more fields. / The river at the time was fallen away" (CPoRF, 56). The speaker witnesses the essential changes by the cycle of seasons in nature. The "fields", "river", "cobblestones", "grassland", "ridges of sand" and "the mountain" etc. attribute to the subjective right of the natural world which is not expected to be reduced to the human's use. "Nothing in nature exists superfluously"[5]. Being a visitor in the neighborhood, the speaker wishes for knowing about the mountain that creates shadow upon the village. In reply to the speaker, the Wordsworthian old man "who moved so slow / With white-faced oxen in a heavy cart" is anxious to promote interest in "a brook".

The old man's excitement- "One of the great sights going to see" – produces a curiosity to know the miraculous incarnation of nature. In his tone, there is a sense of attachment with nature. Such inquisitiveness gets a metaphoric expression "like an ox's breath". The interlocutor's environmental sentiment – "It's always cold in summer, warm in winter" – propels him into wonder and humility towards nature which is the contradictory of a desire to dominate and exploit it. The description offers the qualities of a country tall tale. The sense of revelation in nature "cold in summer, warm in winter" by the old man is a permutation of natural history, philosophical interpretation and personal response to nature.

Frost draws compliment for his skill. He provides the facts for the faith of the readers – "inch-deep with frosty spines" – only to feel the genealogy of the environmental sensibility. It is a demonstration of country quaintnesses and native reverberations. Ecological recuperation constructs a colossal cosmic view of the cosmos. It is also a play between 'artifice and naturalness', between 'transcendence and immanence'. On the other hand, the line "Deer-hunting and trout-fishing" threatens environmental ethics. Here, Frost has not made it clear whether "Deer-hunting" is a pastime or for a survival necessity. Whatever it may be, it is a potential erosion and decay to commonality in environmental principles. The upshot of "trout-fishing" goes against "an occult relation between man and vegetable". The prioritisation of human values in twenty-first century puts problem in ecological balance. "Humans supplant animals; animal is obliterated by human drama"[6]. Nature is silent as per the articulation of human culture. Man's prerogative rarely regards the value of other creatures' life in nature.

Frost's view on life pinpoints a theme in environmental debate. In "Home Burial", there is husband/wife dualism. The tensed and stressed mother cracks up under a weight of woe over her child's death and becomes unbalanced. The couple is trapped inside the house which looks directly on the family graveyard; the graveyard that holds the body of their recently dead child:

> He saw her from the bottom of the stairs
> Before she saw him. She was starting down,
> Looking back over her shoulder at some fear.
> She took a doubtful step and then undid it
> To raise herself and look again. He spoke
> Advancing toward her. 'What is it you see
> From up there always – for I want to know'.
> She turned and sank upon her skirts at that,
> And her face changed from terrified to dull.
> He said to gain time: 'What is it you see',
> Mounting until she cowered under him.
> 'I will find out now – you must tell me, dear.'
> She, in her place, refused him any help
> With the least stiffening of her neck and silence.
> She let him look, sure that he wouldn't see,
> Blind creature; and awhile he didn't see.
> But at last he murmured, 'Oh', and again, 'Oh'.
> 'What is it-what?' she said.
> 'Just that I see'.
> 'You don't,' she challenged. Tell me what it is'.
> 'The wonder is I didn't see at once.
> I never noticed it from here before.
> I must be wonted to it – that's the reason.
> The little graveyard where my people are!
> So small the window frames the whole of it.
> Not so much larger than a bedroom, is it?
> There are three stones of slate and one of marble'
> ....
> But I understand, it is not the stones,

> But the child's mound –'
> 'Don't, don't, don't, don't' she cried. (Oliver, 392-393)

It is a sociobiological issue. The husband and wife are tongue-tied in their acrimonies. There is a sort of suffocation in their ambience. The first line of the poem, – "He saw her from the bottom of the stairs" – presents the husband as a kind of detective. The second line, – "Before she saw him. She was starting down," – justifies a habituated suspicion on her part. In line five, – "To raise herself and look again. He spoke" – stresses on his glance at her as she moves fanatically to the window, unaware of being watched. The depiction of alienation, secretiveness, male intimidation and mutual distrust exposes anti-ecological sphere. Regarding the man/woman dualism, the view of Timothy Clark can be taken into consideration: "The point being made about these dualisms ('man/woman', 'culture/nature', etc.) is that the first term of each pair has often been defined in opposition to and with implicit superiority over the other"[7]. When the husband asks the wife "'Don't-don't go. / Don't carry it to someone else this time'" (L.56-57), he seems to be less domineering to what she shouts: "'Don't, don't, don't, don't' she cried". The similar consequence is also seen in Ernest Hemingway's "Hills Like White Elephants": "Will you please please please please please please please stop talking" (Web)? She asks him not to speak, he tells her not to leave him.

Initially the husband's suspicion over the integrity of his wife and spying on her activity is a sort of male dominating mindset. The source of conflict is the estrangement between husband and wife. The word, "always" in line seven is the demanding version of the husband. On the other hand, in place of showing fear at his "advancing on her", the wife's face changes from "terrified to dull". The words, "until" and "under" in the line, – "Mounting until she cowered under him" – unfold a calculated masculine imposition of will power of the husband. In such context, Greg Garrard mentions the opinion by analysing Val Plumwood:

> Yet, as Val Plumwood's analysis shows, merely differentiating men from women, humans from nature, or reason from emotion, does not itself constitute problematic anthropo-or androcentrism. Rather, the underlying model of mastery shared by these forms of oppression is based upon alienated differentiation and denied dependency: in the dominant Euro-American culture, humans are not distinguished from nature, but opposed to it in ways that make humans radically alienated from and superior to it.[8]

Androcentrism, now and then, inflames sexism and savagism. In consequence, women suffer both physically and psychologically. The masculinity and manliness of the husband combined with appetite is expressed in the line: "I will find out now-you must tell me, dear". The readers may feel the purpose of the words "now" and "dear". Corollary to this, the word "help" signifies a lot: "She, in her place, refused him any help / With the least stiffening of her neck and silence". Such problem needs to acknowledge the statement of Richard Poirier: "Sexuality in Frost has been noted…in a very great number of his poems it figures, as it does here, as a submerged metaphor for his all-consuming interest in the *relational* and *transitional* nature of poetry, of thinking, of talking itself"[9]. The lines, – "She let him look, sure that he wouldn't see, / Blind creature; and awhile he didn't see" – underpin the surges of secret feelings between the two of them but their inability to share any approach with one another.

Obviously, the husband knows the child's grave is out there. But the wife's obstinacy to know, "Tell me what it is" puts differences in between them. It gives a turning point to the situation when the husband says: "Not so much larger than a bedroom, is it"? The husband's comparison of the graveyard to a bedroom is a sign of his coarseness of feelings about what has taken place in their marriage. Marriage is the union of two hearts. If the bedroom is like a graveyard, it is a matter of separation. In this context, David Mazel mentions, "I use consciously to suggest an analogy between the discourses of environmentalism and sexuality. As a variety of feminist critics have pointed out, even though a sexual *penetration* might be thought of as logically complimentary to and simultaneous with, say, an *engulfment* or an *immersion*, the preferred term is of course penetration, which is privileged precisely because it foregrounds male sexual agency. Use of the terms such as engulfment, with their ascription of sexual agency to the female, is all but forbidden by a code that works to efface female sexuality generally"[10]. The conversation between husband and wife seems to form an example of gender discrimination and the very idea of their environment divides them into the action of an inside and an outside.

When the husband asks her, – "Don't – don't go. / Don't carry it to someone else this time", he appears to be less authoritative. Besides, the husband goes on describing as he buries the child- "Three foggy mornings and one rainy day / Will rot the best birch fence a man can build". The weather shows the role of nature in life.

Lastly, he understands his wife and the poem ends on his exclamation "'I *will*!'". The debate between husband and wife comes to an end through the delicacy of mutual understanding. Thus, mutual respect and reciprocity may avoid the boundary between man and woman, between culture and nature. "Home" as a place should maintain the minimum decorum and nature is our "widest home" that should remain in "original decor".

The articulation of action and behavior of women, more or less, unfolds their social, political and economic rights. Exposing the overwrought mother in "Home Burial" or a woman servant in "A Servant to Servants", Frost seems to think of female biology and social experience in managing capability of women. Ecofeminists propound that nature is imagined as a woman and women are closer to nature than men. Besides, the characters in *North of Boston* are apparently abnormal and unbalanced against the background of social and economic disturbance. Corollary to this, morbid disorders crop up in the remote rural locale. A sort of corrosion in life and nature is the cause of the war period. In such context, William Howarth states, "Ecology leads us to recognise that life speaks, communing through encoded streams of information that have direction and purpose, if we learn to translate the messages with fidelity"[11]. It needs to realise that 'the physical world presses in on us from outside and the material anxiety presses in on us from inside'.

The ecological perception of Frost is reflected through the pastoral imagery in "The Black Cottage". The persona and a priest pass by a small black cottage surrounded by "tar-banded ancient cherry trees". The work focuses upon harmony with the natural environment.

> We chanced in passing by that afternoon
> To catch it in a sort of special picture
> Among tar-banded ancient cherry trees,
> Set well back from the road in rank lodged grass,
> The little cottage we were speaking of,
> A front with just a door between two windows,
> Fresh painted by the shower a velvet black.
> We paused, the minister and I, to look.
> He made as if to hold it at arm's length
> Or put the leaves aside that framed it in.
> 'Pretty', he said. 'Come in. No one will care'.
> The path was a vague parting in the grass
> That led us to a weathered window-sill.
> We pressed our faces to the pane. 'You see,' he said,

> 'Everything's as she left it when she died.
> Her sons won't sell the house or things in it.
> They say they mean to come and summer here
> Where they were boys. They haven't come this year.
> They live so far away – one is out west-
> It will be hard for them to keep their word.
> Anyway they won't have the place disturbed'.
> A buttoned hair-cloth lounge spread scrolling arms
> Under a crayon portrait on the wall,
> Done sadly from an old daguerreotype.
> That was the father as he went to war.
> She always, when she talked about the war,
> Sooner or later came and leaned, half knelt
> Against the lounge beside it, though I doubt
> If such unlifelike lines kept power to stir
> Anything in her after all the years. (Oliver, 396)

To keep safe and protect from the attack of pests and insects, the cherry trees have been tar-banded. Coal-tar banding is a natural process. The speaker, possibly, knows that tar-banding will deter caterpillars from living in and eating the trees. Indeed, it underpins the artist's pest management theory that prevents wingless insects from crawling up into trees. It invokes the ancient tradition of farming like Rachel Carson's fairy tale in *Silent Spring*. The word "little cottage" connotes an appealing, pastoral view of rural, peaceful life. This gives the impression of living in a simple, natural ecosphere like life in Thoreau's *Walden*. The cottage is far away from the influences of big cities as Wordsworth writes in "Tintern Abbey": "Thoughts of more deep seclusion; and connect / The landscape with the quiet of the sky" (Wordsworth, 7-8). The expressions – "weathered window-sill", "the leaves aside that framed it" and "Set well back from the road in rank lodged grass" – justify the cottage's quiet connection to nature. Such connection is attributed to "the shower" of rain turning the cottage into "velvet black". Such description demonstrates implicitly or explicitly a contrast to urban living and shows unwillingness towards the modern pace of life. The idyllic setting of "lodged grass" creates the feelings of a remote countryside to live a life in serenity. This sort of life gives message, "we are alive because earth is alive".

On the other hand, the death of the husband in war makes a huge impact on the woman. She is not able to recover herself from the grief and loss of losing her husband. His absence creates an empty space in her family. With such burden and woe, she dies. The outcome of war is decay, degradation, disease and death. Indeed, war is ecocide. The ruinous effect of war is an obstacle for a congenial and healthy biosphere. It disintegrates and destroys the beauty of the biotic community. Regarding the war and change in environment, W. G. O'Donnell writes: "When the Civil War commenced, 12,000,000 acres were under cultivation in New England; fifty years later there were only 7,000,000 acres. During that half century of shrinking agriculture, the population of the region doubled. In short, New England became largely urban and industrialised"[12]. Besides, the expression – "one is out west"- seems to indicate the life from local to global. The globalisation brings a drastic change in environment. In ecocritical point of view, the line – "Her sons won't sell the house or the things in it"-signifies to keep nature safe from commercialism. The poem ends with the line – "Fierce heads looked out; small bodies pivoted". It creates awareness that the "fierce heads" of the bees symbolise the power of nature which will show its fury if it is disrupted or dislocated.

On the other hand, people in *North of Boston* are caught up in a struggle with the basic problems of existence. They lead a way of life to adjust with the environment. In "Blueberries" the artist presents the interaction between two persons passing by a pasture. They become dumbfounded to see blueberry bushes with abundant growth of ripe blueberries "as big as the end of your thumb", "real sky-blue and heavy" producing a drumming sound when they are collected in a pail:

'You ought to have seen what I saw on my way
To the village, through Patterson's pasture today:
Blueberries as big as the end of your thumb,
Real sky-blue, and heavy, and ready to drum
In the cavernous pail of the first one to come!
And all ripe together, not some of them green
And some of them ripe! You ought to have seen!'
....
'I wonder you didn't see Loren about'.
....
'He seems to be thrifty; and hasn't he need,
With the mouths of all those young Lorens to feed?
He has brought them all up on wild berries, they say,
Like birds. They store a great many away.
They eat them the year round, and those they don't eat
They sell in the store and buy shoes for their feet'.
'Who cares what they say? It is a nice way to live,
Just taking what Nature is willing to give,
Not forcing her hand with harrow and plow'. (CPoRF, 78-80)

In their conversation, they expose Loren who feeds so many children mainly on berries throughout the year: "He has brought them all up on wild berries, they say / Like birds". Loren and his family meet the necessities of life with such gift of nature. The fatherly Loren and his brood of young Lorens determine not to be poverty stricken, not asking anything of anyone, just accepting what nature is willing to give. The biocentric vision of Frost is studied in the lines: "It's a nice way to live / Just taking what Nature is willing to give". In such perspective, Ramachandra Guha states: "One of Gandhi's best-known aphorisms is: 'The world has enough for everybody's need, but not enough for one person's greed:' an exquisitely phrased one-line environmental ethic"[13]. The breathless competition emerging from greedy and covetous mindset of man exploits nature what is no more seen in Loren: "Not forcing her hand with harrow and plow". But today's man has been extremely selfish, dangerously competitive, and hideously destructive of nature. To save the environment and make free from pollution, the world needs to follow the path of Gandhiji.

Loren's solace derived from nature is the ecocentric state of thinking. Domination over nature is not his prerequisite. Evidently, humans should develop the intrinsic value to let things get disclosed in nature in their own inimitable ways. In other words, man's survival rests on a fruitful integration with nature, not by a forceful exploitation of it. To avoid the rising threats of ecological holocaust, man should keep integrity, stability and beauty of the natural world. His survival depends upon his capacity to change himself rather than his environment. Nature's laws should not be challenged and man should not wage war against it. If there is any deviation, predicament will arise.

The ecofeministic perception of Frost articulates the plight of women that 'blames the androcentric dualism between man/woman'. Mention may be made of Sharon Doubiago who asserts: "ecology consciousness is traditional woman consciousness"[14]. The woman in "A Servant to Servants" spends her days alone, looking after the house while the men are left. The emptiness prevails upon her. She has been a victim to an insane asylum but is "not afraid of them" who board in her house: "if they're not / Afraid of me. There's two can play at that. / I have my fancies: it runs in the family. / My father's brother wasn't right". The woman's husband Len has rented out these outsiders camping on the land. As it is observed in Frost's poems about isolated women who are hopelessly drab. Here, the view of Pramod K. Nayar can be stated: "Ecofeminists thought emerges from this basic assumption; both women and nature are equally oppressed by male ways of thinking and action"[15].

Everything the woman delivers is touched with an articulation of mad loneliness. Her depiction is full of self-frightening creation:

> And just when he was at the height,
> Father and mother married, and mother came,
> A bride, to help take care of such a creature,
> And accommodate her young life to his.
> That was what marrying father meant to her.
> She had to lie and hear love things made dreadful
> By his shouts in the night. He'd shout and shout
> Until the strength was shouted out of him,
> And his voice died down slowly from exhaustion.
> He'd pull his bars apart like bow and bowstring. (CPoRF, 85-86)

It needs a critique of gender functioning of masculinity and femininity. Androcentric priority of reason over emotion leads to a striking force in ecofeminism. The matter of domination and sexual frustration in childless marriage is noticed here. Love is exhausted in drudgery and the woman's marriage is apparently same to her mother's: "Father and mother married, and mother came, / A bride to help take care of such a creature, / And accommodate her young life to his. / That was what marrying father meant to her". She is deprived of emotional fulfillments of any kind. It fits appropriate to acknowledge the view of Greg Garrard who asserts: "The logic of domination is implicated in discrimination and expression on grounds of race, sexual orientation and class as well as species and gender"[16].

"After Apple-Picking" is a blend of artistry and accuracy to examine the nature-centred system into which human-centred values play the role. Apple itself is sweet, beautiful and intoxicating. In this poem, there is artistic touch of farm life that widely acknowledges Frost as a naturalist. Here, the readers discover him as a harvester in an apple orchard. He narrates the physical and mental weariness after a day of picking through which the scholars get a glimpse of farming practices of that time. His biographer, Jay Parini, mentions: "Few poets in the English language have been so specific in their knowledge of plants and flowers, or filled their poetry with so much flora and fauna"[17]. The poet's accuracy of understanding the natural processes through the outcome of harvesting is reflected in this poem.

> My long two-pointed ladder's sticking through a tree
> Toward heaven still,
> And there's a barrel that I didn't fill
> Beside it, and there may be two or three
> Apples I didn't pick upon some bough.
> But I am done with apple-picking now.
> Essence of winter sleep is on the night,
> The scene of apples: I am drowsing off.
> I cannot rub the strangeness from my sight
> I got from looking through a pane of glass
> I skimmed this morning from the drinking trough
> And held against the world of hoary grass.
> It melted, and I felt it fall and break.
> But I was well
> Upon my way to sleep before it fell,
> And I could tell
> What form my dreaming was about to take. (Norton, 1769)

As the harvester conveys his "drowsing" arresting him, he moves back and forth between the facts of the orchard-the unfilled barrel and the ladder "sticking through a tree"-and the sensations and images of a dream. On account of his day's inclusion of work and his resultant of weariness, he perplexes his sense of time and place. The "essence" of sleep seems to become the "scent of apples". Like the harvest in Keats' "To Autumn": "Or on a half-reap'd furrow sound asleep, / Drowsed with the fume of poppies…" (16-17), Frost seems to vacillate between labour and dream. Besides, the "strangeness" of his "sight", that fascinatingly propounds an imaginative, renovating vision, emerges not only from drowsiness but the morning's real optical illusion. "I skimmed this morning from drinking trough" justifies the poet's environmental sense of late autumn and approach of winter as the overnight temperature is cold enough to freeze solid the top layer of the animals' "drinking trough". The poet furnishes hints of winter through "the world of hoary grass. / It melted, I let it fall and break". This validates the frost covering the ground.

The lines – "Beside it, and there may be two or three / Apples I didn't pick upon some bough" – communicate harvesting of late-bearing apple.

> Magnified apples appear and disappear,
> Stem end and blossom end,
> And every fleck of russet showing clear.

My instep arch not only keeps the ache,
It keeps the pressure of a ladder-round.
I feel the ladder sway as the boughs bend.
And I keep hearing from the cellar bin
The rumbling sound
Of load on load of apples coming in.
For I have had too much
Of apple-picking: I am overtired
Of the great harvest I myself desired.
There were ten thousand thousand fruit to touch,
Cherish in hand, lift down, not let fall.
For all
That struck the earth,
No matter if not bruised or spiked with stubble,
Went surely to the cider-apple heap
As of no worth.
One can see what will trouble
This sleep of mine, whatever sleep it is.
Were he not gone,
The woodchuck could say whether it's like his
Long sleep, as I describe its coming on,
Of just some human sleep. (Norton, 1769-1770)

The mention of "stubble" gives the impression that the apple trees are close to a hay field that has already been cut. Corollary to this, the lines – "I keep hearing from the cellar bin / The rumbling sound / Of load on load of apples" – indicate that the trees are near the farm house. However, the expression – "I feel the ladder sway as the boughs bend." – substantiates that the ladder is not independent and free-standing and must be supported by the branches from which he plucks. As he picks apples, the harvester notes "each russet fleck". The knowledge of botany spells out that russet is a patch or streak of rough brown skin that may be caused by fungus, bacteria, wetness or frost. But he does not spray DDT or any sort of chemicals to protect his apples. It encompasses the speaker's agri-productivity experiences.

Once the reaper picks the apples, he does "cherish in hand, lift down, and not let fall". Such action advocates a precious wonder of loading apples in spite of pains ("ache") and exhaustion ("overtired") from committed labour. A farmer will take care of nature as "Nature is necessary" for him. Because agricultural growth needs the potential support from nature. He does not prefer to rupture it; rather he admits what nature gives: "For I have had too much". Frost's biocentric mindset acclaims that man is essentially a part of nature and hence, no illusion will separate him from it. Thus, mention may be made of Todd A. Borlik: "This yearning for a life in harmony with nature, which finds expression in pastoral, may have political and psychological motivations, but this does not prevent the mode from voicing a real emphatic engagement with the biophysical world"[18]. On the other hand, as the speaker confesses "I have had too much", it also suggests the bountiful harvesting of apples without applying any sort of agro-chemicals. Like the Elizabethan pastoral poets, Frost presumes a "green world". He repeatedly uses the pastoral imagery to protect the virgin land unspoiled. His people in *North of Boston* use lantern in place of electricity or any scientific and industrial products. Even there is no sound of horns in *A Boy's Will* and *North of Boston.*

"The Fear" talks of a farm couple who return home late at night in a horse-drawn buggy in lieu of using any petrol or diesel running-vehicle. His eco-conscious mentality tries to keep the environment free from vehicular emission. When the couple arrives at the barn, the wife stresses on seeing a man's face in the bushes close to the roadside. The supposed stranger may be a danger but the brave wife insists on taking the lantern by herself and finding out the man she has seen. Her courageous manner is justified when she asks her husband not to come rather, she will settle the matter alone. She finds the lurking man and asks him to come within the course of the lantern. The man comes out with a boy who is his son and hence, he is not a robber. The wife addresses her husband Joel to understand the situation but he does not reply. In such graphic circumstances, the wife shows her personhood. A study from this perspective provides a feeling for the developing tradition of women nature. Therefore, it needs to acknowledge the role of feminine nature. In her article, "Heroines of Nature", Vera L. Norwood quotes the analysis of Sherry Ortner and Simone de Beauvoir: "Using Simone de Beauvoir, Ortner argues that woman's psychology, social roles and psychic structure combine to place her in a position perceived to be nearer to nature than man"[19]. Nothing in nature is secret.

But in "Generations of Men" the situation becomes different. The boy and girl get together at the wreck of an old home place and discuss about families and the destroyed place. In the end, they fall in love and make a pact to restore or rebuild what has been lost. In this issue, Marion Montgomery affirms: "This war between man and the natural world did not exist for Wordsworth so positively as it does for Frost. Wordsworth in his early poetry tended to deny all barriers in his effort to become one with the great moving spirit of things, the soul of the world"[20]. Frost tries to unfold the conflictual interferences between man and nature.

The speaker in "The Self-Seeker" illustrates the difficulty and misery of a mill-worker whose feet gets mutilated in an industrial accident. The Frostian man forms a parallel between the lack of positive reception for rare orchids and the low value on a mill-worker's corporeal reliability within the productivity system. In such context, Bonnie Roos and Alex Hunt can be taken into account: "Natural systems and human systems are best understood in the terms by which we experience them – as participatory and inter-activating rather than as opposing forces"[21]. Man creates machine but machine kills man. Machine shows its hegemony of mastering over the world. On the other side, answering to the friend, the mill-worker sums up his helplessness 'to trace the flowers as the loss of all the flowers':

> Of every kind everywhere in this region
> For the next forty summers-call it forty.
> But I'm not selling those, I'm giving them,
> They never earned me so much as one cent:
> Money can't pay me for the loss of them. (CPoRF, 119)

It is a sentimental issue that the mill-worker does get full compensation for the loss. His incapacity does not pursue his infatuation to collect flowers. Industrialism and commercialism can never compensate to the loss what they produce on earth. The mutilated environment produces less of life-sustaining air. The capital-intensive mindset does not bother on it as the labourers become replaced by the progressive system without acknowledging the value of the previous disfigured worker: "Everything goes the same without me there". The impact of market forces makes nature vulnerable. Mankind has to perceive that money cannot buy nature nor repay for the damage: "money can't pay me for the loss of them". There should not be any sort of negotiation between man and nature. 'Nature is non-negotiable'[22]. Ecological understanding of the relationship between human beings and the floral world is subject to realisation when the wayfarer asks: "But what about your flora of the valley"? At one side, there is the work of a man in botanical sphere and on the other, there is the purview of bigger economic power.

"The Wood-Pile" articulates the relationship between the human and the natural world. It mixes up the ontological articulation between the human subject and a mute, passive landscape. The budding synergy between pastoral and environmental ethics gets threatened in a consumptive temperament of felling of trees and making into piles. The persona depicts the environment as he saunters through "the frozen swamp", which is unfamiliar to him. Like the "listener" in Wallace Stevens' "The Snow Man", the walker becomes aware of a wintry barrenness. The Frostian man tries to penetrate into the reality of the surrounding:

> Out walking in the frozen swamp one gray day,
> I paused and said, 'I will turn back from here.
> No, I will go on farther-and we shall see'.
> The hard snow held me, save where now and then
> One foot went through. The view was all in lines
> Straight up and down of tall slim trees
> Too much alike to mark or name a place by
> So as to say for certain I was here
> Or somewhere else: I was just far from home.
> A small bird flew before me, He was careful
> To put a tree between us when he lighted,
> And say no word to tell me who he was
> Who was so foolish as to think what he thought.
> He thought that I was after him for a feather-
> The white one in his tail; like one who takes
> Everything said as personal to himself. (Norton, 1770)

The speaker finds himself in the wintry prospect that relates to the state of ecological consciousness. His mention of "here" means he is away from "home". The speaker's presence in nature ("here") is ultimately suggestive of his distance from human world ("home"). That's why he asserts: "I will turn back from here. / No, I will go on farther". If this is a situation of falling into dilemma between human world and nature, he chooses nature. The voice of this man: "So as to say for certain I was here / Or somewhere else" can be understood from the cause of poor visibility as it was "gray day". He portrays the "swamp" as "frozen" and "gray" and hence, obviously the "snow" is "hard". Such vocabularies can be expected to examine the poetic sensibilities of the weather-beaten landscape. The lines, – "The hard snow held me, save where now and then / One foot went through." – reinforce the climatic conditions of the place. The inoffensive accuracy about the relative hardness of the snow where "one foot went through" validates man's place in the natural world.

The expressions, – "The view was all in lines/Straight up and of tall slim trees/Too much alike to mark or name a place by"-provide the speaker's constant process of inspecting and interpreting nature. He fails to identify or grasp the locality as everything appears "alike". It is due to the weather-condition of the place.

When the speaker is in quest of the distinctiveness of the area, a small bird appears and seems frightened of him: "He was careful / To put a tree between us when he lighted, / And say no word to tell me who he was / Who was so foolish as to think what he thought". It advocates the essential divide between humanity and the natural world. The speaker tries to have the unwanted interference in the world of the bird. The little bird consciously puts a tree between them "when he lighted" as it assumes the speaker as a threat. That's why the creature keeps distance from the bystander. At one side, man's yearning for prying, at the other bird's resentment for protection. This dualism of human and non-human suffuses Frost's ecological vision. He studies man's dominating and dangerous trespasses into the living spaces of other species that destroys the environmental ethics. Here, the poet thinks of a fit environment for both human and non-human. The conflict between human's interest and non-human's survival struggle is the subject of ecological confrontation.

The impression of the bird about the speaker is perhaps his strategy to take the tail feathers from it: "He thought that I was after him for a feather – / The white one in his tail". The self-regard confusion attributed to the bird is obvious if it is judged from the angle of man's greedy and rapacious mindset. Besides, the situation is further suggested by the accusation that the bird is "like one who takes / Everything said as personal to himself". It can be affirmed that on the basis of symbiosis and mutualism, each creature lives in harmony with nature. From ecological perspective, there should be the outlook of mutuality in place of dominance. Frost's creative output tries to originate this idea.

From an ecocentric point of view, the poem builds up a distinction between 'human constructedness' and non-human reality. Maple tree is obviously an autonomous reality of nature's laws. But destroying and cutting down of such trees and turning into a wood-pile is an example of human constructedness.

> And then there was a pile of wood for which
> I forgot him and let his fear

Carry him off the way I might have gone,
Without so much as wishing him good-night.
He went behind it to make his last stand.
It was a cord of maple, cut and split
And piled – and measured, four by four by eight.
And not another like it could I see.
No runner tracks in this year's snow looped near it.
And it was older sure than this year's cutting,
Or even last year's or the year's before.
The wood was gray and the bark warping off it
And the pile somewhat sunken. Clematis
Had wound strings round and round it like a bundle.
What held it though on one side was a tree
Still growing, and on one a stake and prop,
These latter about to fall. I thought that only
Someone who lived in turning to fresh tasks
Could so forget his handiwork on which
He spent himself, the labor of his ax,
And leave it there far from a useful fireplace
To warm the frozen swamp as best it could
With the slow smokeless burning of decay. (Norton, 1770-1771)

The evidence of construct that the readers find is the "wood-pile". It is not nature-made. By disrupting and deteriorating nature, man makes the wood-pile as an investment for his future comfort. The outcome of such exploiting and abusing activities of man damages the planet's basic life-support systems.

The pile of wood lets the speaker instantly forget the bird: "And then there was a pile for which / I forgot him". This anxiousness of the speaker excites him to cut off his relationship with nature: "Without so much as wishing him good-night". But man should believe in the concept of reciprocal relationship with nature. In such context, Joseph W. Meeker mentions: "Human behavior has generally been guided by presumed metaphysical principles which have neglected to recognise that man is a species of animal whose welfare depends upon successful integration with plants, animals and land that make up his environment"[23]. On the contrary, man's anthropocentric vision exploits every natural thing.

The exactitude of man's capacity and potentiality of exploiting nature becomes evident when he cuts down the trees and splits into pieces: "It was a cord of maple, cut and split / And piled – and measured, four by four by eight". Cutting down of trees in later period gave birth to "the Chipko Andolan, a movement of Himalayan peasants against the clear-cutting of forests by timber contractors"[24]. Moreover, it provides a clue to think of a forgotten remnant of earlier efforts as the speaker expresses: "No runner tracks in this year's snow looped near it. / And it was older sure than this year's cutting, / Or even last year's or the year's before". Such remnant reminds a claim of man's presence and mastery over that alien landscape. Man ruptures nature but nature exists ever. Man destroys; nature creates: "And the pile somewhat sunken. Clematis / Had wound strings round and round it like a bundle". Nature cares her creations as a woman does to her babies. When the speaker talks of a "fireplace" and "burning of decay", it enhances to the sense of man's comfort and luxury for getting warmth in winter. Only for such comfort and luxury does man carry an extraordinary power to turn "nature into denature". The terrible impulse born of the will to control over nature is a potential threat to environment.

Notes

1. James M. Cox, *Robert Frost: A Collection of Critical Essays*, Prentice-Hall, Inc. 1962, p.3.
2. John F. Lynen, "Frost as Modern Poet" in *Robert Frost: A Collection of Critical Essays*, edited by James M. Cox, Prentice-Hall, Inc. 1962. P.185.
3. Timothy Clark, in his book *The Cambridge Introduction* to *Literature and the Environment,* Cambridge University Press, 2014, p.118, discusses on Ecofeminism. He is a specialist in Romantic, Heideggerian and post-Heideggerian poetics and in environmental criticism.
4. Greg Garrard unfolds the position of women in his book, *Ecocriticism,* Routledge publication,2012, p.27. He is a senior lecturer in English literature at Bath Spa University, UK.
5. Todd A. Borlik, *Ecocriticism and Early Modern English Literature, Routledge*: Taylor & Francis. 2011. P.7.
6. Graham Huggan and Helen Tiffin, *Postcolonial Ecocriticism: Literature, Animals, Environment,* Routledge, First Indian Reprint,2015, p.185.
7. Timothy Clark, *The Cambridge Introduction* to *Literature and the Environment,* Pp.111-112.
8. Greg Garrard, *Ecocriticism,* Pp.27-28.
9. Richard Poirier, *Robert Frost: The Work of Knowing,* New York, Oxford University Press, 1977. P130.
10. David Mazel, "American Literary Environmentalism as Domestic Orientalism" in *The Ecocriticism Reader,* edited by Cheryll Glotfelty & Harold Fromm, The University of Georgia Press, 1996.p.140. David Mazel is a doctoral candidate in English at Louisiana State university.

11. William Howarth, "Some Principles of Ecocriticism" in *The Ecocriticism Reader,* edited by Cheryll Glotfelty & Harold Fromm, The University of Georgia Press, 1996.p.77. William Howarth is a Professor of English at Princeton university, where he teaches courses in environmental literature and history.

12. W. G. O'Donnell, "Robert Frost and New England: A Revaluation" in *Robert Frost: A Collection of Critical Essays*, edited by James M. Cox, Prentice-Hall, Inc. 1962.p.50.

13. Ramachandra Guha, *Environmentalism: A Global History, A* Penguin Random House India Pvt. Ltd. 2014.p.30

14. Sharon Doubiago 'Mama Coyote Talks to the Boys' in J. Plant (ed) *Healing the Wounds: The Promise of Ecofeminism*, London. 1989. P.41.

15. Pramod K. Nayar, *Contemporary Literary and Cultural Theory,* Pearson, 2015. P.205.

16. Greg Garrard, *Ecocriticism,* p29.

17. Parini, Jay. *Robert Frost, A Life*: Henry Holt and Company, 1999. P.56.

18. Todd A. Borlik, *Ecocriticism and Early Modern English Literature, Routledge*: Taylor & Francis. 2011. P.209.

19. Vera L. Norwood, "Heroines of Nature: Four Women Respond to the American Landscape" in *The Ecocriticism Reader,* edited by Cheryll Glotfelty & Harold Fromm, The University of Georgia Press, 1996.p.324. Norwood is a Professor of American Studies at the University of New Mexico.

20. Marion Montgomery, "Robert Frost and His Use of Barriers: Man vs Nature Toward God" in *Robert Frost: A Collection of Critical Essays*, edited by James M. Cox, Prentice-Hall, Inc. 1962, p.146.

21. Bonnie Roos and Alex Hunt give their views on natural systems and human systems in *The Cambridge Companion to Literature and the Environment*, edited by Louise Westling, Cambridge University Press, 2014. P.187.

22. Harold Fromm, *The Nature of Being Human: From Environmentalism to Consciousness,* The Johns Hopkins University Press, Baltimore,2009. P.47.

23. Joseph M. Meeker, "The Comic Mode" in *The Ecocriticism Reader,* edited by Cheryll Glotfelty & Harold Fromm, The University of Georgia Press, 1996.p.163. Joseph W. Meeker is a human ecologist with a Ph.D. in comparative literature, and master's and postdoctoral studies in wildlife ecology and comparative animal and human behavior.

24. Guha, Ramachandra. *Environmentalism: A Global History,*

CHAPTER 3

Mountain Interval (1916)

Frost's poetic language sketches rurality. Idyllic panorama idealises rural environment. From the perspective of environmental assessment, the pastoral descriptions in his poetry postulate the human psyche either in awe and modesty or in a desire for domination and exploitation. The majority of his poems allow the critics to apply the field's methodology for the assessment of an ethical co-existence between the biotic community and the abiotic world. As it is observed, in larger cases, man is the sole subject; the speaker and also the sovereign of natural phenomena. Attention may be concentrated on "The Road Not Taken", the first poem from the collection *Mountain Interval* (1916) that evokes a plethora of meanings and implications. Regarding such issue, Todd A. Borlik affirms in the discussion of Elizabethan verse: "poetry was valued for its ability to generate an impression of verbal order comparable to an organic order within the biophysical world"[1]. Besides, the poem to some extent is the product of a degenerate state of mind:

> Two roads diverged in a yellow wood,
> And sorry I could not travel both
> And be one traveler, long I stood
> And looked down one as far as I could
> To where it bent in the undergrowth;
> Then took the other, as just as fair,
> And having perhaps the better claim,
> Because it was grassy and wanted wear;
> Though as for that the passing there
> Had worn them really about the same,
> And both that morning equally lay
> In leaves no step had trodden black.
> Oh, I kept the first for another day!
> Yet knowing how way leads on to way,
> I doubted if I should ever come back.
> I shall be telling this with a sigh
> Somewhere ages and ages hence:
> Two roads diverged in a wood, and I –

> I took the one less traveled by,
> And that has made all the difference. (Norton, 1771)

The first line of the poem: "Two roads diverged in a yellow wood" creates environmental awareness of human-construct – "roads" – that stands as an obstacle on nature's autonomy. Such man-made activity disturbs flora and fauna inside the forest. The expression "yellow wood" arouses consciousness of the impact of seasons on earth. Obviously, in winter season, the green leaves of the tree turn into yellow and start falling from the branches. New leaves sprout up in spring. Seasons run in a cyclic way in nature; and hence, in the last line of the poem "Ode to the West Wind", Shelley exhorts, "If Winter comes, can Spring be far behind"? The Shelleyan version is important in order to understand nature's laws.

Upto the Elizabethan period, man had no dominance and supremacy over nature. In course of the development of science and technology, he thought himself to be semi-God and all powerful. From 19th century onwards, in order to fulfill his unlimited wants, he turns nature into "a grocery store of wastes". The over accumulating greedy mindset sometimes keeps humans in Hamletian dilemma. In this eclogue, the speaker confronts the physical facts of reality in a direct way for decision-taking as the diverged of two roads are there. The fact that he has to take one and leave the other pulls him into quandary. The statement of Frederick Turner may be mentioned, "Our bodies and brains are a result of evolution, which is a natural process so paradigmatic that it could almost be said to be synonymous with nature itself"[2]. The evolutionary attitude to achieve more and simultaneously the failure in it makes man to lament: "And sorry I could not travel both". His ability searches for extracting and expecting better from nature: "long I stood / And looked down one as far as I could / To where it bent in the undergrowth". Man's temperament is in the hunt for something new. The powerful visual imageries in "Two roads diverged in a yellow wood / …/ To where it bent in the undergrowth" communicate humans' appropriation of nature for their own interest and nature's silence against such privileged motif.

Man, the prime culprit of nature, always tries to remain in advantage position. In front of his purpose, the natural environment is of secondary importance for him. In his 'lifestyle', he exercises the freedom of choice and for his anthropocentric vision; the wood is simply an optical existence: "Then took the other, as just as fair, /

And having perhaps the better claim". The expressions – "as just as fair" and "the better claim" – need to be examined from the standpoints of environmental ethics. If such tendency for experimenting on nature continues, it will pervert the integrity, stability and sustainability of wilderness. Besides, the desirous and greedy mentality of the traveler is studied as he fumbles in decision and claims: "Because it was grassy and wanted wear". It becomes apparent that man's ambitious outlook to explore and conquer over nature is a threat to ecosystem. The version – "wanted wear" – leads to Adam Smith's concept: "Human wants are unlimited". The concept of "want" incorporates the mankind as a whole. Man sabotages the environment to satisfy his "wants" and keeps nature into "a discount store" to bargain in his desire of "supermarket". It is further suggested by the notion: "Yet knowing how way leads on way". Options are many. On the other hand, the lines – "And both that morning equally lay / In leaves no step had trodden black" – underpin the view that the idea of nature as a green and pleasant space will turn into a black and morbid place for the interference of human beings. The biocentric inspiration of "grassy" road or the road blanketed in leaves loses its significance in the intrusion of human-centred values.

Humans should understand the limits of their intrusion which nature can tolerate. But the traveler exclaims; "Oh, I kept the first for another day"! The choice of the man is not final as his inquisitiveness makes him indecisive. Here, the traveler repents on the choice he made and wistfully he sighs over the decision: "I shall be telling this with a sigh / Somewhere ages and ages hence". Man should understand the true consequences of his action, otherwise he will lament for generation after generation. The ecological view of the current period and the possible future needs redemption from human imposition on nature thereby restricting trials or choice. Nature needs to be free from experimentation.

Trees are related to religious scriptures. Horticulture is devotion. All prominent botanists make study on plants and take care of their survival. Their commitment should not be underestimated. They look after trees not for earning money but to create a clean environment for sustainable living. In nature's economy, the currency is not money, but life. In "Christmas Trees" the country man refuses the city man's valuation of his plantation of Christmas trees. The poem embodies the theme of consumerism and commercialism undergoing the concept of country versus city. The former brings up the trees but the city man thinks of making a profit. The tree-owner prefers to keep his plants and preserve the value of the botany.

Human-centred values replace nature-centred systems and sometimes nature-centred systems impede human-centred values. Man exploits environment but environment at times demands prioritisation. In "An Old Man's Winter Night", the Frostian old man experiences the inner psyche and the outer environment in a winter night. "The thin frost" on the windowpane reflected by the light of an oil lamp creates the image of "almost in separate stars". The outer sounds like "the roar of trees", "crack of branches" and the light of "late-rising" moon enter the inner space of the house but the inner noises are said to "scare" the outside world. The line – "A light he was to no one but himself" – communicates that he is the only one in touch with himself and his existence. Mention may be made of Joseph W. Meeker who states: "Life itself is the most important force there is: the proper study of mankind is survival"[3]. Towards the end of the poem, the speaker advocates winter darkness as a comfort:

> One aged man-one man-can't keep a house,
> A farm, a countryside, or if he can,
> It's thus he does it of a winter night. (Norton, 1772)

Besides, the expression "in clomping here" and "in clomping off" is "nothing so like beating on a box". It regenerates the image of the "treading-treading" of Emily Dickinson's "I Felt a Funeral in My Brain". However, an old man who lives alone and isolated feels the difference between man's apathy and nature's sympathy. One gets comfort from nature, not from self-centred mankind.

The ecological right of the non-humans requires a due share with the humans. Humans are not the sole creatures on earth. They should not destroy and shatter the stability of other creatures' life. Disturbance and displacement in the life of the non-humans are the factors to their survival crisis. In "The Exposed Nest", Frost's shows the sense of care and tender towards the displaced and troubled baby-birds:

> You were forever finding some new play.
> So when I saw you down on hands and knees
> In the meadow, busy with the new-cut hey,
> Trying, I thought, to set it up on end,
> I went to show you how to make it stay,
> If that was your idea, against the breeze,
> And, if you asked me, even help pretend

To make it root again and grow afresh.
But 'twas no make-believe with you day,
Nor was grass itself your real concern,
Though I found your hand full of wilted fern,
Steel-bright June-grass, and the blackening heads of clover.
'Twas a nest full of young birds on the ground
The cutter-bar had just gone champing over
(Miraculously without tasting flesh)
And left defenseless to the heat and light.
You wanted to restore them to their right
Of something interposed between their sight
And too much world at once-could means be found.
The way the nest-full every time we stirred
Stood up to us as to a mother-bird
Whose coming home has been too long deferred,
Made me ask would the mother-bird return
And care for them in such a change of scene
And might our meddling make her more afraid.
That was a thing we could not wait to learn.
We saw the risk we took in doing good,
But dared not spare to do the best we could
Though harm should come of it; so built the screen
You had begun, and gave them back their shade.
All this is to prove we cared. Why is there then
No more to tell? We turned to other things.
I haven't any memory-have you?-
Of ever coming to the place again
To see if the birds lived the first night through,
And so at last to learn to use their things. (CPoRF, 136-137)

A cumulative thrust of an impulse that stems from the very basic level within the persona and his child to restore the baby-birds in the nest unfolds Frost's biocentric vision. Destruction of bird's nest is anti-ecological. The course of time witnesses the extinction of birds. The disastrous action of machine damages the biosystems. The persona reminds the hot summer day when he and his child had sheltered "a nest of full young birds on the ground" against "the heat and light" of the summer sun. The grass-cutting machine that represents the modern technological advancement puts these baby-birds under threat: "The cutter-bar had just gone champing over / (Miraculously without tasting flesh) / And left defenseless to the heat and light". The concern of humans is not to lament over the devastation but the decision to save nature.

The speaker narrates the child's compassion towards the baby-birds: "You wanted to restore them to their right / Of something interposed between their sight / And too much world at once-could means be found". The child's wish to save the baby-birds is significant. The innocent child is not a butcher of the earth. In comparison to avian world, "Humans are in no danger of extinction, and their population would remain healthy and sustainable"[4]. The phrase, "too much world at once" demonstrates the birds' threatened existence. The persona questions himself whether "the mother-bird" would return to her flock and "care for them in such a change of scene". The parent persona's "meddling" with the nest might "make her more afraid". As it is observed in commonplace experiences that some mother birds abandon their offspring if their nests are spoiled by humans or other species of birds. The crucial mode for their existence turns to a problematic issue in biomes. That's why the extinction of birds disturbs the environmentalists.

Mankind has to learn from the child's resolution to help the birds for the sake of their survival. The child's innocence is unaware of the consequences for interference thereby the speaker states: "We saw the risk we took in doing good, / But dared not spare to do the best we could / Though harm should come of it". Human world needs to understand the situation. Regarding the circumstances, Joseph W. Meeker affirms: "Man is a species of animal whose welfare depends upon successful integration with the plants, animals, and land that make up his environment"[5]. The parent persona proceeds to build a shelter for the homeless birds: "so built the screen / You had begun, and gave them back their shade, / All this to prove we cared". It is their obligation for the birds' wellbeing. A feeling of complacency arouses in them as in "Tintern Abbey", William Wordsworth advises his sister, Dorothy: "Nature never did betray / The heart that loved her" (L.122-23). If such tendency of human beings had persisted, the earth could not have turned into 'a carbon sink' nor had dreadful viruses ruled over the world.

The natural spectacle for the climatic cycle thumps on "Hyla Brook". The onset of the peak summer's "heat" is the cause of Hyla Brook's disappearance. The speaker's intimacy with nature recognises the difference that the brook has "run out of song and speed". The post romantic thinking about nature queries that Hyla has "gone groping underground" and "the Hyla breed / That shouted in the mist a month ago" have disappeared. Leaves have blown into the streambed: "Weak foliage that is blown upon and bent / Even against the way its waters went. / Its bed is left a faded paper sheet / Of dead leaves stuck together by the heat". Such dry and void in nature wrought by the hot summer sun reminds the speaker about the old Hyla Brook. The Hyla breeds struggle in the whole scheme of existence. Lastly, the speaker concludes: "We love the things we love for what they are". Wordsworth searches for the same thing in the Lake District, Thomas Hardy looks for "the primitive, primal earth" in Dorset and D.H. Lawrence in the coal fields of the industrial Midlands.

The portrayal of bird is a recurrent image in Frost's poetry. The prominence of birds in Wordsworth's Cuckoo, Keats's Nightingale, Shelley's Skylark and Dickinson's Robin unfurls the human situation and their own existence. Most of the cases witness Frost's bird imageries representing changes in nature, sensitising in aestheticism or arresting his personal issue in the environment. The present poem, "The Oven Bird" focuses on a distorted biota similar to Edward Thomas's "March the Third". "The Oven Bird" became published in 1916 just after Frost's return from England at the outbreak of the World War-I:

> There is a singer everyone has heard,
> Loud, a mid-summer and a mid-wood bird,
> Who makes the solid tree trunks sound again.
> He says that leaves are old and that for flowers
> Mid-summer is to spring as one to ten.
> He says the early petal-fall is past
> When pear and cherry bloom went down in showers
> On sunny days a moment overcast;
> And comes that other fall we name the fall.
> He says the highway dust is over all.
> The bird would cease and be as other birds
> But that he knows in singing not to sing.
> The question that he frames in all but words
> Is that to make of a diminished thing. (Norton, 1772)

The bird is personified communicating the passage of time as one season swaps another, spring moves into summer. It is significant to note that "There is a singer everyone has heard, / Loud, a mid-summer and a mid-wood bird" echoes with Thoreau's *Walden*: 'the oven-birds note is loud and unmistakable, making the hollow woods ring'. From ecological perspectives, the expressions – "we name the fall", "the highway dust is over all", "in singing not to sing" and "a diminished thing"-carry on environmental deterioration. It reinforces the concept – "the solid tree trunks sound" – justifying the meaning that the song is more to the sphere than meeting the ear. During the war period, there was the rapacious industrialism and aggressive commercialism thereby causing "the highway dust… over all". The upshot of industrial discharge and vehicular emission is biocide, "a diminished thing".

Nature opens adaptive strategies but humans choose in order of preferences. In such strategies, one is aesthetic construct that provides different tastes of recreation for nature enthusiasts. Frost creates this sort of enthusiasm preference in "Birches". In the first lines, the persona associates a real scene with aesthetic stance:

> When I see birches bend to left and right
> Across the lines of straighter darker trees,
> I like to think some boy's been swinging them.
> But swinging doesn't bend them down to stay
> As ice storms do. Often you must have seen them
> Loaded with ice a sunny winter morning
> After a rain. They click upon themselves
> As the breeze rises, and turn many-colored
> As the stir cracks and crazes their enamel. (Oliver, 401)

The persona unfolds the enchanting account that seems the similar loom in Wordsworth's "Daffodils": "A host, of golden daffodils. / Beside the lake, beneath the trees / fluttering and dancing in the breeze" (L.4-6). Like "golden daffodils", these enameled trees appear as crafted and ornamental as artistic glass sculpture: "Soon the sun's warmth makes them shed crystal shells / Shattering and avalanching on the snow-crust – / Such heaps of broken glass to sweep away / You'd think the inner dome of heaven had fallen" (L.10-13). The persona's biocentric vision expresses the presence of heaven on earth. Such pastoral aesthetic interplays between the ideal schema and the reality of extracting resource from nature. In such context, Todd A. Borlik states: "But if ecocriticism has inherited the pastoral's aesthetics and ethics, it need not inherit its foibles. We must keep in the mind the dialectic between the world as it is and the world as we might wish it to be-that is, mediate between a georgic view of the world in which human survival is predicated upon extracting energy from the earth and the pastoral's invitation to gently co-exist with (and thus conserve) a pristine, bountiful blue-green planet"[6]. The description in the next lines attests to pastoral invitation through a visual image:

> You may see their trunks arching in the woods
> Years afterwards, trailing their leaves on the ground
> Like girls on hands and knees that throw their hair

> Before them over their heads to dry in the sun.
> But I was going to say when Truth broke in
> With all her matter-of fact about the ice storm
> I should prefer to have some boy bend them
> As he went out and in to fetch the cows – (L.17-24)

From ecocritics' view, women are 'closer to nature' than men through their biological process of motherhood and nurturing as "trees trailing their leaves" "Like girls on hands and knees that throw their hair". The visual imagery of the girl drying her head "in the sun" is important in the sense that threes follow the same way "after a rain". The persona gives emphasis on "Truth" with a capital "T". By personifying truth, the persona returns to his first image of the boy that conveys a figurative value. It is in the sense that the boy is the swinger of birches who knows his power and also the strength of the tree. Before the supremacy of power, the strength of birches bends down. The power of the boy makes him free. He imposes such freedom upon the birches and feels pleasure and thus acclaims: "Earth's the right place for love: / I don't know where it's likely to go better, / I'd like to go by climbing a birch tree" (L. 54-56). Man feels pleasure for exploiting his free will on earth.

At other spectrum of the analysis, "Earth's the right place for love: / I don't know where it's likely to go better" strikes the same note in the Duke in William Shakespeare's *As You Like It.* To enhance the confidence in his fellow exiles in Arden, the Duke asserts: "Hath not old custom made this life more sweet / Than that of painted pomp" (2.1. 2-3)? Here "old custom" refers to pastoral life that feeds support at the adversities. Such ecological anxiety creates an intimate acquaintance with earth that cherishes love for it. But today the ecological anxiety is termed into greedy economy.

Man's understanding of the natural world is necessary. But starting from agricultural background to industrial capitalism, pollution coils up and damages the biosphere. Rachel Carson in *The Silent Spring* stresses out environmental pollution by toxins in agriculture dominated by the indiscriminate use of pesticides and chemical fertilizers. To meet the demands of corporate capitalism, such agri-business is a potential threat to the living-process. Contrary to this, the Frostian man prefers to organic compost. "Putting in the Seed" reveals the persona's mindset to fertilise the soil by burying down the "soft petals fallen from the apple tree":

> You come to fetch me from my work tonight
> When supper's on the table, and we'll see
> If I can leave off burying the white
> (Soft petals, yes, but not so barren quite,
> Mingled with these, smooth bean and wrinkled pea;)
> And go along with you were you lose sight
> Of what you came for and become like me,
> Slave to a springtime passion for the earth.
> How Love burns through the Putting in the Seed
> On through the watching for that early birth
> When, just as the soil tarnishes with weed,
> The sturdy seedling with arched body comes
> Shouldering its way and shedding the earth crumbs. (CPoRF, 155)

The persona asks his wife to call him after the supper is ready as he works to plant the seed. In reply to wife's question about the credibility of the soft petals to fertilise the soil, he asserts that these petals will nourish along with other ingredients in the soil. The farmer expects from his wife to become like him: "you came for and become like me" in the act of preparing the soil for sowing. She should develop the tendency to be a "Slave to a springtime passion for the earth" thereby fostering such passion "Love burns through the Putting in the Seed". It needs to umderstand the birth of plants or the progeny within the seeds. The little tender sprouts from the soil, "The sturdy seedling with arched body comes / Shouldering its way and shedding the earth crumbs" – is a great reward to them. Without endosperm in plants, there can be no life on earth because plants permit life. This action of the Frostian man enriches and nourishes his biocentric vision. Gandhiji was also in favour of organic manure as stated by Ramachandra Guha: "Gandhi also opposed the industrialisation of agriculture, that is, the replacement of the plow by the tractor and the spread of chemical fertilizers, measures which undeniably increased productivity in the short term but which created unemployment and depleted the soil of its nutrients. He warned that 'trading in soil fertility for the sake of quick returns would prove to be a disastrous, short-sighted policy'. He promoted instead the use of organic manure, which enriched the soil, improved village hygiene through the effective disposal of waste, and saved valuable foreign exchange"[7].

Frost outlines the wonderful intricacy of natural systems in "Range-Finding". The poem discusses the fabric of interrelationships in nature that unfurls the cobweb of a spider on a flower and a butterfly becomes a victim to it. Simultaneously, a bird does not mind and maintains to go on about her life:

> The battle rent a cobweb diamond-strung
> And cut a flower beside a ground bird's nest
> Before it stained a single human breast.
> The stricken flower bent double and so hung.
> And still the bird revisited her young.
> A butterfly its fall had dispossessed
> A moment sought in air his flower of rest,
> Then lightly stooped to it and fluttering clung.
> On the bare upland pasture there had spread
> O'ernight 'twixt mullein stalks a wheel of thread
> And straining cables wet with silver dew.
> A sudden passing bullet shook it dry.
> The indwelling spider ran to greet the fly,
> But finding nothing, sullenly withdrew. (CPoRF, 159)

The first line of the poem is a mute response to the war. The word "diamond-strung" seems to speak of a diamond necklace but functions as a trap set. The word "battle" obviously hints about the World War-I that gets justification from "passing bullet". The upshot of war makes impact on nature and also on culture as its only aim is death and destruction. To realise the annihilation of war, the talk between an Indian soldier from Punjab and a British soldier from Midland in the last four lines of T.S. Eliot's poem, "To the Indians Who Died in Africa" can be taken into consideration: "Of action with a common purpose, action / None the less fruitful if neither you nor we / Know, until the judgement after death, / What is the fruit of action"? The line – "Before it stained a single human breast"- draws the image of a wounded, bleeding soldier in the battle field. The non-humans cannot understand the hawkish temperament of humans but struggle to survive: "The indwelling spider ran to greet the fly, / But finding nothing, sullenly withdrew". Nature suffers when war crops up.

War deteriorates life-sustaining air. The outcome of war-related pollutants dangerously affects both biotic and abiotic. Humans' health and mood depend upon the atmospheric condition. The terrific horror of the World War-I instigates three poems: "The Bonfire", "Not to Keep", and "A Soldier" with the mild impact in "Range-Finding". "The Bonfire" emphasizes on awful lessons learned by few as the speaker mentions towards the end of the poem: "*War is for everyone, for children too*". Regarding this, Vivian C. Hopkins quotes John W. Haines in the article, "Robert Frost: Out Far and In Deep":

> You'd think
> Europe might sink, and the wave of her
> Sinking sweep
> And spend itself on our shore and we should
> Not weep,
> Our cities would not even turn in their sleep.*
> In a new and terrifying way this war brought home to Frost the sympathy as well as the antagonism toward England.[8]

The potential dreadfulness of war is the root cause of environmental disaster that brings home all the poison threatening to life and livelihoods of the biota. The emphasis on man's anthropocentric vision is the main source of ecological crisis. It seems pertinent to judge "The Bonfire" from this angle. When man launches war forces in nature, the outcome turns to biocide:

> 'Oh, let's go up the hill and scare ourselves,
> As reckless as the best of them tonight'
> By setting fire to all the brush we piled
> With pitchy hands to wait for rain or snow.
> Oh, let's not wait for rain to make it safe. (CPoRF, 163)

The young father proposes his children to "go up the hill" to be saved from the forces of wildfire. He tries to alarm people to "rouse them all". He creates awareness in the sense that "By letting wildfire loose", it will threaten and endanger themselves. When the children query, "'If it scares you, what will it do to us?'", he replies, "Scare you". The world has seen the actual horror in Hiroshima and Nagasaki. This is the lesson for the mankind to be cautious of its explosion. The father questions his children, "What would you say to war if it should"? Then he contradicts their answer, "Oh, but war's not for children-it's for men". Towards the end of the poem, he responds them, "*War is for everyone, for children too*". They study the message of indiscriminate danger and holocaust to all on account of war. Thus, "The best way is to come up hill with me". Perhaps, "...the web of life could very easily become the web of death"[9]. The ruinous consequences of war are beyond replenishment. But man's ego does not recognise this.

In ancient era man was considering himself as a part of nature but today he is the exploiter of nature. His concern was to think about nature. The psychic revolution in changing culture made man to foster a step-motherly attitude towards nature. But the Frostian man keeps up the past tendency even in agriculture. In "A Girl's Garden" the speaker informs the readers about his daughter's interest "To give her a garden plot". He hands over "an idle bit" of land to the girl and asks her to begin gardening: "That ought to make you / An ideal one-girl farm". Subsistence gardening is presupposition and also eco-friendly.

The Frostian man offers an important message of using dung manure to fertile the land instead of chemical fertilizers and pesticide application. Chemical fertilizers and pesticides are anti-ecological. Dung manure is necessary for land and simultaneously, it encourages taking care of cattle. The passerby may not like the smell, that's why the girl "always ran away and left; / "the dung in the wheelbarrow / Along a stretch of road". Besides, she digs the plot by hand and makes ready the soil, in place of plowing like the hermit in Leo Tolstoy's "Three Questions". Now power-tillers and mega-machines attack the land violently that unfurls brutality towards nature. The peasants use modern technology in a desire for harvesting more crops and more returns.

The girl plants "potatoes, radishes, lettuce, peas / Tomatoes, beets, beans, pumpkins, corn, / And even fruit trees". The interest in the girl for gardening is her aesthetic engagement to nature. The result of her planting a lot of vegetables and fruits accredits her delight in horticulture. In this matter, Todd A. Borlik writes: "Even when setting aside a portion of it for "natural wildness", Bacon speaks of gardening as a "royal ordering" of nature. If Royalist gardens and their commanding "prospects" encouraged proprietary attitudes, Elizabethans knew of Republican gardens as well that required the "sophisticated involvement of a moving spectator". The gardens of Adonis, Kalander's House, and Twickenham all adhere more closely to the Republican-style gardens of Venice, which celebrated harmony, proportion, and a collaboration between art and nature, that is, between the whims of the gardener and the plant-life the soil will support"[10].

Here, the Frostian man acknowledges the girl's love and care for farming and also for the fertility of the land through the natural way. Agrarian persistence carries on the intrinsic value in Frost's poetry. Readers find Frost's commitment to sustainable agriculture and eco-friendly use of land.

Frost's artistic skill in ecological sphere designs seasonal changes and phenomena. The seasonal migratory birds, flora and insects perform the necessary biological arrangements in his poetry. In "The Last Word of a Bluebird", the speaker puts in the discussion of a crow that lets a young girl, named Lesley to know about bluebird's departure: "To tell Lesley (will you?) / That her little Bluebird / Wanted me to bring word". It draws an attentiveness in which plants, animals and humans are related to each other. In this symbiosis, they are approachable to each other that any disturbance in one inexorably disturbs the others. The bluebird must leave the place on account of the cold, north wind and there will be "ice on the trough". The ecological consciousness of the persona awakens the coming of winter:

> That the north wind last night
> That made the stars bright
> And made ice on the trough
> And almost made him cough
> His tail feathers off.
> He just had to fly!
> But he sent her Good-by,
> And said to be good
> And wear her red hood,
> And look for skunk tracks
> In the snow with an ax –
> And do everything!
> And perhaps in the spring
> He would come back and sing. (CPoRF, 170)

Like other species of migratory birds, he would fly from "the north" to the south during winter. He sends messages to Lesley to be "good", safe and nice. Here, the speaker reveals the adaptive strategies and tries to convince that the natural and the human systems are complimentary to each other. Lastly, the bluebird states that he might come back when the weather is warm and comfortable.

Life is dangerous for any creature in an adverse ecosystem. Seasons and weather play a certain role on humans and non-humans both physically and psychologically. The effects of climatic condition influence health, moods and life itself. Therefore, Lawrence Buell asserts: "For seasons, next to the alternations of day and night, are the environmental cycle most perceptible in everyday life"[11]. The bluebird would fly to the south to avoid cold and snow. Through this, the persona claims how the seasonal curve varies greatly by regions.

Frost rarely favours man's relationship with machines. Man creates machines but machines kill man. The rickety buzz – saw in "Out, Out-" leaps from its carriage and severs the hand of an innocently helping boy like the mill-worker in "The Self-Seeker" losing his feet in an industrial accident. The buzz-saw aggressively snarls and rattles as it carries out its work. The noise and dust emitted by the machine pollute the atmosphere when it chops the wood:

> The buzz saw snarled and rattled in the yard
> And made dust and dropped stove-length sticks of wood,
> ....
> That a boy counts so much when saved from work.
> His sister stood beside them in her apron
> To tell them 'Supper'. At the word, the saw,
> As if to prove saws knew what supper meant,
> Leaped out at the boy's hand, or seemed to leap –
> He must have given the hand. However it was,
> Neither refused the meeting. But the hand! (Norton, 1774)

Too much blood spills from him and ultimately, he dies. Humans feel proud for the great status of machines in the era of the scientific and technological advancement. In his article "Historical Roots of Our Ecologic Crisis", Lynn White, Jr. writes: "Since both our technological and our scientific movements got their start, acquired their character, and achieved world dominance in the Middle Ages, it would seem that we cannot understand their nature or their present impact upon ecology without examining fundamental medieval assumptions and developments"[12]. Before the Industrial Revolution, there was a negative connotation to machines. In a sense, Frost's both poems, "Out, Out" and "The Self-Seeker" are much profounder than mere scene in relation to man, machine and ecology.

Tree bleeds on account of trimming and chopping or logging. The outcome of such injury oozes sap, resin or other fluids from beneath the bark of trees. The maximum sources of such injuries are deliberately man-made and rare is of automatic and natural. Humans exploit trees mostly for commercial and resource-extractive purposes. "The Gum-Gatherer" unfolds such issue before the readers. The persona, returning home from "early-morning stride" in "mountain land" is overtaken by "A man with a swinging bag for load / And half the bag wound round his hand". These two people go along together for five miles. "He told me a little about himself". Then the persona comes to know that the gum-gatherer lives in a "shack": "There he had built his stolen shack. / It had to be a stolen shack / Because of the fears of fire and loss / That trouble the sleep of lumber folk: / Visions of half the world burned black / And the sun shrunken yellow in smoke."

Some of the descriptions portray a sketch of rural poverty. The gum-gatherer's shack is illegally erected on timberland. He conveys the persona about the poor farmers who bring the sparest of cash crops like "berries" or "a basket of eggs" to market. But he lives "higher up" in the mountains where the brooks grind granite into moss and the spruce gum brings him little return as it is in slight demand. The ecological problem is entangled into 'Feeding People versus Saving Nature'. In fact, "such conflicts of interest have attracted the attention of both postcolonial and environmentalist critics, who are alert to the dilemmas involved in conserving endangered ecosystems and animals when the livelihoods of local (subaltern) peoples are simultaneously put at risk"[13]. The gum-gatherer is a nomadic who struggles to survive and sets his "breast to the bark of trees" and reaches "up with a little knife, / To loose the resin and take it down". On the other side, trees are exploited, threatened and concurrently their sustainability is endangered.

The breathless imposition of science and scientific devices on earth to make life easy and comfort has been modern man's mindset. The concern for preservation and protection of the natural environment rarely comes to his self-centred attitude. The outcome of this relationship between man and nature is considered as the exploiter and the exploited. Such issue is observed in "The Line-Gang". The loss and damage caused to nature by humans is beyond limit: "Here come the line-gang pioneering by. / They throw a forest down less cut than broken. / They plant dead trees for living, and the dead / They string together with a living thread." The destruction of forest "less cut than broken" by "the line-gang" for setting up the telephone and telegraph poles is ecocide. The line – "They plant dead trees for living, and the dead" – refers to poles that distort and destroy the splendor of wilderness. Technological progress hardly tends to preserve the integrity, stability, sustainability and beauty of the biotic community.

The persona claims how the line-gang is noisy as it works contrasted with "hush" or quietness. The line-gang "shouts" and "laugh[s]" that creates nuisance in the prevalence of peace. The emphasis on urbanisation turns 'Nature into Denature': "An oath of towns that set the wild at naught / They bring the telephone and telegraph". The man-made towns gobble up harmony and serenity present in nature. If such tendency is nourished, the idea of nature as a green and pleasant space will turn into a morbid place opposing the existence of life. "The felling of forests destroys soils and biodiversity"[14]. Humans should be aware of the extinction of plant species. In other words, man lives in nature, 'nature is his body' and hence, he has to maintain a proper affiliation with the planet.

Frost's "The Vanishing Red" talks of racism. The White Miller's hegemony breeds hatred and jealousy over Red John's "poking about the mill". The binaries between the Whites and the Non-Whites, the Americans and the Red-Indians, the exploiter and the exploited create ecological problems. The superiority of the Whites is imposed in direct proportion to the Non-Whites' inferiority. The absolute prioritisation of one's own race puts difficulties for others, even ends in murder: "Some guttural exclamation of surprise / The Red Man gave in poking about the mill /Over the great big thumping shuffling millstone /Disgusted the Miller physically as coming / From one who had no right to be heard from."

The desire to exterminate Red Indians is the theme of the poem. John – the Red – falls into the jaws of exploitation of the White capitalist government represented by the Miller who is the worst culprit and the real beast committing murder. However, it discusses the extinction of a race as "He is said to have been the last Red Man / In Acton. And the Miller is said to have laughed-/ If you like to call such a sound a laugh". The persona unfolds the White supremacy over the Red-Indians and also the other Non-Whites who were 'targets of attack' during the colonial time. Such sociological issue is 'environmental racism'. It needs to acknowledge the definition of Dean Curtin on ecoracism: "as the connection, in theory and practice, of race and environment so that the oppression of one is connected to, and supported by, the oppression of the other"[15]. Sociologically, John's "guttural exclamation of surprise" about "the wheel-pit" disgusts the Miller and out of instinct he thinks that John is "one who had no right to be heard from". His reaction culminates in "You want to see the wheel-pit?" and "showed John the wheel-pit all right". The same prospect is found in Edgar Allan Poe's "The Cask of Amontillado". The murder of John is a socioecological issue as Greg Garrard states: "systems of domination or exploitation of humans by other humans"[16]. Besides, ecological problems may not be clearly divorced from the issues categorising as social problems like racial discrimination.

Natural ecosystem accommodates the life of all, starting from flora and fauna to humans. Each species behaves on their own inimitable way. Among these, trees and humans are complementary to each other in so far as breathing system is concerned. Corollary to this, the perception of trees keeps the harmony between humanity and nature. It can be affirmed that humans neither physically nor psychologically be healthy without trees. The ecological balance is necessary for congenial and conducive existence. In this parameter, man also learns something from trees. Without trees, there can be no other alternatives on earth to sustain life. Frost's last poem of this volume, "The Sound of Trees" exposes wonder about trees:

> I wonder about the trees.
> Why do we wish to bear
> Forever the noise of these
> More than another noise
> So close to our dwelling place?
> We suffer them by the day
> Till we lose all measure of pace,
> And fixity in our joys,
> And acquire a listening air.
> They are that that talks of going
> But never gets away;
> And that talks no less for knowing,
> As it grows wiser and older,
> That now it means to stay. (CPoRF, 195)

Trees produce constant "noise" which is a sort of symphony for the environmentalist but for the persona, it is an acceptance of "knowing" something. The persona thinks such noise is about going away but result ends up staying. They "stay" because of their deep roots. Their talks – "As it grows wiser and louder"-make impact upon people and hence, the persona begins to assume tree-like qualities as he thinks the possibility of going away. Like "Birches", the blowing of wind compels the trees to sway from side to side and rustles their leaves to make the "sound of trees". The ecological bend of mind only can understand this sound. 'Nature is silent in our culture' as exploitation by humans goes on. But it is not so. Regarding this, in his article "Nature and Silence", Christopher Manes writes: "…but also animals, plants, and even "inert" entities such as stones and rivers are perceived as being articulate and at times intelligible subjects, able to communicate and interact with humans for good or ill"[17]. Hence, man has to rethink and refeel nature as alive in order to have a sustainable living. His welfare completely depends upon the integration with plants, animals, and the land of the natural environment.

Notes

* John W. Haines, *The Gloucester Journal*, February2, 1935, reprinted in Richard Thornton, ed, *Recognition of Robert Frost, Twenty-Fifth Anniversary* (New York, 1937), pp. 89-97.

1. Todd A. Borlik, *Ecocriticism and Early Modern English Literature,* Routledge: Taylor & Francis. 2011. p.18.
2. Frederick Turner, "Cultivating the American Garden" in *The Ecocriticism Reader,* edited by Cheryll Glotfelty & Harold Fromm, The University of Georgia Press, 1996.p.42.
3. Joseph W. Meeker, "The Comic Mode" in *The Ecocriticism Reader,* edited by Cheryll Glotfelty & Harold Fromm, The University of Georgia Press, 1996.p.167. Joseph W. Meeker is a human ecologist with a Ph.D. in comparative literature, and master's and postdoctoral studies in wildlife ecology and comparative animal and human behavior.
4. Timothy Clark, *The Cambridge Introduction* to *Literature and the Environment,* Cambridge University Press, 2014, p.181. He is a specialist in Romantic, Heideggerian and post-Heideggerian poetics and in environmental criticism.
5. Joseph W. Meeker, "The Comic Mode" in *The Ecocriticism Reader,* edited by Cheryll Glotfelty & Harold Fromm, The University of Georgia Press, 1996. p.162.
6. Todd A. Borlik, *Ecocriticism and Early Modern English Literature, Routledge*: Taylor & Francis. 2011. p.209.
7. Ramachandra Guha, *Environmentalism: A Global History, A* Penguin Random House India Pvt. Ltd. 2014. p.31.
8. Vivian C. Hopkins, Robert Frost: Out Far and In Deep" in *Interpretations: Essays on American Literature*, edited by R.K. Gupta, American Studies Research Centre, Hyderabad. 1976. p.144.
9. Ramachandra Guha, *Environmentalism: A Global History, A* Penguin Random House India Pvt. Ltd. 2014. p.97.
10. Todd A. Borlik, *Ecocriticism and Early Modern English Literature, Routledge*: Taylor & Francis. 2011. p.19.
11. Lawrence Buell, *The Environmental Imagination: Thoreau, Nature Writing, and the Formation of American Culture,* The Belknap Press of Harvard university Press, 1995. p.220. Buell is a Professor of English at Harvard University.
12. Lynn White, Jr. in his article "The Historical Roots of Our Ecologic Crisis" mentions the activities of humans in their ecology, published in *The Ecocriticism Reader* by Glotfelty & Fromm, The University of Georgia Press, 1996, p.8.
13. Graham Huggan and Helen Tiffin, *Postcolonial Ecocriticism: Literature, Animals, Environment,* Routledge, First Indian Reprint, 2015, p.185.
14. Ramachandra Guha, *Environmentalism: A Global History, A* Penguin Random House India Pvt. Ltd. 2014. p.153.

15. Deane Curtin. *Environmental Ethics for a Postcolonial World*, Lanham, MD; Rowman & Littlefield. 2005. p.145.
16. Greg Garrard, *Ecocriticism,* Routledge publication,2012, p.31. He is a senior lecturer in English literature at Bath Spa University, UK.
17. Christopher Manes, "Nature and Silence" in *The Ecocriticism Reader,* edited by Cheryll Glotfelty & Harold Fromm, The University of Georgia Press, 1996. p.15. Manes is an author, attorney, and Ph.D. candidate in Medieval Literature at the University of Oregon.

CHAPTER 4

New Hampshire (1923)

Environmental threats generate from the acceleration of rapacious commercialism and aggressive capitalism. Hunger for capitalistic-gain and forceful drive for its fulfilment sabotages the ecosystem. Frost studies this type of 'greedy economy' through the observation of local phenomena, position of landscape, association of local to transnational forms of inhabitation and spectacular need of life-style. The first poem of this volume, "New Hampshire" is a long narrative one conversing with a lot of people about the city of New Hampshire. None of these people does speak in favor of the city. In a mild and gentle social satire, the speaker unfolds Americans' dream for big business, commercialism and materialism. About himself, Frost says:

> I'm what is called a sensibilitist,
> Or otherwise an environmentalist.
> I refuse to adapt myself a mite. (CPoRF, 206)

Frost's artistic skill makes a reflection of his mind to place him as an environmentalist. The concept of "selling" or "having anything to sell" is a "disgrace". Besides, the conflict arises to be a "prude" or "puke". If he becomes a "prude", it will degrade his love for nature. Being "puke", it will signify his carelessness about anything except his business. Hence, he is an environmentalist and does not prefer to do anything to harm nature:

> 'Come, but this isn't choosing-puke or prude?'
> Well, if I have to choose one or the other,
> I choose to be a plain New Hampshire farmer
> ....
> It's restful just to think about New Hampshire. (CPoRF, 211-12)

The poem floods with geographical entities, space, life-style of the people from different states and their commercial frame of mind. The Frostian man attaches due importance to places, persons and the happenings in their mindset. In the first stanza, he relates his meeting with "a lady from the South who said /…/ 'None of my family ever worked or hard / A thing to sell"'. It demonstrates her style of living. After this, he faces "a traveler from Arkansas / Who boasted of his state as beautiful / For diamonds and apples. / Diamonds / And apples in commercial quantities?" This tendency reflects commercialism which otherwise devalues nature. Then, the persona meets "a Californian who would / Talk California-a state so blessed, / […] / That's what comes / Of being in the market with a climate". However, someone from Massachusetts satirically opines New Hampshire for its "lofty" inhabitants. Contrasted with the opinion, the persona asserts if choice arises to 'elevate the height of either person of New Hampshire or its mountains', he would prefer to the latter one. This sort of mentality attaches due importance to his love for nature and its magnanimity. Here, the place-value in cultural assumptions interacts with the changing environment. That's why Vera L. Norwood states: "Nature and culture are interactive processes: human culture is affected by the landscape as well as effecting change on it"[1]. The growth of civilisation in unjustified way creates environmental crisis as is observed between the old and New Hampshire.

The poem "The Census-Taker" talks of wasted wildness. The disfigurement in nature displays a desert landscape only with a "black-paper-covered house / Of one room and one window and one door". The speaker's use of "errand" at the beginning of the poem conveys a lot in that seasonless wasteland as "every tree" has been leafless. It poses difficulty for a passerby to identify the seasons. Felling of trees in large number in that landscape is understood "With the pitch-blackened stub of an ax-handle / I picked up off the straw-dust covered floor". The logging roads and railway beds are still visible in the sense that the logs were being transported. Possibly, roads were mechanically built to facilitate the management and harvesting of timber. That's why "every tree up stood a rotting trunk".

> I came an errand one cloud-blowing evening
> To a slab-built, black-paper-covered house
> Of one room and one window and one door,
> The only dwelling in a waste cut over
> A hundred square miles round it in the mountains:
> And that not dwelt in now by men or women.
> ………………………………………………..
> I found no people that dared show themselves,

None not in hiding from the outward eye.
The time was autumn, but how anyone
Could tell the time of year when every tree
That could have dropped a leaf was down itself
And nothing but the stump of it was left
Now bringing out its rings in sugar of pitch;
And every tree up stood a rotting trunk
Without a single leaf to spend on autumn,
Or branch to whistle after what was spent. (CPoRF, 216)

The area has been deforested for "miles" and "every tree" gone, only "stump" remains. Besides, farmers have left the region: "I came as census-taker to the waste / To count the people in it and found none, / None in the hundred miles, none in the house". No habitation, no vegetation, nothing is in that abandoned landscape. The census-taker goes on saying: "Where I came last with some hope, but not too much / After hours' overlooking from the cliffs / An emptiness flayed to the very stone". It is difficult to survive in an adverse ecosystem. Man is responsible for creating this sort of adverse situation. To sustain life and the human community, the preservation of the natural world is necessary.

The census-taker wonders "what to do that could be done – / About the house – about the people not there". Perhaps, these people were the nomads in search of economy. In relation to such type of living in nature, William Howarth discusses Marxist theory: "In Marxist readings, economics determines social history; hence, capitalism becomes the source for all conflict, oppression, and environmental abuse (Crosby). Such views ignore many inconvenient facts: that disturbance is commonplace in nature; that aborigines and socialists often commit ecocide"[2]. In the end of the poem, the census-taker concludes, "Where they grow fewer and fewer every year / Is extreme where they shrink to none at all. / It must be I want life to go on living". The greedy economy decimates nature and both biotic and abiotic face its effect. But the speaker keeps an innate desire to see the survival of people.

In "The Star-splitter", the readers observe a small farming town where McLaughlin, a reluctant and struggling farmer, burns his house down for the "insurance" money. Burning the house is ecocide. The conflict between survival struggle and for buying a telescope "To satisfy a life-long curiosity / About our place among the infinities" creates a compelling story. Besides, the persona describes

McLaughlin's difficulties with farming. Problem arises in between life and livelihood.

In "Maple" a father likes to keep the name of his daughter as Maple. Usually, a maple tree in autumn extends a beautiful birth of colors. Such miracle of beauty recurs every year before the dying of the leaves. For a sustainable development, human identification with the tree needs a wider awareness. However, trees have long been associated with human life and considered sacred by ancient cultures. In this poem, a mother expires in childbirth and suggests her husband to name the infant 'Maple'. When the child asks her father about the meaning of her name, the father replies, "Be a good girl-be like a maple tree". On account of Maple's life span and rebirth through the seasons, the rebirth of mother through the child is same in the cycle of life. Mention may be made of the view of ecocritic Lawrence Buell who asserts: "The nonhuman environment is present not merely as a framing device but as a presence that begins to suggest that human history is implicated in natural history"[3]. It is obvious that human mind confronts an external reality of physical phenomena. Naming the name of someone with the botanical world is nothing new, rather it accords the human world with the physical one to integrate the relationship. Lastly, the persona concludes, "I should say, / As leaving more to nature and happy chance". It is a type of reciprocal relationship that sees natural selection being influenced by social and psychological issues. Really, there is crystallisation of thoughts in Frost's poetry.

The muscular assertiveness of the will power engrosses the speaker in wood chopping in the poem "The Ax-Helve". It presents a first-person account of a short-tempered, self-styled "Yankee" meeting with a country neighbor named Baptiste. Initially, the speaker ridicules Baptiste's broken style of speech, calling it "French-American" and disdainfully remarks on his French manners. Baptiste enters the speaker's yard uninvited, unnoticed and also takes away quickly workman's ax. Such type of trespass is illegal and may bring destruction and loss. It could be colonisation and exploitation. Out of the chaotic confusion and disorder in daily chore of life, there is the necessity of stability. It is possible if life does not tune with a sense of surrender to the material.

Experience may seem an essential part of life what humans recollect as memory in their lifetime. In "Wild Grapes", the woman restates the experience of her youth how her brother led her to a birch tree that was heavy with bunches of grapes. She narrates her story that being a girl "gathered from the birch", "grew to be a little boyish girl" who followed her brother about. "But that beginning was wiped out in fear" the day she did swing on birches as usually boys do, underpins her both masculine and feminine traits. Previously, as it has been discussed in "Birches" in the volume, *Mountain Interval*, the boy climbs the branches of the birch tree until he weighs them down to meet the earth and announces that "Earth's the right place for love" because he does not "know where it's likely to go better". Contrary to this, man exploits the earth for his vested interest.

The boy throws down grapes from the tree at his sister and she eats them. When the boy lowers the branches, he asks her to take hold of the tree with her full strength. She holds the tree but the tree takes hold of her and lifts her into the air. She swings like a fish on a fishpole:

> I said I had the tree. It wasn't true.
> The opposite was true. The tree had me.
> The minute it was left with me alone
> It caught me up as if I were the fish
> And it the fishpole. So I was translated
> To loud cries from my brother of 'Let go!
> Don't you know anything, you girl? Let go!' (CPoRF,241)

The boy shouts for her to let go but she holds on tight. Here, the evolutionary process of womanhood is observed as the mothers "Hung babies out on branches by the hands / To dry or wash or tan". The ecofeministic mindset is understood through such evolutionary traits as she inherits her grip from her femaleness, from mothering and raising babies in the "wildest" of circumstances. In the end of the poem, the speaker concludes:

> I had not learned to let go with the hands,
> As still I have not learned to with heart,
> And have no wish to with the heart-nor need,
> That I can see. The mind – is not the heart.
> I may yet live, as I know others live,
> To wish in vain to let go with the mind-
> Of cares, at night, to sleep; but nothing tells me
> That I need learn to let go with the heart. (CPoRF, 243)

The love of nature faces the battle between mind and heart. In contrast to it, man does not realise that 'nature can never be tamed' or bent to man's own will.

The poem "Two Witches" provides a sharp critique of ecofeminism. As has been highlighted earlier in "A Servant to Servants", in "Two Witches: The Witch of Coos" the readers will meet a woman who is a figure of insane, frustrated and explicit sexuality. There is deprivation of emotional fulfillments in her. During the World-War periods, three things were noticed principally like feminism, apartheidism and patriotism in literary movements. In the poem, "The Ax-Helve" it has been pointed out how there is a sort of racism between the speaker and the French Baptiste. But in the present poem, "Two Witches" there is ecofeministic approach as is found in "The Hill Wife", in "The Fear" and even in "Home Burial". The poem forestalls "The Witch of Coos":

> I stayed the night for shelter at a farm
> Behind the mountain, with a mother and son,
> Two old-believers. They did all the talking. (Williams and Honig, 244)

The "talking" centers upon a good deal of a woman who prefers to continue her neighborhood reputation as a witch: "Summoning spirits isn't 'Button, button, / Who's got the button,' I would have them know". The story is of a skeleton who, in the words of the son:

> It left the cellar forty years ago
> And carried itself like a pile of dishes
> Up one flight from the cellar to the kitchen,
> Another from the kitchen to the bedroom,
> Another from the bedroom to the attic,
> Right past both father and mother, and neither stopped it.
> Father had gone upstairs; mother was downstairs.
> I was a baby: I don't know where I was. (Williams and Honig, 245)

The line – "Father had gone upstairs; mother was downstairs"- indicates a lot to understand the situation. On the other hand, the remarkable skeleton "carried itself like a pile of dishes". The bones are put together "like a chandelier":

> I had a vision of them put together
> Not like a man, but like a chandelier'
> So suddenly I flung the door wide on him.
> A moment he stood balancing with emotion,
> And all but lost himself. (A tongue of fire
> Flashed out and licked along his upper teeth.
> Smoke rolled inside the sockets of his eyes.)
> Then he came at me with one hand outstretched,
> The way he did in life once; but this time
> I struck the hand off brittle on the floor,
> And fell back from him on the floor myself.
> The finger-pieces slid in all directions. (Williams and Honig, 246)

The telltale would not prove that the skeleton was a former lover killed by her husband, Toffile. This married couple seems to be sexless, probably cold and obscene. On the night of her vision:

> The bulkhead double-doors were double-locked
> And swollen tight and buried under snow.
> The cellar windows were banked up with sawdust
> And swollen tight and buried under snow. (Williams and Honig, 245)

The repetition of the line – "And swollen tight and buried under snow"-gives an emotional intensity. The woman admits:

> The only fault my husband found with me-
> I went to sleep before I went to bed'
> Especially in winter when the bed
> Might just as well be ice and the clothes snow.
> The night the bones came up the cellar-stairs
> Toffile had gone to bed alone and left me,
> But left an open door to cool the room off
> So as to sort of turn me out of it. (Williams and Honig, 245)

This vigorous reaction is against domestic confinements. In such context, Richard Poirier finds in the best of Frost's domestic narratives and asserts: "Especially when a woman is the speaker in such poems the bursting out of imagination comes in the form of images at once terrifying, comically macabre, and sexually charged. These are the poems of the mind's extravagance not supported by the feet, of women stuck at home rather than of men wandering beyond the boundaries of the homestead"[4]. Besides, a woman's venture is to have a change in her life but the male-dominated society does not allow it. A woman usually likes a matriarchal governed miscellany centering upon mutual need. But it is not approved by the patriarchal structure. In this issue, P. K. Nayar states: "Both women and nature are equally oppressed by male ways of thinking and action"[5].

The readers will experience the tone of frustration and distortion in "Two Witches: The Pauper Witch of Grafton" as same with the first part. The young witch undergoes inner frustration as she could not believe that the husband loved her. The old pauper of the "noted witch" is plagued by an adulterous generation for a sign and turns into something very different as she recalls the man who first exposed and then married her. The lines – "Up where the trees grow short, the mosses tall, / …/ And he liked everything I made him do" – murmur in 'a perverse voice'. On this basis, Randall Jarrell in the article "To the Laodiceans" asserts: "But here I come to what makes the critic of Frost's poetry groan, and sadden, and almost despair: several of his very best poems, the poems in which he is most magnificent, most characteristic, most nearly incomparable, are far too long to quote. If I could quote "Home Burial", "The Witch of Coos", and "A Servant to Servants", Pharisee and Philistine alike would tiptoe off hand in hand, their shamed eyes starry; anyone who knows these poems well will consider the mere mention of them enough to justify any praise, any extravagance – and anybody who doesn't know them doesn't know some of the summits of our poetry, and is so much to be pitied that it would be foolish to blame him too"[6]. To give a justice to the situation, it seems necessary to quote the view of Timothy Clark who points out: "The association of women and domestic sphere could be reaffirmed as their greater sense of respect for nature as a sort of home ('ecology' being from the Greek 'science of the household'). Few ecofeminists would now agree with such simple assertions".[7]

Environment has a certain impact upon the mood of a person. Environmental conditions and mental health are not altogether separated; rather they are complementary to each other. However, Todd A. Borlik claims: "The word "environment", for instance, does not enter the English language until 1603, and even then, it means "the action of surrounding, the state of being surrounded", rather than the biophysical world per se-a meaning that only comes into its own in the mid-nineteenth century. If early moderns could not reach for a term like "biocentrism", they, nevertheless, had other words and concepts at their beck that we cannot wield today"[8]. This view of Borlik seems appropriate in the context of the poem, "Fragmentary Blue" by Frost:

Why make so much of fragmentary blue
In here and there a bird, or butterfly,
Or flower, or wearing-stone, or open eye,
When heaven presents in sheets the solid hue?
Since earth is earth, perhaps, not heaven (as yet)-
Though some savants make earth include the sky;
And blue so far above us comes so high'
It only gives our wish for blue a whet. (CPoRF, 267)

The poem reveals the persona's love of blue color. The speaker asks why people like so much of the fragments of blue found on the wings of butterfly, in a flower or in a bird or even in human eye, when the whole of the open blue sky satisfies the longings for the color. The persona feels that the humans live on the earth and the sky is too far above to satisfy the desire for the color. Probably, the color of blue clings to heavenly or divinely embodiment in the sphere of earth. Besides, it involves the concept for understanding of the body and temperament as determined by the environment. On the other hand, "Two and a half millennia ago, Pythagoras pioneered what we now recognise as a kind of ecosystemic philosophy that enabled early modern thinkers to erode certain dichotomies between subject and object, human and animal, spirit and matter, God and Nature"[9]. For the persona, the day of universal happiness has not yet come. It would be possible when humans would understand the sky and earth.

The world has witnessed many wars, starting from the First World War to the Second World War, from Gulf War to Desert War, from Chinese Invasion to the Bangladesh War, and from Indo-Pak dispute to the Kargil War. Each time there has been the border issue or expansionism. All the humans know how war is destructive and the seed of such devastation is hatred and violence. Moreover, war creates environmental crisis. The ecological problems spring from man's unconquerable mind structured upon the lion's share of possession and accumulation of wealth. The outcome of greedy capitalism, rapacious commercialism, dominant colonialism and expansionism generates abhorrence, disgust and violence between man and man, and also puts a great divide between man and nature. The poem, "Fire and Ice" by Frost, written in 1920, just after two years of the First World War, talks of cold response and hatred of humans to humans. The speaker asserts how some people are claiming that the world will end in fire while others claim it in ice:

> Some say the world will end in fire,
> Some say in ice.
> From what I've tasted of desire
> I hold with those who favor fire.
> But if it had to perish twice'
> I think I know enough of hate
> To say that for destruction ice
> Is also great
> And would suffice. (Norton, 1774-1775)

As global warming and climate change are appalling, the apprehension for the burning up or freezing up of the world is obvious. The two particular emotions, such as desire for fire and hate for ice, are enough to destroy the world. It is in this sense that humans destroy the universe through hating each other and also through the strongest desire to impose masterly attitude to destroy everything. Moreover, "Fire and Ice" acknowledges desire and passion which are more deadly and destructive than mere hate. Hate may consume both biotic and abiotic through the war but desire shows its power through zeal and irrational attitude that energises to destructive behavior. Besides, the poem was written when revolution, apocalypse, environmental and socio-political disturbance and turmoil were on people's mind after the World War-I. A year earlier, in 1919, W.B. Yeats had written "The Second Coming" in which he has mentioned:

> Things fall apart: the centre cannot hold;
> Mere anarchy is loosed upon the world,
> The blood-dimmed tide is loosed, and everywhere
> The ceremony of innocence is drowned;
> The best lack all conviction, while the worst
> Are full of passionate intensity. (Hieatt & Park, 507)

Corollary to this, T. S. Eliot's "The Hollow Men" which was written in 1925, just after five years of Frost's "Fire and Ice", concludes with the same version of apocalypse: "This is the way the world ends / Not with a bang but a whimper" (Eliot, 78). This is how the poem, "Fire and Ice" projects the world and its futurity.

For an ecocentric bend of mind, a touch of nature makes a powerful impact on mood and thought of a person. The divine beauty of nature plays a certain role to realise peace and solace in life. Human life without reference to nature is incomplete what is understood in "Dust of Snow". The poem is another instance of understanding Frost's biocentric frame of mind. It communicates the relationships between nature and human. Nature heals up negative emotions and blesses the persona as the falling of the dust of snow on his head lifts his mood instantly from negative to positive stance of life. The descriptions of nature, landscape and pastoral sights are the recurrent themes in Frost's poetry:

> The way a crow
> Shook down on me
> The dust of snow
> From a hemlock tree
> Has given my heart
> A change of mood
> And saved some part
> Of a day I had rued. (Oliver, 405)

The poem reveals the curative and healing power of nature. The persona undergoes an unfruitful day when a crow shakes down a "dust of snow" on him "from a hemlock tree". The snow instantly makes him happier and releases him from gloominess of the day. This experience of the persona lies in the deep relationship between man and nature. He perceives the significance of nature that helps him to realise not to waste his day in vain. It exposes a method for living that agrees with biocentrism. Thus, mankind needs to understand that nature is necessary to invigorate life. In his article, "Nature Writing and Environmental Psychology", Scott Slovic writes: "But in order to achieve heightened attentiveness to our place in the natural world- attentiveness to our very existence- we must understand something about the workings of the mind"[10]. Nature constantly appeases human minds but human mind destroys nature.

Nature is destroyed through war and struggle. The potential horror of war is degeneration, destruction and death. The ruinous effect of armed conflicts is ecocide. The binary between the coloniser and the colonised, the exploiter and the exploited, the oppressor and the oppressed unfolds ecological deterioration. The devastation of war raises environmental crisis with all the poison threatening to life and livelihoods of the biota. Its fierceness certainly transmits health hazards as it contaminates biodiversity. The dominant notion of absorption, expansionism and racism causes war, disorder, and death. Besides, the war related death toll shocks and surprises even to the power mongers. Robert Frost unfurls such type ecocatastrophe in the poem "To E.T.", the initials refer to his poet-friend Edward Thomas. The central drive of the poem is about the realisation of the destructiveness of war, especially after experiencing the death of his friend Thomas who died serving in the war. The persona had encouraged and persuaded his friend Thomas to relocate to New England but Edward Thomas preferred to serve in the World War-I but unfortunately, he died in war.

Frost observes natural phenomena and describes nature in relation to human life in "Nothing Gold can Stay". This poem attests to environmental reverence of the poet for the green earth. Physically and psychologically, nature makes an inevitable role on human beings:

> Nature's first green is gold
> Her hardest hue to hold.
> Her early leaf's a flower;
> But only so an hour.
> Then leaf subsides to leaf.
> So Eden sank to grief,

So dawn goes down to day.
Nothing gold can stay. (Norton, 1775)

Written in 1923, the poem underpins how fresh and newly born buds on the trees seem "gold". Due to cyclic process, such color disappears and blossoms turn to flowers. They also disappear quickly. "Then leaf subsides to leaf". The leaves fall to the ground as mankind fell from the paradise of the Garden of Eden. As morning "goes down to day", similarly nothing lasts forever. Then, why humans are busy in war? Man's mind should learn to identify and measure the physical factors that lead to impact the environmental assessment. However, the speaker argues for nature that represents the life-cycle largely being justified with the journey of a "leaf" from infancy to maturity. Directly or indirectly, nature plays a major role in human life. Hence, Lawrence Buell affirms: "In such ways, seasonal representations tease us toward awareness of ourselves as environmental beings"[11].

Each and every creature has own emotions and feelings. In the poem, "The Runaway" the artist expresses the snow falling and his encounter with a young male horse, "Morgan" that exhibits fear at the sight of snow. There is no stress of other creatures in the pasture and the speaker wonders over the care-taker of the "colt" regarding to intimate with snow:

Once when the snow of the year was beginning to fall,
We stopped by a mountain pasture to say, 'Whose colt?'
A little Morgan had one barefoot on the wall,
The other curled at his breast. He dipped his head
And snorted at us. And then he had to bolt.
We heard the miniature thunder where he fled,
And we saw him, or thought we saw him, dim and gray,
Like a shadow against the curtain of falling flakes.
I think the little fellow's afraid of the snow.
He isn't winter-broken. It isn't play
With the little fellow at all. He's running away. (CPoRF, 273)

The speaker's interpretation about "a little Morgan's" features and mannerisms forces the readers to understand the psychology of the animal. It seems to draw a parallel between the horse, a representative from the non-human world and the speaker, an emissary from the human world. As the humans are in thought of safety and security, similarly the "colt" gets fear and looks for a suitable and congenial environment. The reality is that every species tries to accommodate within their own ecosystem. The speaker articulates a strong ecological agenda which is sensitive to the 'symbiotic codependency of the human and non-human creatures' that inhabit in their 'biomes'. It is an example of the behavioral pattern of every species that makes their survival possible.

Frost acknowledges the interrelationship between man and nature that endorses peace, harmony and joy in life. The poem, "Stopping by Woods on a Snowy Evening" precipitates nature not as a dead object but a living entity. Keeping the harmony between man and nature, Frost tries to signify the ecological concept in life. The snow-covered woods on a snowy evening at the remote countryside pervades serenity and calmness. This surrounding unfurls a vista of beauty and tranquility that enthralls the eyes and pacifies the heart. Besides, this picturesque and aesthetic spectacle suffuses the means of solace for the duty-bound mind. Such type of complacency appears to be ecocentric treaties that afford an eco-friendly lifestyle:

> Whose woods these are I think I know.
> His house is in the village though;
> He will not see me stopping here
> To watch his woods fill up with snow.
> My little horse must think it queer
> To stop without a farmhouse near
> Between the woods and frozen lake
> The darkest evening of the year.
> He gives his harness bells a shake
> To ask if there is some mistake.
> The only other sound's the sweep
> Of easy wind and downy flake.
> The woods are lovely, dark and deep,
> But I have promises to keep,
> And miles to go before I sleep,
> And miles to go before I sleep. (Norton, 1775)

Woods play a significant part in Frost's poetry. Despite the increasing urbanisation, the persona presents the remote circumstance in rurality as he speaks: "His house is in the village though". "The woods fill up with snow", "frozen lake", "easy wind and downy flake" etc. unfold the idyllic scene. In such context, Lawrance Thompson states: "A rural traveler is the actor whose brief soliloquy describes the circumstance under which he has stopped his horse-drawn sleigh to enjoy, in spite of cold and loneliness, the strange beauty of white snowflakes falling against a background of dark trees"[12]. At the core of the poem is the mesmerising beauty that enchants strongly to the traveler to stop there, regardless of winter evening and the cold storm. As a conscious esthetic expert, the persona's description of remote wilderness creates a heightened awareness for the natural surroundings. The materialistic mindset believes in the depletion of wilderness that poses threat to the environment.

Contrary to this, the persona mentions: "My little horse must think it queer / To stop without a farmhouse near". From the spell of fascination to the realistic stance, it occurs to the traveler's little horse. Hence, the sleigh-driver is pressed to proceed onwards by the realisation of duties and a considerable distance yet to be travelled; those "promises" which he must keep and the "miles to go" before he completes his journey. The readers come upon the words – "promises", "miles" and "sleep" – with a conscious perception of life in materialistic world as these words are related to the commitments in worldly life. There is a divide between the experience of the rural traveler enjoying beauty in nature and the experience of the worldly traveler undergoing hardships, duties and distances.

Frost intends to express that one will hear and recognise the voice of nature if one comes out of artificial life: "The only other sound's the sweep / Of easy wind and downy flake". To the urban-dweller, nature is at far distance. Besides, Frost's nature awareness focuses on the snow-covered woods on the landscape on a snowy evening unfurls the canopy of serenity. His presentation of a "village" in the evening hour appeals to the aesthetic sensibility. In such context, Ramachandra Guha calls for "a return to the health of village life, with its beauty of surroundings and its contact with nature"[13]. Frost is conscious of the difference between the "promises" in the human world and the panorama of beauty in the natural world. The expression – "promises to keep" and for such commitment, "miles to go before I sleep" is meant for human values but beauty in nature-system thrills the eyes and calms the heart. In relation to this, the opinion of Lawrence Buell can be cited: "The segmentation of "nature" from "civilisation", "country" from "town", already endemic to pastoral becomes even more accentuated"[14].

As a protomodernist, Frost's quest of the moment becomes a pursuit in the Emersonian sense. It is understood with the incidents in his poetry. Like the sleigh-driver in "Stopping by Woods on a Snowy Evening", the single actor in "For Once, Then, Something" unfolds the question of ultimate meanings in human experience. The actor constructs a climactic moment to intensify the question of highest understanding in human concern. The persona seems to be an egocentric who sees the absolute being as the reflection of himself in the water of the well he looks into. If man changes himself from egocentric to ecocentric, he can experience the ultimate reality. The traveler in the snowy woods and the spectator peering down into a well are two examples to understand the mysterious process in life and nature. In relation to this, Lawrence Buell states: "American protomodernist writers like Robinson and Frost were beginning to create lyrics about solipsistic projections of human vision onto nature, like "Luke Havergal" and "For Once, Then, Something"; and these poems were soon to be followed by Wallace Stevens's more sophisticated exercises in skepticism…"[15]. The articulation underpins human's projection in nature. One may feel joy gazing into the bottom of the well through water, but the persona looks there for "truth". Probably, the spectator catches the sight of the hidden mystery itself.

Through certain creatures and agencies, Frost presents the significance of nature in human life. Obviously, butterflies are the beautiful gifts of nature. Their flying in the air sensitizes the sign of divinity in the surroundings that urges human mind to observe an external beautiful reality of the physical phenomena. In the poem, "Blue-Butterfly Day", the poet sketches the image of nature shaping the beautiful scenic views to the spectator if he has the biocentric bend of mind to appreciate it:

> It is blue-butterfly day here in spring,
> And with these sky-flakes down in flurry on flurry
> There is more unmixed color on the wing
> Than flowers will show for days unless they hurry.
> But these are flowers that fly and all but sing:
> And now from having ridden out desire
> They lie closed over in the wind and cling
> Where wheels have freshly sliced the April mire. (CPoRF,277)

The persona compares the blue butterflies to "sky-flakes" that fall to the ground "in flurry on flurry" like snow. More emphatic, at the initial lines he beautifully pronounces the movements of a flock of butterflies. Readers will acknowledge the tone of wonder and astonishment at the view of blue butterflies on a spring day. These insects possess "more unmixed color on the wing" than "flowers will show for days unless they hurry". As it is observed, in early spring few flowers produce blossoms that remain "unmixed". Besides, the flying butterflies are "down" from the sky and flutter to draw attention of the viewer. But there is a twist at the last three lines of the poem. The artist poses the butterflies on the ground due to their behavioral pattern "from having ridden out desire". The "desire" refers to the breeding and reproduction. Unfortunately, on the ground they come to a dark end beneath the "wheels" of moving cars, "freshly sliced the April mire".

The problem demands prioritisation for the safety and security of these butterflies from the basis of ecological and human dimension. Human population is not at extinction but these species of insects are threatened by extinction. Thus, in conservation strategies, plans should be incorporated to save these insects and to flourish their species. However, the identification of nature's beauty and vitality depends upon human psyche. Such identification constructs a positive value of an unalienated union of mind and nature.

Frost's description of nature and natural happenings is pointworthy. By focusing upon the social and environmental interaction between man and nature, Frost tries to rebuild humanistic ideology. In the poem, "The Onset", he expresses the seasonal feelings in different seasons. Very accurately and minutely, he articulates:

> Always the same, when on a fated night
> At last the gathered snow lets down as white
> As may be in dark woods, and with a song
> It shall not make again all winter long
> Of hissing on the yet uncovered ground,
> I almost stumble looking up and round,
> ....
> I know that winter death has never tried
> The earth but it has failed: the snow may heap
> In long storms an undrafted four feet deep
> As measured against maple, birch, and oak,
> It cannot check the peeper's silver croak;
> And I shall see the snow all go down hill
> In water of a slender April rill
> That flashes tail through last year's withered brake
> And dead weeds, like a disappearing snake.
> Nothing will be left white but here a birch,
> And there a clump of houses with a church. (Oliver, 406-407)

The poem reveals the persona's deep and powerful observation of local meteorology and climate during the cyclic changes of seasons in nature. The attribution of value to weather and climate attests to Frost's ecological bend of mind in climatic flexibility during different seasons in nature. The persona talks of a winter storm and the snow falls – "always the same". This proves that nature is a self-regulating system. In the context of environmental pedagogy, Mike Hulme observes: "The idea of climate exists as much in the human mind and in the matrices of cultural practices as it exists as an independent and objective physical category"[16]. Besides, humans know how to adapt to the changing environment as their bodies and brains are subject to evolution. It is, obviously, a natural process. As the question of survival is concerned in the evolutionary process, man's mind and body enlarges to face the challenges. That's why Frederick Turner asserts: "Our bodies and brains are a result of evolution, which is a natural process to paradigmatic that it could almost be said to be synonymous with nature itself"[17]. Possibly, 'the relationship of man with nature is nonnegotiable'.

The "winter death" has failed to bury "the earth" permanently because spring has brought again "the peeper's silver croak". The persona's positive note drives home "the snow all go downhill / In water of a slender April rill". On account of the cycle of seasons, "Nothing will be left white but here a birch, /And there a clump of houses with a church" as Shelley in "Ode to the West Wind" sings: "If Winter comes, can Spring be far behind"? It signifies the subtle relationship that nature shares with human beings. In this issue, Marion Montgomery states: "Man's understanding of the natural world comes slowly"[18].

As it is studied, Frost seems to be an expert to set his poetry in idyllic surroundings. The images of "grapevine", "hill at dusk", "honeysuckle", and "rose petals" etc. invoke pastoral symphony in the poem, "To Earthward". This attests to environmental reverence of the artist for the green earth – "In grass and sand". It is a fact that humans would not get solace, either physically or psychologically, without 'green' things. It is in this sense that the ecological balance is necessary for congenial and conducive existence. Hence, in most of his creations, Frost presents nature in the hope of keeping harmony between humanity and nature. In this poem, the "musk" and "grapevine springs" accumulate taste and smell, otherwise known as gustatory and olfactory sensations. Corollary to this, "honeysuckle" gives the visual imagery combining the sensations of tactile and olfactory. The lips taste and feel all these non-toxic and non-artificial throng of surrounding:

Love at the lips was touch
As sweet as I could bear;
And once that seemed too much;
I lived on air
That crossed me from sweet things
The flow of-was it musk
From hidden grapevine springs
Down hill at dusk?
I had the swirl and ache
From sprays of honeysuckle
That when they're gathered shake
Dew on the knuckle.
I craved strong sweets, but those
Seemed strong when I was young;
The petal of the rose
It was that stung.
....
When stiff and sore and scarred
I take away my hand
From leaning on it hard
In grass and sand,
The hurt is not enough:
I long for weight and strength
To feel the earth as rough
To all my length. (Williams and Honig, 241)

The aesthetic experience of the persona recalls that "lived on air" teasing him with the scent of "musk". It brings to his memory about the confusing "swirl and ache" from the touch of "dew" shaken "on the knuckle". Contrasted with this, Vivian C. Hopkins states: "In "To Earthward", the joys of grapevine, honeysuckle, and rose are pushed aside for contact with the grave. The association of love with burial recalls Emily Dickinson, but goes beyond her in its daring use of sexual imagery"[19]. In the first sixteen lines of the poem, nature consummates intensely with persona's period of youth thereby awakening to the beauty of the earth. In the rest sixteen lines – the last part – the darker mood of the persona studies the actualities of life with his whole being and strength. Explicitly or implicitly, the mood of a person determines his attitude towards nature. The mood also gets reflection with the images of nature. William Wordsworth reveals such moods and the role of nature in "Daffodils":

For oft, when on my couch I lie

> In vacant or in pensive mood,
> They flash upon that inward eye
> Which is the bliss of solitude;
> And then my heart with pleasure fills
> And dances with daffodils. (Hieatt & Park, 305)

The findings of richness and affluence in nature are largely based on one's own moods. Regarding mood, the ecocritic, Harold Fromm affirms: "One is always in a mood and all moods are produced by biochemistry in conjunction with neuroanatomy"[20]. Humans, physically and psychologically come in contact with nature that inbuilds their mood. Their daily life, the sense of the way they feel each day, is mostly determined by the environment they live in.

Ecology needs to examine the succession of plants and animals in their communities. The communities of plants and animals seem to be diverse and complicated. In the poem, "Good-by and Keep Cold", Frost talks of an orchard that was planted "on a northerly slope" near a farm house gets injuries:

> Remind me of all that can happen to harm
> An orchard away at the end of the farm
> All winter, cut off by a hill from the house.
> I don't want it girdled by rabbit and mouse,
> I don't want it dreamily nibbled for browse
> By deer, and I don't want it budded by grouse.
> (If certain it wouldn't be idle to call
> I'd summon grouse, rabbit, and deer to the wall
> And warn them away with a stick for a gun.)
> ....
> I wish I could promise to lie in the night
> And think of an orchard's arboreal plight. (CPoRF, 281)

The buds on the trees and the tender limbs get eaten by rabbit, mouse, deer and grouse. His wish to protect the orchard – "And warn them away with a stick for a gun" – becomes evident and reveals 'the environmental determinants of weather and geography'. The weather – "This saying good-by on the edge of the dark / And the cold to an orchard so young in the bark" – pays good-bye for the winter season. The geography studies the presence of the hill that obscures the view of the orchard. When the persona says: "I wish I could promise to lie in the night / and think of an orchard's arboreal plight", it exposes his biocentric mindset exhibiting a fatherly empathy to protect the plants. This tendency attributes to the vitality of ecological view of life. Judging upon the situation, the ecological view of Joseph W. Meeker can be cited: "In a mature ponderosa pine forest, for instance, thousands of highly specialised types of bacteria maintain stable soil chemistry as each type plays a particular role in the process of decomposition; insects live upon plants and bacteria and are eaten by birds; small mammals breed in the complex vegetation; larger mammals eat certain specific kinds of plants or prey upon smaller animals; the many highly specialised plants, from small ferns to enormous pines, make up the setting for all other life, provide food and shelter, and in turn depend upon the environmental determinants of weather and geography"[21].

The strange beauty of the earth in Frost's poetry helps the readers to develop a conscious perception and recognition of life in emotionally drained materialistic world. He hints that the sense of comfort and pleasure is derived from nurturing nature, not from destroying it. Frost provides evident of man's existence in the natural world. His attitude towards life in nature is one of the armed and amiable truths that one experiences through his poetry. However, Frost consistently tries to examine the networks of communication between humans and non-humans. In "'Two Look at Two", the persona demonstrates the relationships between humans and non-humans and instills an ecological vision of man and animal as parts of a single environment. In this poem, a pair of lovers stand on a mountainside while a doe and buck watch them without any sign of fear:

Two had seen two, whichever side you spoke from.
'This *must* be all' It was all. Still they stood,
A great wave from it going over them,
As if the earth in one unlooked-for favor
Had made them certain earth returned their love. (CPoRF, 283)

The poetic expression unfurls that there is a connection between these "two" looking at "two". In other words, when man and nature are really one, there is the life-sustaining environment. The interconnectedness of all life-forms builds a modest feeling towards nature. It underpins an integrated system of relationship between living things. In his article, "Literature and Ecology", William Rueckert mentions: "The biosphere (or ecosphere) is the home that life has built for itself on the planet's outer surface. In that ecosphere there is a reciprocal interdependence of one life process upon another, and there is a mutual interconnected development of all of the earth's life systems"[22]. For a healthy ecosystem, both human and non-human form equal magnitude. Frost ends the poem by saying that "earth returned their love" and believes that there is an inherent equality between humans and non-humans.

Frost is disturbed by war. The destructiveness of war causes environmental crisis threatening to life and livelihoods of human beings. It pervades health hazards and contaminates biodiversity. Frost is upset due to deployment of soldiers as it becomes almost difficult for families to endure. He expresses the harmful consequences war in the poem, "Not to Keep":

> 'Enough,
> Yet not enough. A bullet through and through,
> High in the breast. Nothing but what good care
> And medicine and rest, and you a week,
> Can cure me of to go again' The same
> Grim giving to do over for them both.
> She dared no more than ask him with her eyes
> How was it with him for a second trial.
> And with his eyes he asked her not to ask.
> They had given him back to her, but not to keep. (CPoRF, 284)

"A bullet through and through / High in the breast" intimidates the dreadfulness of war. "They had given him back to her, but not to keep" precipitates as if the life of a person is a commodity meant for exchange. War is the root cause of ruination. If it goes on, it will construct degeneration, disease and death instead of life and life-supporting variables. It is studied through a wounded soldier's homecoming and his return to war again once his wounds have healed. The poem reveals the thoughts and feelings of the woman, may be a wife or a mother, whose husband /or son has been "sent…back to her" being wounded from the war. The military operation creates apprehension of turning a woman into a widow, or, sonless, or brotherless. The repercussion is biocide as life-supporting viability is destroyed.

Modern man's mindset poisons the whole ecosystem. His superpower mentality separates him from nature. Besides, his supremacy of unnecessary interference with nature-system causes severe consequences on environment. His egocentric attitude hardly thinks of preservation and protection of the natural environment. His sense of 'greed economy' gives birth to the concept of rapacious industrialisation and aggressive urbanisation that despoils nature. In this perspective, Frost's poem, "A Brook in the City" exposes the anthropocentric mindset of modern man causing deterioration in nature-system:

The farmhouse lingers, though averse to square
With the new city street it has to wear
A number in. But what about the brook
That held the house as in an elbow-crook?
I ask as one who knew the brook, its strength
And impulse, having dipped a finger length
And made it leap my knuckle, having tossed
A flower to try its currents where they crossed.
The meadow grass could be cemented down
From growing under pavements of a town,
The apple trees be sent to hearth-stone flame.
Is water wood to serve a brook the same?
How else dispose of an immortal force
No longer needed? Staunch it at its source
With cinder loads dumped down? The brook was thrown
Deep in a sewer dungeon under stone
In fetid darkness still to live and run-
And all for nothing it had ever done
Except forget to go in fear perhaps.
No one would know except for ancient maps
That such a brook ran water. But I wonder
If from its being kept forever under
The thoughts may not have risen that so keep
This new-built city from both work and sleep. (CPoRF,285)

The speaker claims that city has grown with "cemented down / From growing under pavements of a town" in a place where once upon a time there was a brook. Humans have turned that strong brook into a little sewage. "A flower to try its currents where they crossed" proves the futility and strength of the brook. "Its source / With cinder loads dumped down" exposes the anthropocentric vision of man making nature into a dumping yard of wastes. "The apple trees be sent to hearth-stone flame" unfolds the depletion of green cover causing environmental degradation. This poem justifies that the environmental problems are of man's own making.

Competitive commerce and urban pollution are the by-products of human culture compounding environmental threats. The growth of cities, exhaustion of natural spaces and population boom etc. are the factors of ecological disorder. In such context, Timothy W. Luke writes: "After becoming completely ensnared within the mega machinic grids of global production and consumption…Nature is turning into 'Denature'. Much of the earth is a 'built environment', a 'planned habitat', or 'managed range' as pollution modifies atmospheric chemistry, urbanisation restructures weather events, architecture encloses whole biomes in sprawling megacities, and biotechnology reengineers the base codes of existing biomass"[23]. In this poem, Frost exhibits the supremacy of 'human constructedness' over nature's reality. The human-system imprisons the nature-system.

Humans exploit nature and in return nature shows its rage. Humans' self-centredness despoils nature. When man interferes and experiments with the cycles of nature, nature counteracts the austerity of such anthropocentrism. In "Looking for a Sunset Bird in Winter" Frost discusses a harsh winter creating hard times that people face in life. He uses a scene to warn mankind restricted from polluting the environment: "No bird was singing in it now. / A single leaf was on a bough, / And that was all there was to see / In going twice around the tree." Chilly weather has gathered frost. Falling of snow has caused smog atmosphere. The image of fierce winter triggers up the intense suffering of mankind. It is due to man's attempt to breach the laws of nature and inversely gets wrath of nature. In this sense, William Rueckert states: "We are violating the laws of nature, and the retribution from the biosphere will be more terrible than any inflicted on humans by the gods"[24]. Presently, the atmospheric pollution rewrites the fate of the universe. Global warming and climate change have been much discussed studies in today's world. Excess winter, dreadful scorching summer, landslides, untimely heavy rainfall and repeated cyclones etc. witness the climatic disorder.

The power-hankering mind is not ready to accept that nature is eternal, pure, gentle, harmonious and good. It is obvious as the polluters contaminate the environment. To understand nature, man must reestablish his relationship with it. Presently, man has put 'Nature in a cage'. But nature is 'the real touchstone of what is good and right and beautiful'. Nature does know "pretense" or "deceive". The true artist must find solace and beauty in nature. Hence, humans should elevate love and respect towards nature. Readers know nature through the images and words in Frost's poetry. The poem, "A Boundless Moment" unfurls the laws of nature, its slow and gradual change. Nature is automatic in its process. The persona feels the beauty of nature and imaginatively equals the spring bloom to "Paradise". He demonstrates the beautiful and "boundless" moments with full of happiness holding together in observing nature.

The persona minutely delineates that the flowers are happy to get new skin and new petals making them exuberant and "luxuriance of May". But in the end, the persona talks of a wintry tree still holding "its last year's leaves". When it goes on unnoticed by the vast majority of the humans, that comes to the notice of the speaker. Here, the persona gives priority on nature-centered system. In such context, Greg Garrard says: "The shift from a human-centred to a nature-centred system of values is the core of the radicalism attributed to deep ecology"[25]. Probably, Frost keeps in mind that through the mutual and reciprocal relationship, the human and natural can flourish in the biosphere.

The poem "Gathering Leaves" indirectly serves the purpose of fertilising the soil in organic way for farming and yielding good crops. Harvesting heaps of leaves is commonly a work of farm-life. As a farmer, the persona pronounces the shifting of the autumnal leaves into "bags" and storing them in the "shed". He also articulates that gathering leaves is essential for the harvest. At the initial, he admits that gathering leaves is a difficult process:

Spades take up leaves
No better than spoons,
And bags full of leaves
Are light as balloon.
I make a great noise
Of rustling all day
Like rabbit and deer
Running away.
But the mountains I raise
Elude my embrace,
Flowing over my arms
And into my face.
I may load and unload
Again and again
Till I fill the whole shed,
And what have I then?
Next to nothing for weight,
And since they grew duller
From contact with earth,
Next to nothing for color.
Next to nothing for use.
But a crop is a crop,
And who's to say where
The harvest shall stop? (CPoRF, 290)

The persona claims that leaves are extremely uncooperative and avoid his "embrace" and care. This shows the persona's deep attachment with nature. The line – "But the mountains I raise / Elude my embrace" – talks of the 'harmony' of humanity and nature that was in the past, not seen now. Besides, Frost is not in favor of agro-chemicals and pesticide applications. Presently, the experience of agricultural chemicals and pesticide pollution has been a common issue.

In farming or harvesting, leaves are gathered and not expected to stay in bags. Trees produce leaves in cyclic way and they are vital for the earth's survival: "From contact with earth, / Next to nothing for color". The persona concludes by expressing: "a crop is a crop" – means it is an unavoidable process of gathering leaves. It shows a vantage point from which the mutually accepted patterns of lives and interactions take place. In relation to farming and soil, Dona Phillips mentions: "…the soil is our heritage, our history. That is, the soil is also to be read, interpreted, taught, learned from, handed down to the next generation, and kept from becoming mere dirt"[26]. Hence, taking care of earth is necessary.

Nature is the focus in Frost's poetry. He transfers human feelings through the images of nature. His attitude constructs what Todd A. Borlik says: "a more organic, low-impact life style that is respectful and appreciative of nature"[27]. All creatures are acquainted with their natural surroundings. It is, possibly, well known to Frost that man is not above or apart from the natural world. Hence, the cycle of seasons of nature is a recurrent theme for backgrounds in his poetry. He also uses trees and leaves to express humans' emotions and feelings through them. The poem, "Misgiving" is an example of articulating such nature-centred system in human-centred values:

> All crying, 'We will go with you, O Wind!'
> The foliage follow him, leaf and stem,
> But a sleep oppresses them as they go,
> And they end by bidding him stay with them.
> Since ever they flung abroad in spring
> The leaves had promised themselves this flight,
> Who now would fain seek sheltering wall,
> Or thicket, or hollow place for the night. (CPoRF, 292)

The artist compares his lifecycle with the lifecycle of the leaves. He acknowledges that life has similarities with the trees. In other words, nature demonstrates old and new lessons to humans in regard to their life and survival. Possibly, the artist has been familiar with the teachings of nature. That helps him to articulate his thoughts about nature and life through his works. In many numbers of his poems, Frost unfurls a close communion that exists between human life and the cycle of the seasons. This underpins Frost's environmental sentiment and respect for nature.

In the current era, man is thought to be the centre of the universe. The present increasing disruption of the environment is due to man's supremacy and exploiting over nature. His anthropocentric mindset tries to conquer, violate and dominate over every natural thing. In "A Hillside Thaw", Frost shows man's unnecessary interference in the freedom of nature. By catching lizards, man trespasses and tries to take control of nature. The very root of human complacency is to exploit nature and superseding the non-humans. The upshot of such action alienates man from his natural environment. The unnecessarily disturbing the non-humans raises the issue of domination by human sovereignty over them. The non-humans expect to have free movement in wilderness for their survival. But the anthropocentric vision postulated by humans puts barrier on their way of living. A propensity of indifference and hostility challenges to the existence and sustainability of the animals. Therefore, animals are effaced by humans' step-motherly and obnoxious attitude. In such context, Christopher Manes in his article "Nature and Silence" writes: "The distinction, which is borne out by anthropological studies of animistic cultures, throws into stark relief an aspect of our society's relationship with the nonhuman world that has only recently become an express theme in the environmental debate"[28]. Now all the welfare is vested into man as he has been 'the sole subject, speaker and rational sovereign of the natural order'. Man should know that he is a part of nature, not the master of all.

The conflict between mankind's threat to nature and for the cause of defending nature's rage to humans goes on in environmental history. Sometimes the anthropocentric vision loses its significance and the biocentric standpoint becomes strong. In such situations, the human beings and their interests hold little value. In the ensuing state of affairs, nature displaces and denounces any human concern. In the poem, "On a Tree Fallen across the Road", the persona underpins the duel between man versus nature. The barrier between ego-consciousness and eco-consciousness comes into force. The earth-centred system restricts man's aggressive advancement to achieve "the final goal" which might be a vulnerable position for him because of his battle with nature. At the beginning of the poem, the Frostian man acknowledges a voice and vitality of nature to check the trespassing tendency of mankind:

> The tree the tempest with a crash of wood
> Throws down in front of us is not to bar

> Our passage to our journey's end for good,
> But just to ask us who we think we are
> Insisting always on our own way so.
> She likes to halt us in our runner tracks,
> And make us get down in a foot of snow
> Debating what to do without an ax
> And yet she knows obstruction is in vain.
> We will not be put off the final goal
> We have it hidden in us to attain,
> Not though we have to seize earth by the pole
> And, tired of aimless circling in one place,
> Steer straight off after something into space. (CPoRF, 296)

Falling off a tree across the road and obstructing the path indirectly hints to check the progress of the civilisation. Such interference on the part of nature suggests man's limit in his lifestyle, "to bar / Our passage". Then, the speaker says: "But just to ask us who we think we are". This sense advocates, why does man think to be the master of the earth? Humans' enormous sense of self-importance, sometimes, is restricted by the fury of nature, "the tempest". The speaker expresses how a road blocked by a tree strikes his mind in the run of his pursuits and ambitions: "She likes to halt us in our runner tracks, / And make us get down in a foot of snow / Debating what to do without an ax". Man's irresistible desire ventures him to achieve more and more, thereby making him always hurry. Obstructing the path is nature's autonomous identity. In relation to such sense, Timothy Clark's view may be cited: "'Earth' means not just the physical environment without which no human world would exist, but also the very resistance to understanding and knowledge inherent to the non-human"[29]. The contemporary man, with the application of science and technology, shows his 'overlordship' upon nature. His overexploitation of the earth gives rise to survival threatening.

Besides, any obstruction delays man on his way of reaching "the goal". But his thought of being a supreme creature will not allow him to wait. His anthropocentric vision leads him to proceed further: "And yet she knows obstruction is in vain. / We will not be put off the final goal / We have it hidden in us to attain". Such strong impulse of man "to attain" anyhow is his egocentric tendency that causes ecological ills. Regarding this, Wendy Wheeler in her article, "Biosemiotics and the Book of Nature" states: "If we fail to preserve the earth and its biodiversity, we will surely not preserve ourselves in its absence. We are formed by the earth and its ecology-its rocks, rivers, plants and animals"[30]. Hence, the humans have to understand and realise the wrath of nature and think upon the obstruction caused by nature.

Frost's biocentric vision accentuates with seasons, climate, trees, birds, and animals in his poetry. In the poem, "Our Singing Strength", the poet demonstrates the snow in spring covering everything but one road on which migrating birds gather. He studies the presence of birds limited in number because of the late snow confusing them. Regarding the climatic position, he talks of an overnight snowfall that causes heavier consequences on the surroundings:

> Next day the scene was piled and puffed and dead.
> The grass lay flattened under one great tread.
> Borne down until the end almost took root,
> The rangey bough anticipated fruit
> With snowballs cupped in every opening bud.
> The road alone maintained itself in mud,
> Whatever its secret was of greater heat
> From inward fires or brush of passing feet. (CPoRF, 297)

The snowstorm covers everything and even the plants are covered with snowballs "but the road" – "The rangey bough anticipated fruit". On the other hand, the narrator-the human figure-in his domineering mindset forces the birds to disperse as he walks on the road. Man's such attitude troubles the relationship with other creatures. His sovereignty supplants animals represented by birds. At what extent man exploits nature, still nature persists. Because nature is self-regulating and 'non-negotiable'. In his article, "Cultivating the American Garden", Frederick Turner writes: "Nature is the process of increasing self-reference and self-measurement"[31]. To experience the power of nature, the readers observe the exemplary cooperation between birds and plants what the poet mentions at the end of the poem: "And sing the wildflowers up from root and seed". This justifies that nature is strong and alive. However, the speaker gives the birds the appellation of "the country's singing strength" (line-50) that indirectly is a respect for birds and nature. The last part of the poem attests to the conception of nature that makes it ecological in its recognition. It sends environmental awareness to be ecofriendly. In such context, Ramachandra Guha affirms: "…the beauty of nature is the blessedest and most necessary of lessons for men; and that all other efforts in education are futile till you have taught your people to love fields, birds, and flowers"[32].

The last poem of this volume, "The Need of Being Versed in Country Things" explores the relationship between man and nature. It discusses how the wind in the opposite direction of the barn saves it from the fire. It has been left abandoned since the house burned down, no livestock but the birds. They come through the broken windows and sigh about the past and their chirping lacks cheerfulness: "The birds that came to it through the air / At broken windows flew out and in, / Their murmur more like the sigh we sigh / From too much dwelling on what has been."

The images of "the lilac renewed its leaf", "the elm" scarred by fire, "the dry pump", and "the fence post" are still there for a bird to alight upon. The speaker argues that an outsider would think the birds are weeping but a country person knows better. In regard to this, Richard Poirier mentions: "The conclusion of "The Need of Being Versed in Country Things" – "One had to be versed in country things / Not to believe the phoebes wept"-sounds like a formula ready made for the delectation of critics who can then talk, as indeed I do, about poetry in nature, nature in poetry"[33]. From ecological point of view, one needs to be "versed in country things" for understanding the realities. That's why Todd A. Borlik states: "Ecological order does not exist for the sake of human delight"[34]. "The house" on fire that brings "To the midnight sky a sunset glow" refers to the destruction of a man's nesting place but it does not mean the avoidance of the mating of birds. In the past, man had no sovereignty over nature but today, he has made nature into 'a carbon sink'. In order to save himself, man has to promote an understanding of and reverence for nature.

Notes

1. Vera L. Norwood, "Heroines of Nature: Four Women Respond to the American Landscape" in *The Ecocriticism Reader,* edited by Cheryll Glotfelty & Harold Fromm, The University of Georgia Press, 1996.p.334. Norwood is a Professor of American Studies at the University of New Mexico.
2. William Howarth, "Some Principles of Ecocriticism" in *The Ecocriticism Reader,* edited by Cheryll Glotfelty & Harold Fromm, The University of Georgia Press, 1996.p.79. William Howarth is a Professor of English at Princeton university, where he teaches courses in environmental literature and history.
3. Lawrence Buell, *The Environmental Imagination: Thoreau, Nature Writing, and the Formation of American Culture,* The Belknap Press of Harvard university Press, 1995.p.7. Buell is a Professor of English at Harvard University.

4. Richard Poirier, *Robert Frost: The Work of Knowing*, New York, Oxford University Press, 1977. P119.
5. Pramod K. Nayar, *Contemporary Literary and Cultural Theory*, Pearson, 2015. P.250.
6. Randall Jarrell," To the Laodiceans", in *Robert Frost: A Collection of Critical Essays*, edited by James M. Cox Prentice-Hall, Inc. 1962, Pp.99-100.
7. Timothy Clark, *The Cambridge Introduction* to *Literature and the Environment*, Pp.118.
8. Todd A. Borlik, *Ecocriticism and Early Modern English Literature, Routledge*: Taylor & Francis. 2011. P.206.
9. Todd A. Borlik, p205.
10. Scott Slovic, "Nature Writing and Environmental Psychology" in *The Ecocriticism Reader*, edited by Cheryll Glotfelty & Harold Fromm, The University of Georgia Press, 1996.p.351.
11. Lawrence Buell, p.251
12. Lawrance Thompson, "Robert Frost's Theory of Poetry" in *Robert Frost: A Collection of Critical Essays*, edited by James M. Cox Prentice-Hall, Inc. 1962, p.22.
13. Ramachandra Guha, *Environmentalism: A Global History, A* Penguin Random House India Pvt. Ltd. 2014.p.81.
14. Lawrence Buell, p.128.
15. Lawrence Buell, p.199.
16. Mike Hulme, *Why We disagree About Climate Change: Understanding Controversy, Inaction and Opportunity*, Cambridge: Cambridge University Press. 2009. P.28.
17. Frederick Turner, "Cultivating the American Garden" in *Ecocriticism Reader*, edited by Cheryll Glotfelty & Harold Fromm, The University of Georgia Press, 1996.p.42.
18. Marion Montgomery, "Robert Frost and His Use of Barriers: Man vs Nature Toward God" in *Robert Frost: A Collection of Critical Essays*, edited by James M. Cox, Prentice-Hall, Inc. 1962, p.141.
19. Vivian C. Hopkins, Robert Frost: Out Far and In Deep" in *Interpretations: Essays on American Literature*, edited by R.K. Gupta, American Studies Research Centre, Hyderabad. 1976. P.141.
20. Harold Fromm, *The Nature of Being Human: From Environmentalism to Consciousness*, The Johns Hopkins University Press, Baltimore,2009. P.266.
21. Joseph M. Meeker, "The Comic Mode" in *The Ecocriticism Reader*, edited by Cheryll Glotfelty & Harold Fromm, The University of Georgia Press, 1996.p.162. Joseph W. Meeker is a human ecologist with a Ph.D. in comparative literature, and master's and postdoctoral studies in wildlife ecology and comparative animal and human behavior.

22. William Rueckert in his article, "Literature and Ecology" quotes Berry Commoner's first Law of Ecology, published in *The Ecocriticism Reader*, by Glotfelty & Fromm,1996, p.112. He has taught English and American Literature at Russell Sage College, Oberlin College, the University of Illinois at Champaign-Urbana, the University of Rochester, and the State University of New York at Geneseo, from which he retired in 1988.
23. Luke, Timothy W. *Ecocritique: Contesting the Politics of Nature, Economy, and Culture* Minneapolis: University of Minnesota Press, 1997.p.195.
24. William Rueckert in *Ecocriticism Reader*, p.113.
25. Greg Garrard, *Ecocriticism,* Routledge, 2012, p. 24.
26. Dona Phillips, "Is Nature Necessary?" in *The Ecocriticism Reader,* edited by Cheryll Glotfelty & Harold Fromm, The University of Georgia Press, 1996.p.221.
27. Todd A. Borlik, *Ecocriticism and Early Modern English Literature,* Routledge, Indian Reprint 2015, p.12.
28. Christopher Manes, "Nature and Silence" in *The Ecocriticism Reader,* edited by Cheryll Glotfelty & Harold Fromm, The University of Georgia Press, 1996.p.15. Manes is an author, attorney, and Ph.D. candidate in Medieval Literature at the University of Oregon.
29. Timothy Clark, *The Cambridge Introduction* to *Literature and the Environment,* Cambridge University Press, 2014, p.181. He is a specialist in Romantic, Heideggerian and post-Heideggerian poetics and in environmental criticism.
30. Wendy Wheeler, "Biosemiotics and the Book of Nature" in *The Cambridge Companion to Literature and the Environment*, edited by Louise Westling, Cambridge University Press, 2014. P.128.
31. Frederick Turner, "Cultivating the American Garden" in *The Ecocriticism Reader,* edited by Cheryll Glotfelty & Harold Fromm, The University of Georgia Press, 1996.p.44.
32. Ramachandra Guha, *Environmentalism: A Global History, A* Penguin Random House India Pvt. Ltd. 2014.p.21.
33. Richard Poirier, *Robert Frost: The Work of Knowing,* New York, Oxford University Press, 1977. P. x.
34. Todd A. Borlik, *Ecocriticism and Early Modern English Literature,* Routledge, Indian Reprint 2015, p.208.

CHAPTER 5

West-Running Brook (1928)

West-Running Brook is an important work that discusses ecological conception starting from "Spring Pools" to "The Egg and the Machine". In "Spring Pools" the poet delineates that the pools of water in forest are soon to disappear "like the flowers beside them". His biological perception asserts that the pools "chill and shiver" because of the newly budding trees absorb their innards. The speaker's ecocentric vision foresees that the summer wood will be inbred as soon as the leaves start to sprout out, the spring will die, and the topography of the forest will have a change:

These pools that, though in forests, still reflect
The total sky almost without defect,
And like the flowers beside them, chill and shiver,
Will like the flowers beside them soon be gone,
And yet not out by any brook or river,
But up by roots to bring dark foliage on
The trees that have it in their pent-up buds
To darken nature and be summer woods-
Lat them think twice before they use then powers
To blot out and drink up and sweep away
These flowery waters and these watery flowers
From snow that melted only yesterday. (CPoRF, 303)

For sustenance and viability, the trees soak up the pools that provide them to be covered with leaves and "blot out" flowers on the forest floor: "These flowery waters and these watery flowers". Such process in nature exhibits a harmonious, mutually beneficial symbiosis. Hence, William Rueckert views: "In that ecosphere there is a reciprocal interdependence of one life process upon another, and there is a mutual interconnected development of all of the earth's life systems"[1]. It needs to understand the laws of nature. Being a keen observer of the natural world, the Frostian man studies plants, geographical features and the seasons in his poetry. He presents the physical arena of spring pools, winter snows, the sky, the brooks, flowery waters, dark foliage, summer woods, and melting snow before the readers. In relation to it, Lawrence Buell writes: "When Robert Frost looks into such vernal pools, he sees only their beautiful surfaces as they briefly "reflect / The total sky almost without defect" before the thirsty roots dry them up in early summer, but Wallace renders a succinct exposition of the entire food chain without blinking"[2].

Man employs his values and motives to natural phenomena. His sense of supremacy impels unnatural treatment of nature. His ego refuses him to be a part of nature, rather he imagines to be transferred into the image of God. He thinks to have complete control and dominance over nature. The poem, "The Freedom of the Moon" discusses man's free will to control over his surroundings. The speaker reveals the complete freedom and capability to use his mind and body paradoxically to relocate the moon's position. He claims that he has "tried the new moon tilted in the air". He argues that he keeps the moon "anywhere" he pleases. His ability advocates: "I've pulled it from a crate of crooked trees". It proves as if he releases the moon out of "a crate" in which it was trapped. In other words, humans' power to control over nature treats the moon as an earthly object, not a celestial one. In such context, Harold Fromm states: "Before continuing, let us stop for a moment to see where we have been: in the early days man had no power over Nature and turned, instead, to his mind and its gods for consolation. Meanwhile, his mind produces a technology that enables his body to be strong as the gods, rendering the gods superfluous and putting Nature in a cage"[3]. It is indicative of human potentiality to master the universe. If this tendency is respected, it would be difficult to preserve the integrity, stability, sustainability and beauty of the biotic community. Integration of mankind with nature would be helpful to reduce the threat of ecological holocaust. The anthropogenic goes against the nature-centred-systems.

Contrary to this, Frost also exposes the subtle relationship that nature shares with human beings. His imaginative act of identification on nature's beauty and vitality appeals to human psyche. This sort of identification forms a positive sense of an unalienated union of mind and nature. The poem, "The Rose Family" represents an elitist appropriation of nature. It unfurls the love and beauty of nature. Here, Frost's foresight seems to be narrowly anthropocentric and broadly biocentric. The speaker enriches the poem with botanical precision shaping into a floral cloak of beauty:

> The rose is a rose,
> And was always a rose.
> But the theory now goes
> That the apple's a rose,
> And the pear is, and so's
> The plum, I suppose.
> The dear only knows
> What will next prove a rose.
> You, of course, are a rose-
> But were always a rose. (CPoRF, 305)

The poem demonstrates botanical categorisation to assert the beauty of the rose as something classic, a lasting beauty. He claims that the apple tree is a part of the rose family: "That the apple's a rose, / And the pear is, and so's / The plum". The rose, the apple, the pear and the plum – all are beautiful – justifying the speaker's ecocentric mindset. He is not in favor of the scientific classification to acknowledge this. However, Frost is away from capitalistic temperament that evinces his environmental concern and love for nature. The recognition of beauty in nature certifies the artistic talent of Frost that provides him the opportunities for enjoyment.

In some of his poems, Frost creates the relationship between organisms and their environment that substantiates his ecological intuition. The poem, "Fireflies in the Garden" attributes to the ecological system that everyone experiences in day-to-day life. As the dusk approaches, "the real stars" begin to shine in the sky. Corollary to this, on the earth below, the "fireflies" start flitting about with their brightly lit up tails: "Here come real stars to fill the upper skies, / And here on earth come emulating flies." As a keen observer, the poet minutely studies the natural phenomena and leads the readers to think over the autonomy of nature whether the fireflies can accomplish the outstanding role of stars in the night sky. In the end of the poem, he concludes that fireflies cannot be equal with the stars: "they can't sustain the part." But from ecological conception, there is the interconnectedness between the rising of stars and the flying of fireflies. In such context, Graham Huggan and Helen Tiffin can be cited: "Simply to import such condensed ecological formula as Berry Commoner's First Law of Ecology that "everything is connected to everything else" […] into a literary-critical context…"[4].

In our biosphere, there are complex interactions and interrelationships with one another.

Nature shapes its own image if there is no interference of artificiality. Every creation is automatic in the absence of human-centred- systems. In the poem, "Devotion", the way of the water of the ocean thrashing against the land's shore conveys the idea of nature-made. Besides, it is nature's love and loyalty that formulates devotion for "supernatural naturalism". It is the true devotion that demonstrates the infinite wash of the water against the shore in "an endless repetition" like the sun's rising and setting and the moon's monthly shining and fading. Humans know the cosmos through images and words but their anthropocentric mindset disturbs them to understand the eternal truth. The Frostian man sings: "The heart can think of no devotion / Greater than being shore to the ocean-/ Holding the curve of one position, / Counting an endless repetition." Man should inject this biocentric idea into his materialistic mind to realise the importance of his relationship with nature like the ocean and the shore. Human technology devastates that relationship. Mention may be made of Louise Westling's views who states: "Ecocriticism grows out of this context, in some ways reviving pastoral and romantic attitudes toward the natural world, but informed by modern science and responding to alarm about the fragility of biological environments increasingly devastated by human technologies"[5]. Humans should reintegrate with nature for a sustainable living. They should rethink of its importance.

Nature in Frost's poetry, as readers feel, contributes to his awareness of self and non-self. It is in this sense that he makes communication between the inner self and the outer world, between mind and body (mind is culture; body is nature). Most of the time, a poignant debate goes on between inner consciousness and external nature. He sketches the sense of harmony, even identity in vividness with a person's own surroundings. His constant process of inspecting and interpreting nature astounds the readers to think many times upon the creation. In "The Cocoon", he presents "one poor house alone" that puts a question about its existence when there are almost no signs of life around it. Readers feel as if the observer is present on the spot: "As far as I can see" to conclude with scarcely a sign of habitation.

The images like "the autumn haze", "the evening air", "the new moon", "pours the elm-tree meadow full of bloom", "one poor house", "one chimney", and "smoke" shape pastoral view in the biophysical world. The absolute serenity tunes the cosmic symphony of the spheres that is inaudible but subject to feel. "The Cocoon" bears the stamp of pastoral aesthetics and ethics. In this context, Todd A. Borlik mentions: "This yearning for a life in harmony with nature, which finds expression in pastoral, may have political and psychological motivations, but this does not prevent the mode from voicing a real empathetic engagement with the biophysical world"[6]. Frost's description of "the elm-tree meadow full of blue" underpins a pastoral invitation to a bountiful blue-green planet. Today, pastoral has been poisoned due to evil-spell of greedy, rapacious industrialism and commercialism. Nature-lovers hardly find opportunity to observe pastoral view.

Advanced technology obstacles man to enjoy the aesthetic view in nature. Nature sparkles with divine energies and beauties. Through his poems, Frost tries to make connectivity between man and nature. The poem, "A Passing Glimpse" displays the fleeting glimpses of flowers seen from "a passing car" of "the train". Flower is nature-made that bestows beauty. Train is man-made that talks of technology. Nature systems and human systems are in binary opposition thereby the Frostian man loses personal contact with nature: "I often see flowers from a passing car / That are gone before I can tell what they are / I want to get out of the train and go back / To see what they were beside the track / I name all the flowers I am sure they weren't. / […] / Heaven gives its glimpses only to those / Not in position to look too close." The binary opposition contextualises the concept of the machine created by man versus the living beauty of nature, the artificial versus the natural. Train's prerogative contrasts with nature's delicate, beautiful flowers. Man creates the machine but machine enslaves the man. The contemporary life-style directed by capitalism and consumerism tends to divorce humans from nature. In this matter, Timothy Clark advocates: "Modern people treat the natural world with such brutality because their culture is based on the view that humanity is separate from and superior to it"[7] . But the Frostian man is not in the run of 'greed economy', rather he thinks of beauty that multiplies when one steps back and looks at it from a distance. Thus, man has to return back from the machine-world and revalue nature.

The materialistic way of living is defined by its quantum of pollution and waste. Regarding this, Greg Garrard declares:

"Pollution: it's a crying shame"[8]. The increasing modernisation in competitive economy is the cause of environmental deterioration. The hustle and bustle of life for wealth accumulation turns the surroundings into 'a carbon sink'. The capitalistic mindset runs after the fulfilment of insatiable wishes thereby producing a troubled and chaotic environment. In the poem, "A Peck of Gold", the poet presents humans' greed that pervades upheavals in the life-sustaining air:

> Dust always blowing about the town,
> Except when sea-fog laid it down,
> And I was one of the children told
> Some of the blowing dust was gold.
> All the dust the wind blew high
> Appeared like gold in the sunset sky,
> But I was one of the children told
> Some of the dust was really gold.
> Such was life in the Golden Gate.
> Gold dusted all we drank and ate,
> And I was one of the children told,
> 'We all must eat our peck of gold'. (CPoRF, 312)

The poem strikes Frost's ecocentric vision that assesses the prevalent social system, lifestyle and attitudes of people. He draws attention to harmful contamination of air that "we drank and ate". In the name of progress and materialistic success, as the speaker claims, the people of San Francisco alienate themselves from nature, turning it into a hill of "dust". The emphasis on capitalistic ideology is the principal cause of man's tragic flaw that damages the environment. In such context, Ramachandra Guha advocates: "The ecology crisis is insoluble under capitalism. We have to get rid of the capitalist manner of regulating the economy, and above all of the capitalist driving mechanism, for a start at least bringing it under control"[9] . For a stable and sustainable living, anthropocentrism should be restricted. Humans and environment are absolutely inter-related. Besides, environmental conditions and mental health are reciprocal to each other. "All the dust the wind blew high / Appeared like gold in the sunset sky" creates socio-ecological challenges arising from man's response to materialistic bent of mind. Hence, he is the product of his own suffering.

Man is the only knowledgeous creature who can understand the other biological communities that surround him. As a literary and well-conscious mortal, he is aware of the cyclical notion of time. In the sonnet, "Acceptance", the artist reacts on nature's unconcern for the passing of light and the passing of time: "When the spent sun throws up its rays on cloud / And goes down burning into the gulf below, / No voice in nature is heard to cry aloud /At what has happened. Birds, at least, must know /It is the change to darkness in the sky." The human world contrasts with the natural world. The other creatures try to accept the self-regulating system of nature. The birds and other creatures accept that the sun has gone and will return again. But man cannot take it easily and thinks upon it as a difficult task for acceptance. Nightfall is a natural occurrence and hence, man has to admit nature's autonomy. In this parameter, Alison Byerly in her article, "The Uses of Landscape" quotes Pete Gunther who "has pointed out that man and nature bear different relations to time: "Man lives in a progressive, expressive, non-repetitive time; ecology is the science of cyclical repetition" (112)[*]. One way to reconcile these two opposing movements, the arrow and the circle, is to freeze them both"[10]. Man should not expect that nature will be tamed or bent down to his own will.

The appropriate reading of nature is to acknowledge its power and sovereignty. Man should know that he is simply a part of nature, not the master of all. All is well until man's unnecessary interference intrudes to upset this order. The ocean seems to be innocent but due to man's interfering in its natural flow, it makes a death-dance. Frost's attitude of care and wonder towards nature turns him to be more biocentric than anthropocentric. The poem, "Once by the Pacific" in the traditional form of the sonnet, demonstrates the destructive rage of the ocean against mankind. Man exploits nature and nature shows its ferocity. The shore, cliff and continent all are against the threat of the forthcoming storm; the destructive force of the ocean:

> The shattered water made a misty din.
> Great waves looked over others coming in,
> And thought of doing something to the shore
> That water never did to land before.
> The clouds were low and hairy in the skies,
> Like locks blown forward in the gleam of eyes.
> You could not tell, and yet it looked as if
> The shore was lucky in being backed by cliff,
> The cliff in being backed by continent;
> It looked as if a night of dark intent
> Was coming, and not only a night, an age.
> Someone had better be prepared for rage.
> There would be more than ocean-water broken
> Before God's last *Put out the Light* was spoken. (Norton, 1775-1776)

The Frostian man is in a sense of urgency about the demise of the world. In fear and hope of impending apocalypse, he wonders about the source of the ocean's destructive "rage". The lines-"It looked as if a night of dark intent / Was coming, and not only a night, an age"- unfurl as if the end of the world is imminent. Shakespearean tragi-hero Othello, in Act-V, Scene-II, expresses in soliloquy: "Put out the light and then Put out the light" on account of suspecting Desdemona's honesty and killing her on her contaminated bed as the darkest villain Iago has poisoned his mind. Frost concludes the sonnet by emphasising on "Put out the light". With this in mind, Greg Garrard exponents: "But most importantly, for our purposes, apocalypticism is inevitably bound up with imagination, because it has yet to come into being"[11]. However, the waves are the outcomes of the changing weather systems that make them most terrifying. The sonnet ends with God's supererogatory power to abandon the humanity completely because of man's evil. Man's possessiveness is the cause of his sufferings.

God has created a perfect environment for His creatures. He has arranged everything to their benefit. But man's greediness disobeys God and ruptures the environment created by Him. With the knowledge of science and technology, man thinks to be immortal. Such will of the man is not accepted, rather he faces troubles and predicaments for violating the order. In the poem, "Lodged", Frost uses the symbols of rain and wind to expose man's struggle in life. In these struggles, when his predicaments multiply, he feels "pushing" and "pelting" like the wind and rain against "the garden bed":

> The rain to the wind said
> 'You push and I'll pelt'
> They so smote the garden bed
> That the flowers actually knelt,
> And lay lodged-though not dead.
> I know how the flowers felt. (CPoRF, 315)

As the flowers are lodged, or flattened by the force of rain and wind, man should turn to God for disobeying the law of nature. Regarding this type of situation, Paula Gunn Allen in her article "The Sacred Hoop" states: "God is known as the All Spirit, and other beings are also spirit – more spirit than body, more spirit than intellect, more spirit than mind. The natural state of existence is whole"[12]. Each and every creature is portion of a living whole.

Man is obviously anthropocentric. He shows little regard or concern for other species and focuses on his own activities. His existence and his interests are of solely value and constantly take priority over those of other species. Nature is necessarily beautiful but man's anthropocentrism distances him from enjoying it. Frost's poem, "A Minor Bird" underpins man's ego-consciousness that restricts him to appreciate nature. Driving away the bird with the sound of clapping hands propounds man's hegemony over nature:

I have wished a bird would fly away,
And not sing by my house all day;
Have clapped my hands at him from the door
When it seemed as if I could bear no more.
The fault must partly have been in me.
The bird was not to blame for his key.
And of course, there must be something wrong
In wanting to silence any song. (CPoRF, 316)

In the last four lines of the poem, the speaker returns from ego-consciousness to eco-consciousness. He realises that bird's singing was not fault of the bird: "The fault must partly have been in me / The bird was not to blame for his key". In the end, he confesses his mistake "to silence" the bird's song. The first four lines demonstrate man's anthropocentric vision and the last four lines reveal the biocentric bend of mind. In regard to this, Harold Fromm writes: "At the high end of the ecological conversation, we are confronted with several antinomies that roughly define the specialised subsets of the discourse:deep vs. shallow ecology, biocentrism vs. anthropocentrism, reform vs. radical ecology; and there are myriad terms that shape and shade the major positions, such as conservationist, preservationist, liberal, leftist, bioregional, New Age, mainstream and so forth"[13]. The statement of Fromm is enough to acknowledge the position of Frost.

In earlier days, there was no spectacular development of science and technology. In those times, man had been part of nature but now he is estranged from nature. God had created Adam and then Eve to give company to man. During such eras, it was in man's mind that God is all-Powerful who has created day and night, the earth and all other biotic and abiotic. God had given him plants, animals, birds, fishes, and everything for man's benefit. But in course of time, man took advantage of such benefits in wrong way. He attributed antagonistic qualities to his natural surroundings thereby the outcome was his psychological tension. He felt as if everybody and everything is against him. In such paranoiac fear, man sees the leaves of the trees as snakes rising to strike him; to what Frost unfolds in "Bereft":

> Leaves got up in a coil and hissed,
> Blindly struck at my knee and missed.
> Something sinister in the tone
> Told me my secret must be known:
> Word I was in the house alone
> Somehow must have gotten abroad,
> Word I was in my life alone,
> Word I had no one left but God. (CPoRF, 317)

In isolation and loneliness, man thinks of God in the hope of getting consolation. Unless does man understand himself and recognise his love for nature, he cannot find a home in nature, nor can live outside of it. It needs to acknowledge the view of Harold Fromm who affirms: "In the early days, humankind had no power over Nature and turned, instead, to its mind and its gods for consolation. Meanwhile, this mind produces a technology that enables its body to be as strong as the gods, rendering the gods superfluous and putting Nature in a cage"[14]. Psychologically and physically man is in disturbed conditions. He should rethink of his life in nature.

For a healthy life and peace of mind, man should have contact with the beauty of the surroundings and with nature. To live sustainably man should emphasise on idyllic settings. The ecological balance is necessary for congenial and conducive existence. Frost's poems attest to environmental reverence for the green earth. The poem, "Tree at My Window" is the paradigm for understanding man's proper relation to nature. The Frostian man wakes up from his sleep and gazes at the tree outside his bedroom window. The branches of the tree frivolously tap against the window pane thereby the speaker compares: "Your head so much concerned with outer, / Mine with inner, weather". It explains that man can neither physically nor psychologically get amity without green things:

> Tree at my window, window tree,
> My sash is lowered when night comes on,
> But let there never be curtain drawn
> Between you and me
> Vague dream-head lifted out of the ground,
> And thing next most diffuse to cloud,
> Not all your light tongues talking aloud
> Could be profound.
> But, there, I have seen you taken and tossed,

And if you have seen me when I slept,
You have seen me when I was taken and swept
And all but lost
That day she put our heads together,
Fate had her imagination about her,
Your head so much concerned with outer,
Mine with inner, weather. (Oliver, 408)

As it is observed, Frost intentionally keeps and speaks of man when he speaks about nature. Nature exists and man has to experience it. Examining the role of nature and particularly its applicability in the above poem, it needs to acknowledge the opinion of Joseph W. Meeker who states: "Human values could no longer be based on the assumption that man is alone at the center of creation; allowance would have to be made for the welfare of all the plants, animals, and land of the natural environment"[15]. It is a strategy for living which needs the harmony between humanity and nature.

Environmental problems also stem from the systems of domination and exploitation of humans by other humans. Focusing on the grounds of political, economic and social exploitation, "man have warred" among themselves. Besides, religious dogmas, anarchism and communism, etc. raise binary in social strictures. In other words, the current state of the world undergoes a lot of difficulties and problems resulting from differences and variances in religious beliefs, social ideology, political leadership, and feelings of inequity. The disturbance in society also disturbs the environment. Frost's poem, "The Peaceful Shepherd" talks of such disorders that turn into war and hostility. The "Crown", "Scales", and "Cross" signify different facets of society; government, economy, and religion respectively. It is a fact that environmental problems cannot be separated from social problems; both are interrelated. In such context, Greg Garrard clarifies: "Eco-Marxists and social ecologists are therefore neither monists nor dualists. One of the consequences of this view is that environmental problems cannot be clearly divorced from things more usually defined as social problems"[16]. Environmental deterioration is connected with conflict and war in society.

Survival sustainability undergoes a threat when humans exploit over non-humans. When they interface with each other, it turns to a struggle for existence, especially for the non-humans and such trespass of humans push them into the way of extinction. Humans' enormous sense of self-importance creates vulnerable situation for the non-humans which is observed and experienced in Frost's poem, "The Thatch": "So low I brushed the straw with my sleeves, / I flushed birds out of hole after hole, / Into the darkness." The speaker disturbs and unsettles the birds from their nests in the roof thatch and his egocentric brutality injects him to flush "birds out of hole, / into the darkness". Properly understood from ecological point of view, man does not have the right to do anything whimsically with the usual process of nature. As it is studied, humans prefer to supersede the non-humans thereby such problem often seems uncompromising. This sentiment obviously generates problems for ecological balance of the planet. To save the ecosystem, human laws should make preservation and protection of the non-humans. By these activities, it will not mean man's bending of mind or surrender before non-humans; rather it will be man's mind-expanding and generosity. From that perspective, the speaker's realisation for making the birds dislodged – "It grieved my soul" – turns him into a different one from egocentric to ecocentric. It becomes more promulgated when he says: "They could not go flying about in search / Of their nest again, nor find a perch". By this temperament, it would create a harmonious, mutually beneficial relationships between man and nature. Therefore, man has to present himself as a microscopic part of nature, not the master of all. He has to learn that getting along with one's fellow creatures is the most driving force for sustainability.

The pedagogic context of the cycle of seasons seems to be very strong and powerful drive in Frost's poetry. The image of nature constructs the beautiful scenic views of a lush green paradise like Eden to the spectator. If one is far away from all sorts of capitalistic achievements and devalues materialistic importance in life, one will tend towards nature and appreciate the glory of nature. Capitalism is the source of all conflicts, oppressions and environmental crises that create a divide between man and nature. Nature is not a dead object but a living entity. It unfurls a vista of beauty that enthralls the eyes and pacifies the heart. The poem, "A Winter Eden" visualises a beautiful snowy landscape with bushes wrapped in "berries shining scarlet red". As one looks closer, one is a step closer to heaven. Besides, a picturesque and aesthetic spectacle becomes a means of solace for man's restless mind. A sense of complacency takes place in observing images of buds and berries abound:

A winter garden in alder swamp,
Where conies now come out to shun and romp,
As near a paradise as it can be
And not melt snow or start a dormant tree.
It lifts existence on a plane of snow
One level higher than the earth below,
One level nearer heaven overhead,
And last year's berries shining scarlet red.
It lifts a gaunt luxuriating beast
Where he can stretch and hold his highest feast
On some wild apple tree's young tender bark,
What well may prove the year's high girdle mark.
So near to paradise all pairing ends:
Here loveless birds now flock as winter friends,
Content with bud-inspecting. They presume
To say which buds are leaf and which are bloom.
A feather-hammer gives a double knock
This Eden day is done at two o'clock.
An hour of winter day might seem too short
To make it worth life's while to wake and sport. (CPoRF, 322)

The poem discusses "winter day" in the cycle of seasons that symbolises the transition to rebirth. Nature, gendered female, associates the fertility to have rebirth in spring. The poem refurbishes of Milton's *The Nativity Ode* that fabricates an 'explanation for why Christ was born in Winter'.

Nature in awe to him
Had doff't her gaudy trim
With her great Master so to sympathise:
It was no season then for her
To wanton with the Sun, her lusty Paramour. (32-36)

Milton emphasises on nature's submission to God because God had created the garden of Eden and also Adam and Eve. The mankind disobeyed God but nature welcomed the savior's birth. In such context, Paul Gunn Allen states: "In Paradise, God created a perfect environment for his creatures. He arranged it to their benefit, asking only that they forebear from eating the fruit of one particular tree"[17]. Due to exploring curiosity and greediness, man disobeyed God and estranged from nature. But nature is not barred from preserving the seeds in winter and nurturing them in spring. Man's interference in nature's self-regulating system is ecocide.

The submerged thematic undercurrent of racial supremacy of the Whites over the Non-Whites is also experienced in Frost's poetry. The binary between the Whites and the Non-Whites, the oppressor and the oppressed enhances to ecological problems. Racial incongruity constructs socio-ecological problems through favoritism, discrimination and economic exploitation. Frost's poem, "The Flood" published in 1928, talks of the natural disaster of the great Mississippi River flood of 1927 that had killed thousands of African Americans. And most of these races were rootless and homeless. Herbert Hoover, at that time President in U.S.A. supervised the rescue efforts. "His betrayal of African – American victims of the flood led blacks to leave the Republican party..." (Google: https://www.lehigh.edu > ~amsp >2005/09 > flood-by-...). The conflict – between a race that undergoes depravity, tyranny, exploitation and evil by another race which is essentially an exploiter and the looter---damages the ecosystem. In this poem, Frost makes a response to such racism between the White and the Black and also the Non-Whites' victimisation in natural calamity: "But power of blood itself releases blood / It goes by might of being such a flood / Held high at so unnatural a level."

That flood in 1927 had destroyed the lives and livelihoods of the millions of people, mostly the poor and the African-American who could have been evacuated and rescued. From ecocritical perspective, man's carbon economy sabotages nature but that tendency cannot control nature's fury. Besides, the socio-economy-racial problem between haves and have-nots becomes acute in post-disaster. That's why the American environmental philosopher Deane Curtin states: "the connection, in theory and practice, of race and the environment so that the oppression of one is connected to, and supported by, the oppression of the other"[18].

Among all the species of the universe, man is, undoubtedly, an adaptive animal. His survival and sustenance depend upon his mind and ability to change himself rather than his environment. Hence, he should be modest and unheroic, not egocentric, to have a fruitful integration with nature. In the poem, "Acquainted with the Night", the artist declares: "I have been one acquainted with the night. / I have walked out in rain – and back in rain". Man's mind learns to identify and measure the physical factors for the environmental assessment thereby the artist proclaims: "the time was neither wrong nor right. / I have been one acquainted with the night". Therefore, man has to cultivate such type of mentality that will make him capable of understanding the intricate processes between himself and nature. This understanding will generate eco-friendly tendency in man.

Frost's gender-conscious prospectus attributes to ecofeminism. Obviously, women are connected with motherhood and nurturing that make them closer to nature. Contrasted with this, men are involved with culture. Such discourse pinpoints that the exploitation of the environment and the oppression of women are deeply interlinked. In his poem, "The Lovely Shall Be Choosers", Frost articulates the imposed patterns of male power and female powerlessness. The speaker inquiries into the stages or "joys" in women's lives that may be nothing more than punishment for loving and serving others. The image of a woman's womanhood lies in the extent of tolerance, care and innocence. The speaker talks of the seven "joys" that coincide with the traditional events in a woman's life. Each "joy" undergoes a secret sorrow in the sense that the woman sublimates the wishes to fulfil her role as wife and mother. At each stage, she "almost speaks", but the circumscribed circumstance puts obstacles on communication. Her "silence" is the only source of resistance. Besides, the reductive identification of women with passive nature is an indirect act of exploitation.

Man's existence runs like water in the flow of time, otherwise his fate will be of dinosaurs. The poem, "West-Running Brook", which furnishes the title for Frost's fifth volume, bases upon a dialogue between a wife and her husband. The woman, who is closer to nature for her biology, talks about nature while the man, who represents culture, emphasises on time. Besides, it has a certain implicit reference about racism. The racial disparity between the Whites and the Blacks becomes an issue to give the environment a backward turn like the brook that runs down to the West and differentiates itself from all other brooks flowing East to the ocean:

> 'Fred, where is north?'
> 'North? North is there, my love.
> The brook runs west.'
> 'West-running Brook then call it.'
> (West-running Brook men call it to this day)
> 'What does it think it's doing running west
> When all the country brooks flow east
> To reach the ocean?
> ....
> 'Why, my dear,
> That wave's been standing off this jut of shore'-
> (The black stream, catching on a sunken rock,

Flung backward on itself in one white wave,
And the white water rode the black forever,
Not gaining but not losing, like a bird
White feathers from the struggle of whose breast
Flecked the dark stream and flecked the darker pool
Below the point, and were at last driven wrinkled
In a white scarf against the far shore alders)
That wave's been standing off this jut of shore. (Oliver, 409)

The Whites' domination over the Blacks was one of the factors behind the partition of the Northern and Southern states in America. In this matter, Lawrance Thompson states: "We may go on to play the age-old game of analogies and say that the poet's hunger for creating a sense of stability and of crystallisation from the flux of things has in it a sacred regret of its own – and a sense of triumph in his accomplishment, for this very reason"[19]. The bio-social context of racism constructs environmental hazards. The cruelty of supremacy of one race by another paves the way to conflicts that pollutes the biosphere. Regarding this, Harold Fromm quotes: "It is no easy matter to extricate oneself from these biases, to arrive at a more ecocentric state of thinking than western culture now sustains, without falling into other biases like environmental racism"[20]. It portrays the phenomena of discriminatory treatment of socially marginalised and economically disadvantaged peoples.

Ecocritical perspective discusses the confrontation between man's power and nature's force. Both man and nature try to locate the importance of their own way of existence. The poem, "Sand Dunes" sketches the sea and the sand representing nature's force that defends not only man's ego and exploitive attitude but also attempts to destroy mankind. The artist delves into the dualism between the anthropocentric position and the biocentric standpoint:

Sea waves are green and wet,
But up from where they die,
Rise others vaster yet,
And those are brown and dry.
They are the sea made land
To come at the fisher town,
And bury in solid sand
The men she could not drown.
She may know cove and cape,
But she does not know mankind
If by any change of shape,
She hopes to cut off mind.
Men left her a ship to sink:

> They can leave her a hut as well;
> And be but more free to think
> For the one more cast-off shell. (CPoRF, 330)

The destructive force of nature is exemplified when the speaker exposes: "And bury in solid sand / The men she could not drown". To take revenge upon mankind, – "she hopes to cut off mind" – nature imposes physical death to man. But nature is unaware of the sophistication of human mind; the way in which it works: "But she does not know mankind". The conflict arises between nature-centred systems and human-centred values. Human-centred values supersede nature.

Readers can understand the poet's mind and his potential intimacy with nature through his poems. The way in which he demonstrates the day-to-day happenings of human life in nature that justifies his profound understanding of the interrelationship between man and nature. The poem, "The Times Table" displays his ecological vision and environmental attentiveness: "More than halfway up the pass / Was a spring with a broken drinking glass, / And whether the farmer drank or not / His mare was sure to observe the spot / By cramping the wheel on a water-bar." The socio-ecological balance is necessary for the sustainability of the universe. To maintain the balance, it requires a deeper understanding and extensive probing into the various aspects of the ecosystem. Population explosion generates environmental crisis. It makes nature miserable: "Was a spring with a broken drinking glass". Besides, the growth in population needs to be controlled and checked for the betterment of less interference and keeping nature safe and secured from pollution thereby the artist concludes: "Reduce the births of the human race, / And bring back nature in people's place". In such context, Timothy Clark proclaims: "In the 1960s and 1970s the exponential growth in the human population became the often-leading concern of environmental movements. The human population is still soaring today, moving from about 6 billion in 2000 towards a projected 9 billion by 2060, a trend ecologists would see in any other species as leading inevitably to a crash"[21]. The earth has a limited capacity to bear the pressure of mankind. Frost tries to curb that growth.

Nature seems to be uninteresting and boring when the materialistic society attaches importance to sophistication and luxurious lifestyle. This short-sighted vision does not concern with the pollution and the spoilation of the ecosystem. The poem, "The Investment" displays – "an old, old house renewed with paint", a "man and wife", "an impulse not to care", "extravagance" – the testimony of acquisitiveness that underpins ecological ruination. Besides, man's relation to the soil – the lonely figure of "a digger" in a desolate landscape, "the plowed ground in the cold", and "unearthed potatoes" – becomes changed as "some money suddenly come into". Paganism loses significance in materialism.

Frost experiences the botanical forms of life in nature. The delightful grassy glade overgrows into wilderness in the cycle of seasons if there is no "mowing". His traditional ground knowledge as a rural farmer is well-equipped in "The Last Mowing". The poem designates a "Far-away Meadow" that is abandoned, takes over by the wild flowers before turning into a massive wilderness:

> There's a place called Far-away Meadow
> We never shall mow in again,
> Or such is the talk at the farmhouse:
> The meadow is finished with men.
> Then now is the chance for the flowers
> That can't stand mowers and plowers.
> It must be now, though, in season
> Before the not mowing brings trees on,
> Before trees, seeing the opening,
> March into a shadowy claim.
> The trees are all I'm afraid of,
> That flowers can't bloom in the shade of;
> It's no more men I'm afraid of;
> The meadow is done with the tame.
> The place for the moment is ours
> For you, oh tumultuous flowers,
> To go to waste and go wild in,
> All shapes and colors of flowers,
> I needn't call you by name. (CPoRF, 338)

The line, – "All shapes and colors of flowers" – demonstrates nature's triumph over the supererogatory of man. The farmer leaves the meadow to turn wild "in season" or to change into apparently an untamed landscape while "The meadow is done with the tame". However, Yvor Winters propounds: "Shape and color are named as pure abstractions; no particular shape or color is given; and what we get is an image of the shapeless and the shadowy, of haunting confusion, of longing for something unrealisable, of the fields of asphodel"[22]. On the other hand, wilderness is nature's construct. It has a 'sacramental value'. It opens up a relation between humanity and the earth. In such context, Greg Garrard exposes: "The idea of wilderness, signifying nature in a state uncontaminated by civilisation, is the most potent construction of nature available to New World environmentalism"[23].

Frost keeps a strong affinity for his native place. In one's self-awareness, the place that one loves, spontaneously feeds ingredients to the heart. That place becomes the prime source of values, meaning and purpose in one's state of mind. Obviously, such an impulse arises from the basic level of desires to be a part of the surroundings that simplifies the improvement of life in the ecosystem and also articulates each one's place-consciousness. Therefore, Richard Nelson expresses: "What makes a place special is the way it buries itself inside the heart, not whether it's flat or rugged, rich or austere, wet or arid, gentle or harsh, warm or cold, wild or tame. Every place, like every person, is elevated by the love and respect shown toward it, and by the way in which its bounty is received"[24]. Frost unfolds the same feeling and the same thought in "The Birthplace" that values the love and relation between man and nature:

Here further up the mountain slope
Than there was ever any hope,
My father built, enclosed a spring,
Strong chains of wall round everything,
Subdued the growth of earth to grass,
And brought our various lives to pass.
A dozen girls and boys we were.
The mountain seemed to like the stir,
And made of us a little while-
With always something in her smile,
Today she wouldn't know our name
(No girl's, of course, has stayed the same.)
The mountain pushed us off her knees.
And now her lap is full of trees. (CPoRF, 339)

The visual imageries of "the mountain slope", "a spring", "the growth of earth to grass" and "full of trees" etc. portray the emotional relation of the artist with nature and construct the survival value on earth. He tries to communicate that nature is alive as changes take place. He delves into the deeper realms of meaning underlying the forms of the physical world. Out of some nostalgia for the past of childhood days, the artist becomes emotional and then becomes convinced of the laws of nature that is automatic. Besides, Leslie Marmon Silko expresses: "Survival depended upon harmony and cooperation not only among human beings, but among all things – the animate and the less animate"[25]. The artist concludes the poem in emotional way: "The mountain pushed us off her knees. /And now her lap is full of trees". But it is necessary for the pure, clean, life-sustaining air.

In the carbon dominated world, it seems difficult to get clean-air. Commercialism, capitalism, consumerism and expansionism etc. disrupt the earth that is lost to the cataclysm of global warming and the appalling climate change. Exposure to the sun's ultraviolet radiation disfigures the skin by creating dark spots, dry, rough and wrinkle. Man's proper care for nature, instead of exploiting, will save him from sunburnt as Frost describes in his poem, "Sitting by a Bush in Broad Sunlight". Sunlight cannot penetrate his fingers as he sits by a bush: "When I spread out my hand here today, / I catch no more than a ray / To feel of between thumb and fingers, / No lasting effect of it lingers." In the first stanza, the speaker unfolds nature's role to give protection to man from sunburnt. But in the second stanza, he presumes how life originated "When dust really took the sun". The line – "Again come to life and crawl off" – signifies Darwinian theory, "survival of the fittest". It reminds the readers of Thoreau's biological ideas in *Walden*. In these issues, Frederick Turner states: "Nature is the process of increasing self-reference and self-measurement. Evolution is how nature finds out what it is. In the first moment of the Big Bang, it didn't have the faintest idea"[26]. The artist's version of "sun-smitten slime" and "crawl off" is biological.

Man struggles for material possessions that underpins Darwin's phrase, "struggle for existence". The poem, "The Armful" incubates the network of man's greed to acquire more and more although something is beyond his capacity. Such type of mentality descopes aesthetic pleasures in life. Frost consistently tries to expose the channels of confrontation and communication between man and nature. Man, in his whims and caprices, attempts to use and abuse nature thereby rupturing the subtle and ingenious relationship between himself and the earth. In the poem, "Riders", the speaker delves into man-nature confrontation:

> The surest thing there is we are riders,
> And though none too successful at it, guiders,
> Through everything presented, land and tide
> And the very air, of what we ride.
> What is this talked-of mystery of birth
> But being mounted bareback on the earth?
> We can just see the infant up astride,

His small fist buried in the bushy hide.
There is our wildest mount-a headless horse.
But though it runs unbridled off its course,
And all our blandishment would seem defied,
We have ideas yet that we haven't tried. (CPoRF, 345)

Humans try to control the earth and prefer to lead in a direction as per their will. That's why the relationship between man and nature is viewed as exploiter and exploited. The distortion and deformation of the earth is man's own product. In such context, Harold H. Watts speaks: "That is, we are-in Frost's sense of the word – "environmentalists" and more intelligently with the beast (process) which carries us, a beast that Frost calls, in this same poem, "our wildest mount – a headless horse" [...] one among the many aspects of the confrontation of man with nature"[27].

Human world is chaotic and environmental threats operate from modern civilisation. Man is thought to be the center of the universe thereby he presents himself as a triumphant creature among all. But he lacks the value of permanence and tranquility what heaven has. "On Looking up by Chance at the Constellations" discusses the speaker's comparison between human world and the heavenly bodies. The sky is calm and nothing sensational happens there. Every disturbance is in human world. Hence, nature and culture are different to each other.

Living is the most vital force as it needs adaptability and accountability to each one's environment. It is assumed that nature cares about the lives of each creature. The ecological view of life acknowledges to be simple, modest and unheroic. It is a strategy for living like Frost's "The Bear". The poem discusses how the bear acts and reacts in its natural environment. The animal pulls down the tree branches to collect some food and after retrieving the fruit, it lets the branch to go "upright in the sky":

The bear puts both arms around the tree above her
And draws it down as if it were a lover
And its choke cherries lips to kiss good-by,
Then lets it snap back upright in the sky.
Her next step rocks a boulder on the wall
(She's making her cross-country in the fall).
Her great weight creaks the barbed-wire in its staples
As she flings over and off down through the maples,
Leaving on one wire tooth a lock of hair.
Such is the uncaged progress of the bear. (CPoRF, 347)

Such sensuous movement of the bear draws the observer to contemplate it as a thing of beauty. Its skilled movement shapes a majestic manner when it feeds. Nature is the platform whereby life stands with the prime source of values, meaning and purpose. All creatures are bound to depend upon their natural surroundings for their sustainability.

But man's aesthetic sensitivity to the idea of good and beautiful got changed due to advanced technologies and mushrooming populations. Besides, the concept of rapacious industrialism and competitive commerce is the cause of global ecological collapse. From day-to-day, nature undergoes a startling alternation as human technologies astoundingly rupture and disintegrate the biological environments. "The Egg and the Machine", the last poem of this volume, studies technology's harmful impact on nature. The speaker reacts against the techno-product of the rail track that destroys a turtle's nest. He shows his hatred and anger towards a locomotive and in retaliation throws turtle's eggs at it:

> He gave the solid rail a hateful kick.
> From far away there came an answering tick
> And then another tick He knew the code
> His hate had roused an engine up the road.
> He wished when he had had the track alone
> He had attacked it with a club or stone
> And bent some rail wide open like a switch
> So as to wreck the engine in the ditch. (CPoRF, 349)

Frost assumes for a complacent form of harmony and integrity in the human relationship with nature. He is disturbed at environmental pillage and biosystems that are being destroyed. Regarding this, Louise Westling affirms: "Ecocriticism grows out of this context, in some ways reviving pastoral and romantic attitudes toward the natural world, but informed by modern science and responding to alarm about the fragility of biological environments increasingly devastated by human technologies"[28]. Through technologies, man seems to acquire almost limitless power to dominate over the planet. Frost's ecological vision is against that technological power. His artistic talent dislikes the inexorable increase of human exploitation over nature.

Notes

* Gunther, Pete A.Y. "Creativity and Ecology". In *Creativity in Art, Religion, and Culture*, ed. Michael H. Mitas. Wurzburg: Konighausen Neumann, 1985. 107-16.

1. William Rueckert in his article, "Literature and Ecology" quotes Berry Commoner's first Law of Ecology, published in *The Ecocriticism Reader*, by Glotfelty & Fromm, 1996, p.112. He has taught English and American Literature at Russell Sage College, Oberlin College, the University of Illinois at Champaign-Urbana, the University of Rochester, and the State University of New York at Geneseo, from which he retired in 1988.
2. Lawrence Buell, *The Environmental Imagination: Thoreau, Nature Writing, and the Formation of American Culture,* The Belknap Press of Harvard university Press, 1995.p.259. Buell is a Professor of English at Harvard University.
3. Harold Fromm, *The Nature of Being Human: From Environmentalism to Consciousness,* The Johns Hopkins University Press, Baltimore,2009. P.43.
4. Graham Huggan and Helen Tiffin, *Postcolonial Ecocriticism: Literature, Animals, Environment,* Routledge, First Indian Reprint, 2015, p.71.
5. Louise Westling, *The Cambridge Companion to Literature and the Environment,* Cambridge University Press, 2014. p.5.
6. Todd A. Borlik, *Ecocriticism and Early Modern English Literature, Routledge*: Taylor & Francis. 2011. p.209.
7. Timothy Clark, *The Cambridge Introduction* to *Literature and the Environment,* Cambridge University Press, 2014, p.23. He is a specialist in Romantic, Heideggerian and post-Heideggerian poetics and in environmental criticism
8. Greg Garrard, *Ecocriticism*, Routledge, 2015, p.130.
9. Ramachandra Guha, *Environmentalism: A Global History*, Penguin Books, 2014. p.129.
10. Alison Byerly, "The Uses of Landscape: The Picturesque aesthetic and the National Park System" in *The Ecocriticism Reader,* edited by Cheryll Glotfelty & Harold Fromm, The University of Georgia Press, 1996.p.54. Byerly is assistant Professor of English at Middlebury College, where she teaches an English/Environmental Studies course, "Visions of Nature".
11. Greg Garrard, *Ecocriticism,* Routledge, 2015, p. 95.
12. Paula Gunn Allen, "The Sacred Hoop" in *The Ecocriticism Reader,* edited by Cheryll Glotfelty & Harold Fromm, The University of Georgia Press, 1996.p.247. Allen is Professor of English at the University of California, Los Angeles.
13. Harold Fromm, *The Nature of Being Human: From Environmentalism to Consciousness,* The Johns Hopkins University Press, Baltimore, 2009. p.66.
14. Harold Fromm, *The Nature of Being Human: From Environmentalism to Consciousness,* The Johns Hopkins University Press, Baltimore, 2009. p.43.

15. Joseph M. Meeker, "The Comic Mode" in *The Ecocriticism Reader,* edited by Cheryll Glotfelty & Harold Fromm, The University of Georgia Press, 1996.p.168. Joseph W. Meeker is a human ecologist with a Ph.D. in comparative literature, and master's and postdoctoral studies in wildlife ecology and comparative animal and human behavior.
16. Greg Garrard, *Ecocriticism,* Routledge, 2015, p. 32.
17. Paula Gunn Allen, "The Sacred Hoop" in *The Ecocriticism Reader,* p.244.
18. Deane Curtin. *Environmental Ethics for a Postcolonial World,* Lanham, MD; Rowman & Littlefield. 2005. p.145.
19. Lawrance Thompson, "Robert Frost's Theory of Poetry" in *Robert Frost: A Collection of Critical Essays,* edited by James M. Cox Prentice-Hall, Inc. 1962, p.29.
20. Harold Fromm, *The Nature of Being Human: From Environmentalism to Consciousness,* p.*90*.
21. Timothy Clark, *The Cambridge Introduction* to *Literature and the Environment,* Cambridge University Press, 2014, Pp.127-128. He is a specialist in Romantic, Heideggerian and post-Heideggerian poetics and in environmental criticism.
22. Yvor Winters, "Robert Frost: or, the Spiritual Drifter as Poet" in *Robert Frost: A Collection of Critical Essays,* edited by James M. Cox Prentice-Hall, Inc. 1962, p.77.
23. Greg Garrard, *Ecocriticism,* Routledge, 2015, p.66.
24. Nelson, Richard. *The Island Within.* San Francisco: North Point Press 1989. p. xii.
25. Leslie Marmon Silko, "Landscape, History, and Pueblo Imagination" in *The Ecocriticism Reader,* edited by Cheryll Glotfelty & Harold Fromm, The University of Georgia Press, 1996.p.267.
26. Frederick Turner, "Cultivating the American Garden" in *The Ecocriticism Reader,* edited by Cheryll Glotfelty & Harold Fromm, The University of Georgia Press, 1996.p.44.
27. Harold H. Watts, "Robert Frost and the Interrupted Dialogue" in *Robert Frost: A Collection of Critical Essays,* edited by James M. Cox Prentice-Hall, Inc. 1962, p.107.
28. Louise Westling, *The Cambridge Companion to Literature and the Environment,* Cambridge University Press, 2014. p.5.

CHAPTER 6

A Further Range (1936)

Humans rarely understand or think of the harmful impact of scientific and technological movements upon the ecosystem. Without examining the basic or fundamental concepts, they apply such movements into their life-style to make it easier, comfort and accessible. The breathless labor one does in factory needs some rest and comfort but the technological world gives little comfort. The real comfort lies in nature. Frost's study of factory life in "A Lone Striker", subtitled as "Without Prejudice to Industry" communicates the replacement of the pastoral way of life by the machine-dominated industrial life-style. The artist recalls a young woman who works in the factory: "Her deft hand showed with finger rings / Among the harp-like spread of strings." The "finger rings" indicate, as if, her marriage to the machine rather than to a man. The rattle of machine replaces the heavenly music represented by "harp". The natural and normal way of living turns into mechanical life-style that is completely artificial, emotionless and rigid:

The swinging mill bell changed its rate
To tolling like the count of fate,
And though at that the tardy ran,
One failed to make the closing gate.
There was a law of God or man
That on the one who came too late
The gate for half an hour be locked,
His time be lost, his pittance docked.
He stood rebuked and unemployed. (CPoRF, 355)

Aggressive industrialism and competitive commercialism despoil freedom, peace, and comfort thereby making man timebound and serious. The trend of greedy economy accelerates life through time and space and simultaneously uproots the intimacy between man and nature. In relation to industrialisation in the form of mills or factories, Ramachandra Guha mentions: "Having protected large chunks of wilderness from the threat of 'development', the

American environmental movement has increasingly turned its attention to controlling the hazardous byproducts of industrialisation: air and water pollution, and the production of toxic or radioactive wastes"[1]. Frost's "tardy" worker prefers to have comfort and goodness in "a wood" represented by nature. He decides to take a walk in the woods:

He knew another place, a wood,
And in it, tall as trees, were cliffs;
And if he stood on one of these,
'T would be among the tops of trees,
Their upper branches round him wreathing,
Their breathing mingled with his breathing. (CPoRF, 356)

Frost's ecological perception must be praiseworthy as he delves into the universal truth of the breathing of trees "mingled with" the breathing of humans. Both are interdependent to each other and any disturbance in one, inevitably disturbs the other. Factory drains out everything from the worker and makes him exhausted but nature feeds sustenance to him.:

He knew a path that wanted walking;
He knew a spring that wanted drinking,
A thought that wanted further thinking;
A love that wanted re-renewing. (CPoRF, 356)

Frost's ecological vision articulates his ultimate and ulterior preoccupation to integrate a balanced and harmonious relationship between man and nature that does not arise in technological mindset. In contrast to the mill that is technological product, nature inspires holistic "thinking" represented by woods. In such context, Harold H. Watts expresses: "As Frost, speaking for himself and for the worker, says of the machines in the factory. It is easy to resist provided there is a forest one knows. It is a sound preference that puts contemplation of process ahead of work at a spinning machine. At least, Frost says of this defense that leads the worker along a woodland path"[2]. The lone striker desires for cliffs, trees, water from spring, and clean-air for breathing. Hence, time has come to revisit, revalue, and re-renew the relationship of man with nature.

The readers observe environmental implications in the artistic output of Robert Frost. They feel its importance as the grip of global warming and climate change gets strong and intensified from day to day. Frost expresses climate fluctuation in New England region in "Two Tramps in Mud Time", subtitled as "A Full-Time Interest". He portrays the natural phenomena in the month of April when "the sun was warm but the wind was chill". Such a sunny day in April reminds one about the presence of weather in the month of May. It is difficult to predict about the vagaries of the climate. An unexpected change of weather may occur, even before one speculates anything or forecasts something. The sunlit or clear blue sky amazingly overcasts with a cloud and simultaneously a chilly "wind comes off a frozen peak". Then, one feels as if one is "two months back in the middle of March":

> The sun was warm but the wind was chill.
> You know how it is with an April day
> When the sun is out and the wind is still,
> You're one month on in the middle of May.
> But if you so much as dare to speak,
> A cloud comes over the sunlit arch,
> A wind comes off a frozen peak,
> And you're two months back in the middle of March.
> A bluebird comes tenderly up to alight
> And turns to the wind to unruffle a plume
> His song so pitched as not to excite
> A single flower as yet to bloom. (Williams and Honig, 242-243)

One experiences the indeterminate climatic conditions in environmentally threatened world. Serious effects of climate change are perceived today as a challenge for the contemporary world. Ecological crisis creates problems for both humans and non-humans. The bluebird who comes to alight, tries to keep its feathers composed and unruffled because of chilly wind. The bird realises that it is not yet spring and hence, sings a song in such a tone that does not excite "A single flower as yet to bloom". It justifies that cold season is still continuing although it creates the impression of spring. Presently, climate change is acknowledged as a grave issue. Judging upon the seriousness of the current situation, Joni Adamson in her article, "Environmental Justice, Cosmopolitics, and Climate Change" points out: "As a growing number of writers, ethnographers, literary critics, and scientists have observed, it is becoming increasingly clear that humans are the primary agents driving climate change"[3]. On the month of April, New England climate is poised with cold and warm, winter and spring. Frost shows the impact of climate change but does not discuss the structures and systems that cause the change.

Contrasted with this, Frost also argues that nature seems to be against man. He articulates that man is a stranger in the universe. He is no more than the other creatures who share the natural world with him. In "The White-Tailed Hornet", man's position is reduced and his proper place is destroyed. His fallibility indirectly articulates man's surrender to natural law. Regarding this, Yvor Winters examines the poem "in which Frost describes the activities of a hornet and the errors it commits under the guidance of instinct, and he reprehends mankind for having engaged in downward comparisons".[4]

Before the eighteenth century, it was in the belief that man derives the power from God. But by the eighteenth century, the growth of industrialism in the West made a steady decline in that belief. The earlier was experiencing any calamity as the cruelty of nature and to be saved from it, the belief was in the kindness of God. In such context, Harold Fromm advocates: "If humans were indeed made in the image God, then it was reasonable to assume that only God could fully appreciate "man's unconquerable mind", while a just assessment of reality required that the field of the body be given up-as how could one do otherwise? – to Nature"[5]. On the other hand, Frost exposes how humans behave in exploiting the world in "A Drumlin Woodchuck", subtitled as "Be Sure to Locate": "As one who shrewdly pretends / That he and the world are friends." The woodchuck's eyes search for the area where it would build its home. The area is a drumlin and the wood is scattered around that "make[s] up for its lack of size" and provides it "cozier skies". The sense also connects to humans' construction of their homes. All creatures build their homes for safety, security and comfort to their life. Thus, the woodchuck chooses a place where "two rocks almost meet" and between those rocks "a two-door burrow" is dug. A woodchuck is conscious of its protection.

Regarding the poem, Lawrance Thompson gives the opinion: "…in the ambiguous animal fable entitled "A Drumlin Woodchuck", wherein the creature which makes his home in the sandbank left by the ice-age glacier explains to his mate in tones of snug and smug pride that he has adequately constructed their home as a defense against at least the foreseeable forms of destruction"[6]. The world and the biotic in it are in an incessant struggle of wills. Hence, for sustainability, caution is necessary. In the current world, when virus rewrites the fate of the universe, the significance of Frost's poetry is highly applicable.

Frost's ecological perception attributes to the knowledge on plants and animal biology, the experiences on climate and weather, and also practical understanding in orchard management. As an eco-scientist, he delves into the matters of biotic and abiotic. Having a full-phased farming practices, Frost presents "The Gold Hesperidee", otherwise known as "How to Take a Loss" discusses on a season in the life of a special apple tree from blossoming to bearing the fruit and the emotional attachment of a dedicated farmer, Square Matthew Hale to it. The emotional investment of Hale turns into fury when he realises that his precious apples have been stolen. The accuracy of his description on the life cycle of an apple from blossom to fruit justifies Frost's botanical knowledge. The expression of "young grafted apple tree" communicates the idea of grafting a stem from the desired species onto the trunk of a host tree:

> Square Matthew Hale's young grafted apple tree
> Began to blossom at the age of five,
> And after having entertained the bee,
> And cast its flowers and all the stems but three,
> It set itself to keep those three alive;
> And downy wax the three began to thrive. (CPoRF, 367)

Frost's botanic expertise acknowledges that tree blooms for the first time at the age of five as it needs, obviously, the length of time to grow into the minimum size to produce flowers. Besides, a tree needs the duration of time to be capable of bearing flowers and fruits that depends upon the type of rootstock or the percentage of graft to rootstock. However, Frost's sense of pollination is wonderful as most apple trees cannot self-pollinate. Hence, an agent like bee is necessary to carry the pollen to fertilize the ovum. Without fertilisation, flower cannot be turned into fruit.

The farmer minutely observes how each growing apple turns "from looking up" on its stem and then hangs downward as it becomes heavy for the stem to support: "They had just given themselves a little twist / And turned from looking up and being kissed / To looking down and yet not being sad." Frost knows that this downward position is necessary because it will help the fruit to grow and ripe. However, he anticipates the enemies like the "codlin moth" and the "rusty parasite" are the widespread pest that damage the apple. In such context, Neil Evernden writes: "Creatures can "infect" each other with evolutionary transformations. And finally, most remarkable of all is the fact that these elements appear to be transmissible not only between individuals of the same species, but between species as well. This means it is conceivable that group of species, perhaps even whole communities of organisms, could, in a sense, co-evolve. They are all quite literally inter-related"[7]. In autumn on "the verge of frost" the apples get ripe but, on his way to church one morning, Hale notices that the apple tree has been ransacked and the precious apples are gone. To put into other words, an orchard is an ecosystem that needs to be taken care of and handled properly by humans. Natural ecosystem is under threat.

Frost talks of geological and ecological processes in his poetry. As it is studied, these processes project the geographical distribution of plants, animals, and other creatures. The poem "In Time of Cloudburst", subtitled as "The Long View" discusses the geological study of the speaker in relation to soil erosion by the heavy "downpour", restoration of the lost topsoil in a tectonic disorder that will leave "The bottom of seas raised dry – / The slope of the earth reversed." When forests are destroyed for agricultural purposes, the great rain falls on the hills obviously beat down the loosened soil and make erosion. Agriculturists should think of preventing the waste of soil:

> Let the downpour roil and toil!
> The worst it can do to me
> Is carry some garden soil
> A little nearer the sea.
> 'Tis the world-old way of the rain
> When it comes to a mountain farm
> To exact for a present gain
> A little of future harm.
> ....
> Some force has but to apply,
> And summits shall be immersed,
> The bottom of seas raised dry-
> The slope of the earth reversed.
> Then all I need do is run
> To the other end of the slope,
> And on tracts laid new to the sun,
> Begin all over to hope. (CPoRF, 369)

Usually, in monsoon, torrential rain quickly washes away soil but in current era, due to global warming and climate change, abnormally great rain falls causes landslides in hilly areas. In such sense, Ramachandra Guha mentions: "Destitution of the mountains will result in destitution of the realm"[8]. The speaker thinks of nature's repeated cycles; even if he could "Begin all over" on the "tracts laid new to the sun" at "the other end of the slope", he would only "to hope". The fulfilment of the targets for harvesting goes into uncertainty.

On the other hand, Frost is well conscious of social inequalities and class distinction that attune to economic exploitation. Such exploitation creates imbalances and polarity that commonly affects the ecosystem. The capitalistic mindset causes environmental degradation and exploits the freedom of the poor in the globalised world. Fundamentally, capitalism sensitizes to the contemporary realities of social inequality. In such context, Pramod K. Nayar states: "Eco-socialists argue that class inequalities influence the experience of the environment"[9]. Corollary to this, the capitalistic society is extremely selfish, competitive and grossly destructive of the universe. In the poem, "A Roadside Stand", subtitled as "On Being Put Out of Our Misery", Frost studies the binaries that exist between the rich and the poor, the haves and the have-nots, the full-belly and the empty-stomach, and the exploiter and the exploited. These divisional forms are not eco-friendly. The poem studies the failure of country folk to survive in the midst of economic depression. It portrays the plight and misery of the poor and the complex undercurrents of their existence.

Frost seems to claim that the poor should have the same access as the wealthy have. The rich people enjoy and the poor remain deprived. The poor farmer puts "a little new shed" in front of his house "at the edge of the road" in a hope for selling "wild berries", "squash", and other products. He needs money but several thousands of cars speedily pass and people in vehicle give a cursory glance at his stall. And if few of them, occasionally, happen to look at the stall, they are only for being confused with the letters N and S that had been turned wrong. The rich people, obviously, do not think of the struggling life of the poor nor care about the environment. Mention may be made of Axel Goodbody who writes in his article, "Ecocritical Theory: Romantic Roots and Impulses from Twentieth-Century European Thinkers": "Marxism depicts humans as inextricably connected to nature, and "nature" as socially mediated and constructed. It posits human's self-realisation through "metabolic" interaction with the natural environment, and critiques the capitalist structures leading to inequality as responsible for environmental destruction. For our environmental problems to be solved, capitalist production for the accumulation of wealth must be replaced by meeting people's real needs"[10]. Class-struggle disrupts the social and ecological relations and dangerously affects the environment. Money is the cause of contamination and pollution in ecosystem.

The poet as a socio-ecologist reacts on the selfish activities of the city-dwellers who drive a U-turn of their cars and spoil the grass in poor farmer's yard. They ask for petrol but the farmer does not sell that. Eco-Marxists argue that there is a strong connection between poverty and ecological deterioration. Frost exposes how the "greedy good-doers" and "beneficent beasts of prey" befool the poor village folk and make their life miserable and pitiable. In this issue, Harold H. Watts affirms: "It must be said that Frost discovers no apt alternate unless laissez faire be an alternate. (Does Frost have clue for this from Adam Smith or from process?) Frost presents us, in "The Roadside Stand", the pathetic hopes of country folk who set up their stands to snare the nickels and dimes of passing city folk. Such country folk are in graver danger than comes from financial disappointment"[11]. Economic exploitation suffocates the society through the conflicts between the rich and the poor. Sometimes it causes war that leads to environmental disruption, as is witnessed by the current scenario of the world.

Nature tolerates the nuisance of humans' intentional activities. For his vested interests, man makes a startling alternation in nature's identity. Wiping out of the forest is lack of ecological consciousness and also deficiency in preservationist outlook. Deforestation is one of the major causes for global warming, climate change, and the loss of biodiversity. Frost's environmental awareness is pertinent when he thinks of timber management in "The Old Barn at the Bottom of the Fogs", subtitled as "Class Prejudice Afoot". He discusses on the destruction of chestnut as a useable wood. The wooden door locks on the barn are "specimens": "Their label Prop-locks, only specimens / In chestnut now become a precious wood / As a relic of a vanished race of trees – / When these go there will be none to replace them". The loss and damage man makes to nature, can never be compensated and replenished. Everyone should realise the importance of plants and trees for the protection and preservation of the biosphere. Felling off the trees will be a stress on the environment. Therefore, Todd A. Borlik mentions: "As a crisper picture of the ecological history of the early modern world has developed in recent scholarship, it has become evident that [...] a population boom and widespread deforestation provoked anxieties about a looming energy crisis"[12].

Man is the only literary creature among all the species in the world. He has to decide cautiously and conscientiously his role-play for the welfare and survival of mankind. He has to examine his act honestly and carefully and to put insight into his relationship with other species. But his enormous sense of self-importance creates vulnerable bionetwork. Humans' huge ego for science and technology imposes supremacy over the non-humans. God has made man a rational being and given mind to use knowledge in noble way but he uses that power to destroy the good. Instead of being rational, he becomes irrational. In place of wisdom, he foolishly exhibits his super-ego to harm other creatures. The misuse of his wisdom abuses nature and the natural world. In the poem, "At Woodward's Garden", subtitled as "Resourcefulness Is More Than Understanding", Frost discusses how the misuse of the magnifying glass is to burn the monkeys rather than to see small print. Here is the abuse of power rather than the use for its true end.

The Frostian boy, from his study of science, learns to use the magnify glass not only for better vision but also to distillate the rays of the sun to get heat and fire. "Presuming on his intellect", he applies that glass to torment "monkeys in a cage". Indirectly, Frost hints about the scientists who are gifted with the power of knowledge make experimentations upon the animals. The superseding mentality of humans puts problems for the survival of non-humans. Non-humans are effaced by humans' activities.

The boy uses the glass as a weapon on the noses of monkeys for concentrating the rays of the sun through the lens:

> He made the sun a pin-point on the nose
> Of first one, then the other till it brought
> A look of puzzled dimness to their eyes
> That blinking could not seem to blink away.
> They stood arms laced together at the bars,
> And exchanged troubled glances over life.
> ....
> There was a sudden flash of arm, a snatch,
> And the glass was the monkeys', not the boy's.
> Precipitately they retired back cage
> And instituted an investigation
> On their part, though without the needed insight.
> They bit the glass and listened for the flavor.
> They broke the handle and the binding off it. (CPoRF, 379)

The monkeys apprehending danger and reacting with animal instinct of touching their noses, snatch away the glass from the boy.

They have no knowledge for the use of the magnifying glass, although they make "investigation" to make sense of this new thing. Ultimately, they bit, break and listen "for the flavor", and "hid it in their bedding straw". They demonstrate more common sense and good judgement by implying their animal instincts than the educated boy in the sense that they know it is evil and reject it. Hence, the poet concludes the poem by approving monkey's knowledge: "What monkeys did or didn't understand? / They might not understand a burning-glass. / They might not understand the sun itself. / It's knowing what to do with things that counts." In the context of human and non-human drama, humans do not compromise the non-humans and vice versa. Apathy and hostility seem to be a continuous texture between man and animal. Obviously, it is a complex web of conflicts. Regarding such conflicts, in his article "Nature, Post Nature", Timothy Clark pinpoints: "In response, human beings will, as they always have, continue to act on a stage dominated by unpredictable nonhuman agency, but this time increasingly divested of illusions of sovereignty"[13]. Frost examines the interface of human and non-human community that subsists in ecosystem. The behavioral action of humans trespassing the border of non-humans is the root cause of disturbances.

Man's predicament is his misuse of nature. Humans' goodness is possible if they accept nature and treasure its value as it is, without making further spoil. They should understand nature through the images and words, a process that shapes the question of truth in their survival. Man's self-consciousness should acknowledge not to tame or bend nature. The poem "Lost in Heaven" sketches the poet's contemplations into the heavenly bodies as "the clouds" part "one stormy night" that makes him unable to identify any familiar "skymarks in the blue". Initially, he feels "consternation" but, afterwards accepts his "lostness", welcoming a transcendental feeling of surrender to "overwhelm" him: "The clouds, the source of rain, one stormy night / Offered an opening to the source of dew, / Which I accepted with impatient sight, / Looking for my old skymarks in the blue." Frost's study of the natural theology opens up his divine mentality. He tries to understand the cosmic power how nature's creation operates. The speaker's celestial intention sweeps the things into the net of divine meaning. Such intention talks of a genuine attachment with nature. This attitude is not his mind-bending, rather mind-expanding.

Frost experiences the impact of nature on human beings. His description of snowfall night and pervasive loneliness caused by it cannot be overlooked and underestimated. In the poem, "Desert Places", he portrays loneliness and silence in nature as a lot of snow has almost covered everything. At the approach of the night, with animals gone to their burrows, it turns to "A blanker whiteness of benighted snow". Such snow covers "the ground" and "the woods" that denies the presence of plant life or anything else. On the other hand, weather affects humans physically and psychologically. There is the influence of weather upon man's health, moods and life itself. As man's physical health declines, his psyche also undergoes a change. In such context, Vivian C. Hopkins writes: "Snow, which has appeared in these poems as peace and mystery, a threat to life, a delight in violent force, pervades "Desert Places" with an atmosphere of despair"[14]. A lonely man walking alone in a landscape of snow says: "The loneliness includes me unawares". The outside nature responds to the inside psyche:

> Snow falling and night falling fast, oh, fast
> In a field I looked into going past,
> And the ground almost covered smooth in snow,
> But a few weeds and stubble showing last.
> The woods around it have it-it is theirs.
> All animals are smothered in their liars.
> I am too absent-spirited to count;
> The loneliness includes me unawares.
> And lonely as it is that loneliness
> Will be more lonely ere it will be less-
> A blanker whiteness of benighted snow
> With no expression, nothing to express.
> They cannot scare me with their empty spaces
> Between stars-on stars where no human race is.
> I have it in me so much nearer home
> To scare myself with my own desert places. (Norton, 1777)

There is the interface between anthropocentric position and biocentric standpoint as the poet announces: "They cannot scare me with their empty spaces". Besides, man is a part of nature, he can never be separated from it. It is wise to adapt with the natural environment instead of challenging it. Because nature is unchallenged and non-negotiable.

The external reality of physical phenomena makes impact within human mind. Hope for survival stems from the mysterious realm of natural phenomena. The images of external nature through which man experiences by applying his senses boost him to take a stand in ecosystem. Such powerful insight Frost makes into "A Leaf-Treader" that pinpoints his attitude towards life and his belief in natural cycle. His choice of life over death is revitalised from the cycling process of nature. His deep understanding of the natural world fortifies his poetic vision. He discusses how the seasons make topsy turvy to the world in each year; what was "overhead" is now "underfoot". Possibly, he tries to equate the life-cycle of leaf with his own life.

Frost's observation into nature and the natural world is unique. Nature integrates the psychic content of man to come out of dilemmas. It attests to the mood of an individual that decides the significance of selection. If there is no aesthetic bend of mind, one cannot understand nature. In "Leaves Compared with Flowers", Frost asks: "Which is fairer, flower or leaf". Nature-lovers would say in favor of flowers during the day as they see and appreciate leaves as they rustle in night. Besides, flowers are temporary but leaves are a constant process, though they have no beauty like flowers. Besides, a tree needs the right nutrients in order to flower and flourish. The accuracy of his study of nature articulates the things for what actually they are. His ecological vision underpins the images of trees, and with timing of seasons they bear flowers and fruits to provide nutrition and sustenance to human beings that he presents many times in his poetry. However, leaves on a tree function to perform photosynthesis through sunlight, oxygen and carbon dioxide that are necessary for the existence of mankind:

> A tree's leaves may be ever so good,
> So may its bark, so may its wood,
> But unless you put the right thing to its root
> It never will show much flower or fruit.
> But I may be one who does not care
> Ever to have tree bloom or bear.
> Leaves for smooth and bark for rough,
> Leaves and bark may be tree enough.
> Some giant trees have bloom so small
> They might as well have none at all.
> Late in life I have come on fern
> Now lichens are due to have their turn.
> I bade men tell me which in brief,
> Which is fairer, flower or leaf.
> They did not have the wit to say,
> Leaves by night and flowers by day.
> Leaves and bark, leaves and bark,
> To learn against and hear in the dark.

Petals I may have once pursued.
Leaves are all my darker mood. (CPoRF, 387)

Frost's ecological perception is studied when he thinks of the tree that will never "show much flower or fruit" if humans don't "put the right thing to its root". As it is examined, the algae group usually provides photosynthetic ability and nutrient uptake. Thus, the root, bark, and leaves contribute their specific role for the survival of the tree. The poet's botanical knowledge is praiseworthy as he delves into "lichens are due to have their turn". In such context, Neil Evernden states: "But now it appears that the chloroplasts within the plant cell behave quite independently of the rest of the cell, and may originally have been separate organisms, like the algae and fungi in lichen"[15]. Besides, the speaker's psychological mood gets compatible with "flower" and "leaves". Man, and tree both are equated with the same natural process.

The simplest solution for man's problems and to derive benefit is his harmonious relationship with nature. Snow, woods, stones, birds, flowers, leaves, seasons, and moon rays are connected to Frost's poetic emotions underlying with ecological significance. Most of the time, he resembles Henry Thoreau.

The image of a cone moon rays in "Moon Compasses" spreading down a mountain, between showers, moves slowly into his artistic output: "The mountain stood exalted in its place. / So love will take between the hands a face..." The association of love with nature creates a 'blessed spirit' to lead on a happy life in a sustainable environment.

Man's anthropocentric vision underestimates the power of nature thereby putting challenge against it. His ego for being the supreme creature makes him proud and arrogant. The poem, "On Taking from the Top to Broaden the Base", shows the challenge man issues ultimately turns to be his tragic flaw. "Roll stones down on our head!" – itself is a challenge from man's defiance. The Frostian man scolds the "old mountain" as a "squat old pyramid" that has got its "last good avalanche". Man does not know even the old mountain can bring down an "avalanche": "A pebble hit the roof". Derisive the mountain can generate a mudslide that would bury the man: "The mud came in one cold / Unleavened batch". If man overtakes nature, predicament is obvious. In such context, William Rueckert mentions: "In ecology, man's tragic flaw is his anthropocentric (as opposed to biocentric) vision, and his compulsion to conquer, humanise, domesticate, violate, and exploit every natural thing"[16].

Frost's biological vision unfolds the living creatures' interface with each other and their own way of survival. He focuses on a struggle for existence and a redemptive behavioral condition of the creatures' particular biospace in his poem "Design". Hence, Randall Jarrell remarks: "The most awful of Frost's smaller poems is one called "Design"[17]. The moth does not know that danger and death lurk for it on "a white heal-all" – a common flower. Nature displays the role of both the killer and the killed. Frost's interminable insight registers the forceful competition for survival into the concept of the predator and the prey. The predator is shrewd, powerful, and also intelligent. The elemental force of nature designs this web of life and death:

> I found a dimpled spider, fat and white,
> On a white heal-all, holding up a moth
> Like a white piece of rigid satin cloth-
> Assorted characters of death and blight
> Mixed ready to begin the morning right,
> Like the ingredients of a witches' broth-
> A snow-drop spider, a flower like a froth,
> And dead wings carried like a paper kite.
> What had that flower to do with being white,
> The wayside blue and innocent heal-all?
> What brought the kindred spider to that height,
> Then steered the white moth thither in the night?
> What but design of darkness to appall? –
> If design govern in a thing so small. (Norton, 1777-1778)

The flower embraces the moth but the dark forces, represented by the hungry spider, push the moth into "the ingredients of a witches' broth" that ends in the web of "death and blight". The proper study of life is to struggle and survive. In relation to this, Lawrence Buell states: "Cooper's *Deerslayer*, Faulkner's "Bear", Bryant's poem "To the Fringed Gentian", Whitman's "Out of the Cradle", Robert Frost's "Design" – of such is the core of these traditions comprised. It is easy to persuade oneself on the basis of the average critical discussion of these works that the literary naturescape exists for its formal or symbolic or ideological properties rather than as a place of literal reference or as an object of retrieval or contemplation for its own sake. It is unthinkable that Bryant could have sought to immerse himself in the natural history of the gentian, or Frost in observing spiders"[18]. Besides, nature's process is instinctive. The plant needs the visits of the moths as they contribute to fertilisation and pollination. The moth predator-spider-waits for its prey. The whole process goes on a chain system.

Corollary to this, each creature thinks of safety and security for its survival. The predator and the prey both are on the same platform and hence, any deviation or breach in it will invite death. The place-consciousness is necessary for congenial and sustainable living. Frost draws the attention of the readers regarding place-consciousness and behavioral psychology in the poem, "On a Bird Singing in Its Sleep". The artist wonders whether a bird feels endangered when it sings out in night thereby reducing the risk, it takes position low in a bush: "that from no special bush's height". Regarding the behavioral psychology, the voice the bird creates is difficult to locate: "it sang ventriloquist". It is well aware of its safeness. Besides, in the genetic system, it happens obviously: "On the long bead chain of repeated birth". The bird is conscious of not trespassing the Darwinian laws.

A bird half wakened in the lunar noon
Sang halfway through its little inborn tune.
Partly because it sang but once all night
And that from no special bush's height;
Partly because it sang ventriloquist
And had the inspiration to desist
Almost before the prick of hostile ears,
It ventured less in peril than appears.
It could not have come down to us so far
Through the interstices of things ajar
On the long bead chain of repeated birth
To be a bird while we are men on earth
If singing out of sleep and dream that way
Had made it much more easily a prey. (CPoRF, 397)

Frost is an expert of Darwinian thinking. If such behavior of singing aims at confusing the predators, hence, it is the best adaption. Adaption with the changing environment will help to survive. It needs a deep understanding and extensive probing into the different aspects of the ecosystem.

Frost's ecological conception, sometimes, penetrates into the climatological condition of the region. His study on weather, seasons, cloud, rainfall, snowfall, and storm makes him a keen observer in meteorology. He seems to be capable of understanding the intricacy of nature. In the poem, "Afterflakes", he observes nature during "the thick of a teeming snowfall" and asks "why / Of everything below". He witnesses how the thick snowstorm at the beginning unexpectedly turns into a light snowfall at the end. As he looks "back up at the sky", the snowstorm is over. In evolutionary process, nature changes abruptly. It is difficult to understand nature: "In the thick of a teeming snowfall / I saw my shadow on snow. / I turned and looked back up at the sky, / Where we still look to ask the why / Of everything below." The shadow of the storm is commonly "shapeless" and the only "form" one can perceive in nature. But the poet casts his shadow that gives form to the scene: "the shadow of mine should show in form / Against the shapeless shadow of storm, / How swarthy I must be". Mystery lies in nature and to understand it varies from person to person. However, Frost makes an insight into the diametric change of climatic condition what everyone feels today across the globe.

Man thinks of to be beneficial for biotic and abiotic. Hence, his brain makes it possible to modify his behavior consistent with conceptual plans. Frost seems to express this sort of mindset in "Unharvested". It cannot be ignored that fruits are the essential part for both humans and non-humans in ecosystem. On fruits, the birds and other creatures expect to have a duly share with humans. Corollary to this, it is necessary to acknowledge the symbiosis between human and non-human in order to have a comprehensive understanding of ecosystem. Regarding this, Joseph W. Meeker states: "Human behavior has generally been guided by presumed metaphysical principles which have neglected to recognise that man is a species of animal whose welfare depends upon successful integration with plants, animals, and land that make up his environment"[19]. The speaker displays "an apple tree" with "unharvested" "solid red" apples scattered on the "ground". From ecological point of view, birds and other herbivorous can enjoy what has been "left" by man. A balanced ecosystem is possible when biocentric vision will equate with anthropocentric mindset and it is necessary for a sustainable living.

Man's sovereignty to conquer over the process of nature commits ecocide. His egocentric mentality as a supreme creature instigates him to violate the laws of nature by rupturing its systems. Generally, nature keeps open the adaptive strategies that the human mind would devise. But the construction of artificial condition to win over nature is the cause of ecological deterioration. In "There are Roughly Zones", Frost examines into man's self-centredness that unnecessarily abuses nature. The apposition of "indoors" and "outside" at the beginning of the poem unfolds the speaker's self-centredness that they comfortably "sit indoors" and "talk" of the imported "peach tree". The tree is in "the cold outside" being ravaged by the storm. Besides, it has been altered by man. Obviously, trees represent the ecology of place. Trees need a certain environment for their growth and sustainability. Ecological understanding of the relationship between human world and the botanical world is a kind of blessed spirit. Trees are the vital energies that shape the spirit of the earth thereby animals, birds, and even insects get benefit from them.

From ecocentric angle, the poem builds up a distinction between human constructedness and nature's reality: "And every gust that gathers strength and heaves / Is a threat to the house". The conflict goes on between human supremacy and nature's fury:

> We sit indoors and talk of the cold outside.
> And every gust that gathers strength and heaves
> Is a threat to the house. But the house has long been tried.
> We think of the tree. If it never again has leaves,
> We'll know, we say, that this was the night it died.
> It is very far north, we admit, to have brought the peach.
> What comes over a man, is it soul or mind-
> That to no limits and bounds he can stay confined?
> You would say his ambition was to extend the reach
> Clear to the Arctic of every living kind.
> Why is his nature forever so hard to teach
> That though there is no fixed line between wrong and right,
> ....
> But if it is destined never again to grow,
> It can blame this limitless trait in the hearts of men. (CPoRF, 401)

Man does not have the right to do anything whimsically with the life of a tree. Tree is obviously the autonomous body of nature's laws but the human interference creates problem for it. Acquisitiveness serves as a cumulative thrust of an impulse that stems from the very basic level within human mind to possess more and more. Hence, the speaker questions: "What comes over a man, is it soul or mind – / That to no limits and bounds he can stay confined?" Mind is culture, body is nature. Culture dominates over nature. In mind-body dualism, Harold Fromm writes: "In the course of human history until the twentieth century, there was never any serious likelihood that the body-mind battle could be won on the field of the body"[20]. Man's disastrous impulse born of will does not allow him to think that he is simply a microscopic part of nature, but not the master of all.

Frost's ecocentric mindset is not in favor of technology. All mega machines born of technology are the spectacular demonstrations of man's power over nature. They are the potential horrors for pollution and spoliation of the biosphere. The poem "A Trial Run" displays man's relationship with machine. Man creates machine but it keeps man under stress and strain. Instead of being the master, he turns to be a slave to machine. Man, who created the machine, is now frightened by its power and his fear urges him almost to say a "prayer" to himself. The machine does not get identification but is understood to be used "in war". As it has the capacity to produce "a homicidal roar", it is surely an atmospheric disturbance and pollution. If it were to "wreck", it will build up "a thunder-clap" which is not eco-friendly. Its disrupting and devastating outcome is against nature's peace, harmony and tranquility. Until does it "stop", man cannot take "rest". This is how humans face the consequence of their advanced technology. Humans' faith in science and technology and their consequences bring about disaster on environment.

Frost's ecological conception injects him to be a natural habitat instead of being a planned habitat. He prefers to live in nature than to lead on life in city. In this sense, Harold H. Watts states: "This insight is put to one side when Frost suggests that the beliefs that societies have lived by are not "natural" but "artificial". It is as though one should say, "God made nature and man-made the town"- the town or, more inclusively, the whole course of human history, the close-woven mesh of human values"[21]. The huge buildings in megacities swallow up the biomes. In "Not Quite Social", the poet disapproves city life:

> To punish me overcruelly wouldn't be right
> For merely giving you once more gentle proof
> That the city's hold on a man is no more tight
> Than when its walls rose higher than any roof. (CPoRF, 403)

City boosts to commercialism and capitalism that the poet does not like. One should not blame him choosing nature over industry. Corollary to this, Timothy W. Luke writes: "...architecture encloses whole biomes in sprawling megacities, and biotechnology reengineers the base codes of existing biomass"[22]. The Frostian man speculates if "anyone is free to condemn" him "to death", he will leave "it to nature to carry out the sentence". His conscience dictates that nature will allow him to grow old and die of natural causes as opposed to artificial ones. Besides, he loves nature and he cannot conform to an urban society. If such tendency is fostered and respected, the earth will be revitalised. Humans should rethink upon it.

In "Evil Tendencies Cancel", Frost discusses that the plants suffer but they still struggle to grow and survive. The farmers "guess" that they will not die unless something else comes along to kill it. The farmers think of the environmental effects and the sustainability of plants. Linking with this piece of poem, the next one is "Pertinax" that predicts the future of "Let chaos storm! / Let cloud shapes swarm! / I wait for storm." Natural disaster or calamity is uncontrollable and hence, man has to see and "wait". In another piece of a three-line poem, "One Guess", Frost delves into the sound of an insect and lets his readers to contemplate and try to figure out what it is. The insect dwells near dusty places but carries on attractive qualities like legs that can make song, and "fan" like "wing". It seems to be some form of grasshopper or cricket. Like an entomologist, he studies on the life of the insect and concludes how the insect spews dye out of its mouth to defend itself instead of biting or stinging: "He has dust in his eyes and a fan for a wing, / A leg akimbo with which he can sing, / And a mouthful of dye stuff instead of a sting".

In the last three pieces, "The Hardship of Accounting", "Not All There", and "In Dives' Dive", the speaker sketches the distorting picture of existence. In "Not All There", the artist explains the miserable conditions of everything: "About the world's despair; / But to make bad matters worse". In "Dives' Dive", he suggests that one should not complain though conditions are poor. It articulates the role of the marginalised voice. The less-known or the less-fortunate people are deprived of coming into the mainstream of environmental organisations. Their silence is the only source of resisting oppression.

Notes

1. Ramachandra Guha, *Environmentalism: A Global History,* A Penguin Random House India Pvt. Ltd. 2014.p.2.
2. Harold H. Watts, "Robert Frost and the Interrupted Dialogue" in *Robert Frost: A Collection of Critical Essays*, edited by James M. Cox Prentice-Hall, Inc. 1962, p.113.
3. Joni Adamson, "Environmental Justice, Cosmopolitics and Climate Change" in *The Cambridge Companion to Literature and the Environment*, edited by Louise Westling, Cambridge University Press, 2014. P.181. Adamson is Associate Professor of English and Environmental Studies at Arizona State University.

4. Yvor Winters, "Robert Frost: or, the Spiritual Drifter as Poet" in *Robert Frost: A Collection of Critical Essays*, edited by James M. Cox Prentice-Hall, Inc. 1962, p.65.
5. Harold Fromm, *The Nature of Being Human: From Environmentalism to Consciousness,* The Johns Hopkins University Press, Baltimore,2009. p.39.
6. Thompson, Lawrance. *Robert Frost, University of Minnesota Pamphlets on American Literature, Vol.2.* University of Minnesota Press, Minnesota-55455, U.S.A., 1959. P.23.
7. Neil Evernden, "Beyond Ecology: Self, Place, and The Pathetic Fallacy" published in *The Ecocriticism Reader* edited by Cheryll Glotfelty & Harold Fromm, The University of Georgia Press, 1996. P.95. Neil Evernden is the Faculty of Environmental Studies at York University.
8. Ramachandra Guha, *Environmentalism: A Global History,* A Penguin Random House India Pvt. Ltd. 2014.p.60.
9. Pramod K. Nayar, *Contemporary Literary and Cultural Theory,* Pearson, 2015. P.247.
10. Axel Goodbody, "Ecocritical Theory: Romantic Roots and Impulses from Twentieth-Century European Thinkers" in *The Cambridge Companion to Literature and the Environment*, edited by Louise Westling, Cambridge University Press, 2014. P.67.
11. Harold H. Watts, "Robert Frost and the Interrupted Dialogue" in *Robert Frost: A Collection of Critical Essays,* edited by James M. Cox Prentice-Hall, Inc. 1962, p.116.
12. Todd A. Borlik, *Ecocriticism and Early Modern English Literature,* Routledge, Indian Reprint, 2015, p.2.
13. Timothy Clark, "Nature, Post Nature" in *The Cambridge Companion to Literature and the Environment,* edited by Louise Westling, Cambridge University Press, 2014. P.87.
14. Vivian C. Hopkins, Robert Frost: Out Far and In Deep" in *Interpretations: Essays on American Literature,* edited by R.K. Gupta, American Studies Research Centre, Hyderabad. 1976. P.142.
15. Neil Evernden, "Beyond Ecology: Self, Place, and The Pathetic Fallacy" published in *The Ecocriticism Reader* edited by Cheryll Glotfelty & Harold Fromm, The University of Georgia Press, 1996. P.94.
16. William Rueckert in his article, "Literature and Ecology" quotes Berry Commoner's first Law of Ecology, published in *The Ecocriticism Reader,* by Glotfelty & Fromm,1996, p.113.
17. Randall Jarrell, "To the Laodiceans" in *Robert Frost: A Collection of Critical Essays,* edited by James M. Cox Prentice-Hall, Inc. 1962, p.88.
18. Lawrence Buell, *The Environmental Imagination: Thoreau, Nature Writing, and the Formation of American Culture,* The Belknap Press of Harvard university Press, 1995.p.85. Buell is a Professor of English at Harvard University.

19. Joseph M. Meeker, "The Comic Mode" in *The Ecocriticism Reader,* edited by Cheryll Glotfelty & Harold Fromm, The University of Georgia Press, 1996.p.163. Joseph W. Meeker is a human ecologist with a Ph.D. in comparative literature, and master's and postdoctoral studies in wildlife ecology and comparative animal and human behavior.
20. Harold Fromm, *The Nature of Being Human: From Environmentalism to Consciousness,* The Johns Hopkins University Press, Baltimore,2009. p.38.
21. Harold H. Watts, "Robert Frost and the Interrupted Dialogue" in *Robert Frost: A Collection of Critical Essays*, edited by James M. Cox Prentice-Hall, Inc. 1962, p.111.
22. Luke, Timothy W. *Ecocritique: Contesting the Politics of Nature, Economy, and Culture* Minneapolis: University of Minnesota Press, 1997.p.195.

CHAPTER 7

A Witness Tree (1942)

The significance of ecological balance is comprehended when one feels the need of a congenial and conducive existence. Such perception acknowledges the environmental reverence for the green earth. Frost's two poems, "Beech" and "Sycamore" that stand as title poems for this volume, understandably suffer from neglect: "Where these are driven in and piled, / One tree, by being deeply wounded, / Has been impressed as Witness Tree".

In order to understand nature, it seems necessary to acknowledge the role of a woman. The recognition of 'feminine essence' that makes women 'closer to nature' is one of the attributes of Frost's poetry that he says in "The Silken Tent": "By countless silken ties of love and thought / To everything on earth the compass round". To value or devalue femininity depends upon the structure of the societies – matriarchal or patriarchal. The poem, having the form of the Shakespearean sonnet, is set in rural surroundings that witnesses Frost's love for nature. Leaving busy metropolitan cities in order to live his life in the countryside, Frost presents the view of a summer's day that is bright and "sunny" with a pleasant and joyous "summer breeze". This breeze stirs the tent and dries the dew thereby loosening the "ropes", moving easily and gently. As the poet compares the tent with the woman, like the movement of tent, the woman freely moves when she gets free from her domestic chores. Man is scarcely conscious of the necessity of a woman's freedom. The "central cedar pole" is a strong support to erect the tent. In the same way, societies should support and recognise the power and dignity of women. As the tent is tied with a number of "ropes", similarly, a woman is bound with "ties of love and thought" in the role of nurturing and motherhood. Regarding this, Richard Poirier mentions: "By the time we learn that its "silken ties" are "countless" we have been readied also to accept the information that these are "ties of love and thought" and to guess that this is much more than a real tent, silken or otherwise"[1]. Besides, women like nature believe in motherhood that runs parallel with nature's nourishment of human beings.

She is as in a field a silken tent
At midday when a sunny summer breeze
Has dried the dew and all its ropes relent,
So that in guys it gently sways at ease,
And its supporting central cedar pole,
That is its pinnacle to heavenward
And signifies the sureness of the soul,
Seems to owe naught to any single cord,
But strictly held by none, is loosely bound
By countless silken ties of love and thought
To everything on earth the compass round,
And only by one's going slightly taut
In the capriciousness of summer air
Is of the slightest bondage made aware. (CPoRF, 443)

The reference to "bondage made aware" pinpoints the condition of woman as a wife under the dominance or influence of domestication. In such context, Greg Garrard states: "The logic of domination is implicated in discrimination and oppression on grounds of race, sexual orientation and class as well as species and gender"[2]. The gendered dichotomy of 'masculine wildness and feminine domesticity' is a kind of exploitation over women and nature.

Humans' mind and body are related to the air or weather in the lap of nature. The kind of weather shapes the quality of moods or feelings in a person. One's mood varies in observing a beautiful clear sky and a "stormy" weather. Happily, or unhappily, one's mood depends upon one's own understanding of the weather. In "Happiness Makes Up in Height for What It Lacks in Length", the speaker says: "Oh, stormy stormy world, / The days you were not swirled / Around with mist and cloud, / Or wrapped as in a shroud." In cloudy or stormy weather, the visibility of the sun is poor. If such weather continues for a longer time due to climate change, health hazards may occur. In relation to this, the view of Harold Fromm may be quoted: "But if one is feeling physically out of sorts, if one is unable to focus, feels lazy and vaguely wrong, one's frame of mind is altered, and one's interest in things is not what it would otherwise be"[3]. Humans cannot be separated from the weather: "Around with mist and cloud". As the effects of weather upon humans decide their moods, in same proportion, it determines the quality of their actions.

Vivian C. Hopkins, in such context, states: "Most precious in the poet's experience are the few ecstatic moments when, under the stress of emotion, the subjunctive mood becomes indicative, and the dividing line dissolves"[4].

It needs to admit that physical environment creates the platform for artistic purposes. Understanding of the natural phenomena helps the artist to create something that signifies his state of mind and the outer world. The eccentric output emerges from the connection of the signifier and the signified, that may be the self-absorption of P.B. Shelley's persona in "To a Skylark", John Keats's "Ode to a Nightingale", William Wordsworth's "To the Cuckoo", or Thomas Hardy's "The Darkling Thrush", and Robert Frost's "Come In". The 'environmental essence' feeds their 'subjective feelings of rejuvenation and anxiety' to rethink upon life in human world and the world of nature. Frost feels an enjoyable moment when he hears a thrush singing in full-throated ease. The song was serving the purpose of "almost like a call" but the listener answers "I would not come in". Such mindset underpins the loosely ecological sense of interconnection as the place is "dark". The outer green circles don't agree with the "inside" blackness:

> As I came to the edge of woods,
> Thrush music-hark!
> Now if it was dusk outside,
> Inside it was dark.
> Too dark in the woods for a bird
> By sleight of wing
> To better its perch for the night,
> Though it still could sing.
> The last of the light of the sun
> That had died in the west
> Still lived for one song more
> In a thrush's breast.
> Far in the pillared dark
> Thrush music went-
> Almost like a call to come in
> To the dark and lament.
> But no, I was out for stars:
> I would not come in.
> I meant not even if asked,
> And I hadn't been. (Oliver, 415)

The self-centred attitude of the listener is incompatible with the self-sacrificial tendency of a thrush who is not in thought of the safeness for the night, – "By sleight of wing / To better its perch for the night" – rather prefers to continue music to make the earth more beautified. The bird's song reveals a new world rising from the seeming darkness in listener's eyes that represent the human world. Thrush belongs to the green world thereby remaining away from the concern of fear and death. Besides, the music in nature never dies. The listener's expression: "I was out for stars" is not new because human life experiences the reality of astronomical distance. But in the current era, such distance is reduced by violating the laws of nature through the advancement of science and technology. The listener distinguishes himself from nature by refusing the call of the bird. This action galvanises that nature and man are not one. Such mentality is harmful for a sustainable world.

On the other hand, man's expectation is more but nature's response to fulfil such expectations is limited. Man is so engrossed in his insatiable desires that makes him to feel the 'brute indifference' of nature denying to respond. The speaker in "The Most of It" wants more from nature than it ordinarily provides: "He thought he kept the universe alone". In relation to this, Yvor Winters expresses: "In the seventh volume, *A Witness Tree*, there is an even more impressive piece entitled "The Most of It". This poem represents a momentary insight into the vast and brute indifference of nature, the nature toward which Frost has cherished so sentimental a feeling through so many poems"[5]. Man expects that the world would provide too much for him and he would enjoy to his satisfaction:

> He thought he kept the universe alone;
> For all the voice in answer he could wake
> Was but the mocking echo of his own
> From some tree-hidden cliff across the lake
> Some morning from the boulder-broken beach
> He would cry out on life, that what it wants
> Is not its own love back in copy speech,
> But counter-love, original response. (CPoRF, 451)

The speaker longs for a reply from nature but the reply what it comes is not the one he had expected. The human centered values and the nature centered systems contradict with each other. In such context, Roy Harvey Pearce states: "Crucially, there is the word "kept" in the first line. Although at the end the poet-protagonist surely does not "keep" the "universe alone", still cannot be said to "share" it with the buck. Being a "natural" as opposed to a "human" universe, it is neither to be kept nor shared"[6]. Man should remain within his limit.

Man's flaw is his own product. He disobeys the law of the universe. Frost reminds his readers about the expulsion of Adam and Eve from the Garden of Eden in his poem, "Never Again Would Birds' Song Be the Same". Adam and Eve represent human world and birds stand for nature. The consequences of the Fall attribute to their uncontrollable desires. Besides, Richard Poirier points out: "Mythological identification in this poem consists of voices finding a way to acknowledge and also to transcend historical differences and historical catastrophes"[7]. Adam and Eve were well aware of their difference from nature. Like Milton, Frost does not study the event from the same angle. However, the appropriation and absorption of nature through Adam is the beginning history of mankind thereby "human history is implicated in natural history"[8].

Humans need to understand the natural biosphere upon what their life depends. Place and circumstances define man's life and livelihoods. The intimate and vital involvement of self with the place of living is an adhesive to eco-friendly environment. The recognition of nature and natural forces is more important for adaptability and adjustability than the stubbornness for opposing. Adjustability is the motto of life. The beauty and the complexity of nature are both for human beings. In the poem, "Willful Homing", the Frostian man experiences the complexity of nature as he is caught in "the blizzard" that "blinds him to any house" in a winter dark: "It is getting dark and time he drew to a house, / But the blizzard blinds him to any house ahead. / The storm gets down his neck in an icy souse / That sucks his breath like a wicked cat in bed." Man's proper understanding of nature and recognition of natural "force" offer a comprehensive account of ecological vision and stipulate instant ecological conscience and consciousness. The Frostian man feels the snow goes down the neck of his shirt and the terrible cold snatches away his breath "like a wicked cat in bed". Nature's elements obscure to find his way home. But his adjustability with such environment feeds confidence into his persistence to get that eventual success. Man as a creature of pioneer species knows to accustom with the changes in the environment.

The new environmentalism acknowledges the significant contributions of botanists, zoologists and ornithologists as they are basically alert to the interests of plants, animals, and birds undergoing environmental threats. Frost, as a home-grown botanist, looks for plant life-forms in relation to place and time. In "The Quest of the

Purple-Fringed", he botanizes the purple-fringed orchis that blooms in late spring or early summer. Ecological succession of the purple-fringed flower faces difficulty as the "headlong bee" does not play the role. Agrarianism studies "the buds in the copse's depth / That were pale as a ghost". Besides, some flowers are the indicators of the arrival of seasons. The Frostian man "felt the chill of the meadow underfoot". The chill meadow pinpoints that winter is at hand but "the sun overhead" talks of the early summer. This is the time for the purple-fringed orchis to bloom. The floral motif of the artist evidences reverence for nature.

Man's long commitment to a place is his affectionate bonding with the ecology of the landscape. The bond between people and place obviously determines humans' love and concern for the natural environment. Literally, people and place are inter-related. The reciprocal relationships between human and land establishes the concept that humans are alive because the earth is alive. Frost expresses the same view in "The Gift Outright":

> The land was ours before we were the land's.
> She was our land more than a hundred years
> Before we were her people. She was ours
> In Massachusetts, in Virginia,
> But we were England's, still colonials,
> Possessing what we still were unpossessed by,
> Possessed by what we now no more possessed.
> Something we were withholding made us weak
> Until we found out that it was ourselves
> We were withholding from our land of living,
> And forthwith found salvation in surrender
> Such as we were we gave ourselves outright
> (The deed of gift was many deeds of war)
> To the land vaguely realising westward,
> But still unstoried, artless, unenhanced,
> Such as she was, such as she would become. (Norton, 1779)

The beginning line, "The land was ours before we were the land's" indicates the complementary relationships between human and place. The speaker asserts and claims that America was "our land" for over "a hundred years / Before we were her people". Immediately he reacts: "But we were England's, still colonials". The dominant colonialism and expansionism generate war, threatening the ecosphere. The lion's share of possession and accumulation by the colonisers makes the colonised to be deprived of their own rights. The exploited are "unpossessed". The binary between the coloniser and the colonised, the exploiter and the exploited create environmental crisis as the violent notion of absorption ultimately turns into war and disorder: "The deed of gift was many deeds of war". The speaker bespeaks military language "deeds of war" to fight for their own land. Gluttonous expansionism and hungry colonialism are ecocide making the earth into a storehouse of pollution and waste. Randall Jarrell mentions: "One sees this extraordinary command in the composed, thoughtful, and traditional rhetoric of "The Gift Outright", one of the best of Frost's smaller poems, and perhaps the best "patriotic" poem ever written about our own country"[9]. Each one has the right to survive and feel proud for his own country. He has to formulate his relation with the ecosystem at the place of his living. He should be free from the tyranny of the tyrants. Environmental conditions and mental health are co-related; any disturbance in one, inevitably disturbs the other.

The connection between one's native place and psyche plays a significant role in environmental science as the body gets acquainted with the local climate. Beyond this, wherever one goes, he tries to be adapted and adjusted with the place and the climate. Therefore, most of the people don't prefer to have an alternative view of existence. They become reluctant to leave their forefather's land. Living in their own land, as they feel, is their right choice for a sustainable living. This provides an ethical and conceptual basis for their bonding with the place. In such context, Lawrence Buell states: "Anglo-American celebrants of the bond to place enact the rite of passage that Robert Frost made famous in "The Gift Outright". "The land was ours before we were the land's", after which we must learn how to belong to it""[10]. Frost attaches value to the living-place that is psychologically oriented with his love and liking. Human life without the importance on the living-place is incomplete. The place of living is the medium in which life transpires and its purpose finds the meaning.

Life is important for all. Each one struggles to survive and hence, tries to defend against the hurdles on the way of living. Whatever may threaten, the continuity of life comes under different modifications. Humans are well conscious of their safety and security. Frost's "Triple Bronze" discusses the question of protection that a person needs: "The Infinite's being so wide / Is the reason the Powers provide / For inner defense my hide. / For next defense outside…". "The Infinite" represents the cosmos, the universe or "the Powers" talking of eternity. The artist is communicated that a triple bronze is necessary for his existence. The first one relates to his personal: "For inner defense my hide". As the pollutants destroy and create hole in the Ozon layer, the solar radiation burns the skin that causes cancer. "The next defense outside" is the protection of the dwelling place that is made "Of wood or granite or lime". Humans dwelling place gets converted into 'a carbon sink'. The third is the protection of "a national boundary" that receives threat from colonialism and expansionism causing crisis to environment.

Nature is always present in Frost's artistic output. Sometimes he unfurls man versus nature and vice versa. The descriptions of nature, landscape and pastoral sights demonstrate the poet's ecological vision. It is necessary to acknowledge the symbiosis between man and nature in order to have a comprehensive understanding of ecosystem. There is the subject-object relationship between nature and man. But man's appropriation of nature for his own sake disturbs the relationship of losing the balance. The anthropocentric arrogance ruptures nature and sabotages the bionetwork. Being the ceaseless consumer in greed economy, man kills nature. Self-centred anthropocentric interest is apathetic to biocentric concepts. But nature is not answerable to human greed.

Man threatens nature and for the cause of defending, nature exhibits its fury to man. Frost focuses on such issues in "Our Hold on the Planet". Man's limitless expectations and nature's harsh reality interface with each other: "We asked for rain. It didn't flash and roar. / It didn't lose its temper at our demand / And blow a gale." The last two lines portray the exponential growth in human population that is even soaring today and putting pressure on the planet. Population explosion is not possible if nature does not favor as a friend. But ultimately it is responsible for environmental degradation. Besides, "proportion of good to ill" is directly linked with the proportion to man's exploitation and domination over nature. John T. Napier mentions: "If we venture into the too-common practice of giving poets credit for unqualified endorsement of attitudes exhibited in their poems, we should be called upon to recognise in Frost a hard-won optimism. "Our Hold on the Planet" appears to state the careful balancing of probabilities, [...] Through all his pondering on the infinitesimal zing magnitudes of space, Frost has kept his gift for song as man his hold on the planet"[11]. Nature bears all sorts of nuisances created by man but it has a certain limit of carrying capacity. When man's exploitation crosses nature's carrying capacity, it shows rage to mankind. It displays the role of both friend and foe together, preserver and destroyer in respect of man's activities. Man despoils nature and nature affects man. Mankind has to rethink whether nature will be turned into the possibility of danger or the potential for beauty.

Nature will nourish mankind if humans become well aware of the importance of natural things. But humans' lifestyle in different occasions exhausts the basic ecological health of the planet like cutting down of trees for the celebration of the Christmas. For a sustainable environment, campaign goes for the plantation of trees. In the poem, "To a Young Wretch (Boethian)", Frost relates to the act of cutting down of the tree is an evil. He narrates how a young man chops down a "spruce" tree from his "woods" and drags it home to use as a Christmas tree. Tree should not be wasted in petty entertainment:

> But tree by charity is not the same
> As tree by enterprise and expedition.
> I must not spoil your Christmas with contrition.
> It is your Christmas against my woods. (CPoRF, 470)

The spruce is precious to nature. Humans should attach due importance to the trees and restrain themselves from the depletion of forests. Cutting down of tree whimsically is an environmental abuse and a crime against nature.

In the name of 'progress', humans turn nature into 'Denature'. The most ambitious effort of man to lead on a high luxurious life turns the earth into 'a grocery store of garbages'. The mindset for getting more and more injects him to violate the laws of nature thereby retribution comes from the biosphere in the form of epidemics or the inflicted malaise that Frost discusses in "The Lesson for Today":

> Space ails us moderns: we are sick with space.
> Its contemplation makes us out as small
> As a brief epidemic of microbes
> That in a good glass may be seen to crawl
> The patina of this the least of globes. (CPoRF, 473)

Man's anthropocentric attitude is the cause of the degeneracy of the age for which the speaker alleges: "If this uncertain age in which we dwell / Were really as dark as I hear sages tell". He believes that the time is bad on account of war and corruption. He tries to create awareness of space in modern times by dint of acknowledging how tiny and insignificant humanity is, as Heidegger's philosophy states: "Man is not the lord of beings. Man is the shepherd of Being"[12].

Frost's presentation of nature, landscape and pastoral sights in his poetry primarily demonstrates his interest in environmental aesthetics. His artistic skill acknowledges the divine beauty of nature. Besides, his poems seem to reveal human values and nature systems in participatory action. Obviously, the perception of aesthetics arouses the subject-object relationship between the viewer and the viewed, between man and nature. The spectacularisation of nature's panoramic views thrills the eyes, calms the heart, pacifies the mind and sets the reaction against the background of toxic intoxicated city life. Acknowledgement of such sensibility is Frost's ecological concern. In "Time Out" the "pause" is so abrupt that articulates to stop at "the slant" and see "the mountain". Nature is "a book held up before his eyes". If the mountain is a book for the climber, "he followingly fingered as he read". The projection of mountain and book is a transposal in the sense that the climb is brought to a halt with the sights of the mountain to be read. The reading of the mountain is a serene speculation – "obstinately gentle" – and "it will have its moment to reflect". It indicates the involvement of an individual with nature: "It took that pause to make him realise / The mountain he was climbing had the slant / As of a book held up before his eyes / (And was a text albeit done in plant)."

The natural surroundings with iridescent brilliance of living entity are threatened "from the hard and level stare / Of enemies defied and battles fought". Instead of harmonising the humans with nature and expecting for a life-sustaining environment, war puts mankind in jeopardy. Battle ravages both biotic and abiotic beyond replenishment and despoils life-sustaining systems. The outcome of battle is ecocide. Its devastation fetches environmental disaster with all the poison threatening to life of the biota. Health hazards crop up as the biodiversity is contaminated.

Each creature strives to survive. Environmental disorder causes vulnerability to the existence of life. Survival problem is same for all creatures, may be a moth or a man. In the poem, "To a Moth Seen in Winter", the narrator speaks of his own condition with the life of a moth in the dead of winter. Both the moth and the narrator struggle against the same forces to survive. The narrator can "touch" the moth but cannot fully touch its life as each one's has own yearnings. Life is dangerous for any creature if time and place go against it.

Natural ecosystem accommodates the life of every species within it. In the name of progress with time, the ecosystem deteriorates and the landscape changes into "the riskscape". Hence, 'everything depends on timing, and time is responsible for everything'. The loss and damage caused to the environment is also due to the flow of time thereby survival becomes a challenge. The moth and the man are on the same platform.

Corollary to this, "A Considerable Speck (Microscopic)" discusses the narrator's pleasure of looking closely to the activity of "a living mite" that runs across on a piece of his written paper. He first thinks of killing it, then realises it is intelligent. this realization is like Hemingway's Santiago with the marlin in *The Old Man and the Sea.* The mite needs the right to live and to take the place like the narrator. Besides, the mite doesn't make any harm to him. In the facts of ecology, balance is necessary. It may be a microscopic creature, but the Frostian Man attaches due importance to it. From ecological perspective, it is considerable for what it signifies. Some categories of mites are the most abundant in spring and the least in autumn. For the narrator, it is only a considerable time. Thus, humans have to understand that killing of the non-humans is foolish, it is wise to preserve them. Each one should get the opportunity to live. Regarding the poem, Marion Montgomery writes: "But this is motion of natural objects and not emotion, human simile but not human feeling. In "A Considerable Speck" Frost says, after examining the microscopic creature, "Plainly with an intelligence I dealt"[13]. The problem is man's understanding of the natural world that arises rarely to think of the welfare of the other creatures in ecosystem. His ego-consciousness bars the eco-consciousness.

Humans' egocentric mentality induces war that always keeps life at stake. Each moment paves potential threat to humans and non-humans. Life lives in fear of getting killed as environment is pushed into a precarious state. Physically and psychologically, war experiences are hard to pinpoint. Frost points out such experience in "November". The artist uses "leaves" as a metaphor for the soldiers. As the leaves fall from the trees in autumn, war brings down the soldiers in a "rain" of bullets:

> We saw leaves go to glory,
> Then almost migratory
> Go part way down the lane,
> And then to end the story
> Get beaten down and pasted

In one wild day of rain.
We heard ''Tis over' roaring
A year of leaves was wasted.
Oh, we make a boast of storing,
Of saving and of keeping,
But only by ignoring
The waste of moments sleeping,
The waste of pleasure weeping,
By denying and ignoring
The waste of nations warring
1938 (CPoRF, 485)

The sense "to glory" obviously "go[es] part way down the lane, / And then to end the story". Humans "boast of storing, / Of saving and of keeping", but neglect to judge what they "waste". Accumulation, possession, and expansion are nature-defying mindset causing ecocide. The hellish turn of war is the waste of life and "waste of nations". The ruinous consequences of war should be avoided to save life and to save earth as the war legacy contaminants make death-dance and invoke the phenomena of apocalypse.

Humans enormous sense of arrogance and huge ego create vulnerability to the survival of the non-humans. Their sovereignty prioritises over the non-humans thereby the non-humans are effaced by apathy and hostility of human actions. In the poem, "The Rabbit Hunter", the poet talks of the unnecessary killing of the innocent rabbits by the superseding temperament of humans. Man's potentiality makes him careless to the life of animals: "Careless and still / The hunter lurks / With gun depressed, / Facing alone / The alder swamps / Ghastly snow-white". The complex web of conflicts between man and animal is difficult to comprehend: "And deal a death / That he nor it / (Nor I) have wit / To comprehend". If such tendency of humans to kill the animals continues, the extinction of animal species will be obvious. It will be ecologically well when man will restrain from killing animals and love to preserve them.

Man's scientific and technological bend of mind makes him a strong and superpower creature. He feels himself to be the master, 'the sole subject' and sovereign of natural order but he is not so. In the poem, "A Loose Mountain", the poet displays man's ego versus nature's fury. The meteors "Leonid" are weapons used in an attack on humans: "Did you stay up last night (the Magi did) / To see the star shower known as Leonid / That once a year by hand or apparatus / Is so mysteriously pelted at us"? Humans have to rethink upon their precarious situation within the realm of "heartless and enormous Outer Black". The "artificial light" cannot stand against the moment of eclipse of nature's darkness. Hence, the speaker suggests, it is "best to have us in our orbit". Humans have to redecide their plan of action not to impose their supreme power for abusing nature, otherwise they will witness the violent and imminent destruction of the planet.

Modern technology discards the importance of nature. It has made man the lord of everything. But the poet reminds of the past in "It is Almost the Year Two Thousand": "To start the world of old / We had one age of gold". It refers to a mythical age when humans were happy and in harmony with nature. Lynn White, Jr. states: "Formerly man had been part of nature; now he was the exploiter of nature"[14]. At that time, there was no need to work as nature was providing fruits without man's cultivation of the ground: "Not labored out of mines, / And some say there are signs / The second such has come, / The true Millennium". The myth of the Golden Age will re-return and everyone will enjoy: "We well may raise our heads / From weeding garden beds". They will stop pulling out weeds. The artist's expectation for the Golden Age seems parallel to W.B. Yeats's "The Second Coming". Most of the time, Frost assesses nature as something mysterious and its secrets somehow unknowable. His presentation of the human place in the planet seems to be a paradigm of ecophilosophy.

The hegemonic supremacy of capturing another's property is an act of exploitation and oppression that makes impact upon environment. The violent appropriation of the land shows the motif of conquest and land acquisition. In the poem, "Trespass", the speaker exposes:

> No, I had set no prohibiting sign,
> And yes, my land was hardly fenced.
> Nevertheless the land was mine.
> I was being trespassed on and against. (CPoRF, 503)

Trespass is a severe offence in the country's systems. Everyone has the right to have the land. But the capitalists forcibly capture the land of the poor.

Frost's artistic skill creates a sense of familial relationship with the flora and fauna that attunes to his awareness in the natural community. Besides, he is a pioneer in studying birds' life that contributes to the knowledge of the nesting, mating, feeding and migration in seasons. Such experience acknowledges him to be a teller of ornithology. Through his poetry he shows enthusiasm, a genuine love and concern for birds. He demonstrates the activity of Whippoorwills in "A Nature Note":

Four or five whippoorwills
Have come down from their native ledge
To the open country edge
To give us a piece of their bills
Two in June were a pair-
You'd say sufficiently loud,
But this was a family crowd,
A full-fledged family affair.
All out of time pell-mell!
I wasn't in on the joke
Unless it was coming to folk
To bid us a mock farewell.
I took note of when it occurred,
The twenty-third of September,
Their latest that I remember,
September the twenty-third. (CPoRF, 504)

The pastoral enjoyment of nature is a propensity for eco-friendly sentimentality. Birds are obviously a liking picturesque in natural scenery.

Notes

1. Richard Poirier, *Robert Frost: The Work of Knowing*, New York, Oxford University Press, 1977. p. xv.
2. Greg Garrard, *Ecocriticism,* Routledge, 2012, p. 29.
3. Harold Fromm, *The Nature of Being Human: From Environmentalism to Consciousness,* The Johns Hopkins University Press, Baltimore, 2009. p.34.
4. Vivian C. Hopkins, Robert Frost: Out Far and In Deep" in *Interpretations: Essays on American Literature*, edited by R.K. Gupta, American Studies Research Centre, Hyderabad. 1976. p.133.
5. Yvor Winters, "Robert Frost: or, the Spiritual Drifter as Poet" in *Robert Frost: A Collection of Critical Essays*, edited by James M. Cox Prentice-Hall, Inc. 1962, p.78.
6. Pearce, Roy Harvey. *The Continuity of American Poetry*. Princeton, New Jersey: Princeton University Press, 1961.p.280.
7. Richard Poirier, *Robert Frost: The Work of Knowing*, New York, Oxford University Press, 1977. p. 171.
8. Lawrence Buell, *The Environmental Imagination: Thoreau, Nature Writing, and the Formation of American Culture,* The Belknap Press of Harvard university Press, 1995.p.7. Buell is a Professor of English at Harvard University.

9. Randall Jarrell, "To the Laodiceans" in *Robert Frost: A Collection of Critical Essays*, edited by James M. Cox Prentice-Hall, Inc. 1962, p.95.
10. Lawrence Buell, *The Environmental Imagination: Thoreau, Nature Writing, and the Formation of American Culture,* p.210.
11. John T. Napier, "A Momentary Stay Against Confusion" in *Robert Frost: A Collection of Critical Essays*, edited by James M. Cox Prentice-Hall, Inc. 1962, p.134.
12. Greg Garrard, *Ecocriticism,* Routledge, 2012, p. 35.
13. Marion Montgomery, "Robert Frost and His Use of Barriers: Man vs Nature Toward God" in *Robert Frost: A Collection of Critical Essays*, edited by James M. Cox, Prentice-Hall, Inc. 1962, p.140.
14. Lynn White, Jr. in his article "The Historical Roots of Our Ecologic Crisis" mentions the activities of humans in their ecology, published in *The Ecocriticism Reader* by Glotfelty & Fromm, 1996, p.8.

CHAPTER 8

Steeple Bush (1947)

The importance of nature in the life of human beings is certainly great. 'The individual-in-environment' is a component of the survival value. From biocentric stance, man is not distinct from nature. If emphasis is given on the concept that humans are natural, it will adhere to a theory of human nature that asserts life to be beautiful but death is unavoidable. In the poem "A Young Birch", Frost describes the struggle of the birch tree to survive and be beautiful but death is the riding force on its existence. From such perspective, man is not different from the birch to face the domineering death in life. In the next poem "Something for Hope", Frost unfolds the concept of ecological succession that carries on the possibility of change and evolution:

> So busy yourself with other things
> While the trees put on their wooden rings
> And with long-sleeved branches hold their sway
> Then cut down the trees when lumber grown,
> And there's your pristine earth all freed
> From lovely blooming but wasteful weed
> And ready again for the grass to own.
> ....
> Patience and looking away ahead,
> And leaving some things to take their course.
> Hope may not nourish a cow or horse,
> But spes alit agricolam 'tis said. (CPoRF, 518)

The choice is not "steeple bush" but "the edible grass". It relates to the individual growth of species through the evolutionary process. The poem is concluded with: "Hope may not nourish a cow or horse, / But spes alit agricolam 'tis said." In relation to this, William Rueckert may be quoted: "We must remember Commoner's first Law of Ecology: "Everything is connected to everything else." The biosphere (or ecosphere) is the home that life has built for itself on the planet's outer surface. In that ecosphere there is a reciprocal interdependence of one life process upon another, and there is a mutual interconnected development of all of the earth's life systems"[1]. Besides, all creatures try to adapt to circumstance, otherwise it would be difficult to survive.

Environmental crisis is the product of human culture. Ecocritics make observation, and speculation into the changes in environment. In relation to things around them, humans assume the ecological condition in which they have to live. In the poem, "One Step Backward Taken", Frost discusses the geological allegory of unstable ground that is risky to stand upon. For one's safety and security, one has to take the right move to avoid the "crisis": "In the universal crisis / But with one step backward taken / I saved myself from going. / A world torn loose went by me." The world is in crisis. If one takes a step in the right direction, one can find something good: "with one step backward taken / I saved myself from going." But man fails to see the right path, and blames nature to be responsible for everything. The poem establishes the artist's ecological vision that suggests the mankind to take a backward step from the catastrophic developments undergoing toxic effluents. Humans have to rethink on the current state of crisis due to global warming and climate change. Man's prerogative makes nature exploited and extracted everything from it.

Besides, the modernist mindset, in the name of progress and development, turns nature into inhospitable place. All existence is manipulated through a number of diverse and contradictory positions. Frost exposes such contradictory positions in "Directive". To trace environmental degradation caused by modern life, the artist posits:

> Back out of all this now too much for us,
> Back in a time made simple by the loss
> Of detail, burned, dissolved, and broken off
> Like graveyard marble sculpture in the weather,
> There is a house that is no more a house
> Upon a farm that is no more a farm
> And in a town that is no more a town. (Norton, 1779)

A change for better in the mind of the mechanistic and scientific man apparently undergoes into the life of void, emptiness, desolation, and confusion. Physical geographies take an alternative shape putting stress on environment. The house, and its "village culture", "both of them are lost".

Humans and nature, both are interrelated. Any disturbance in one, inevitably disturbs the other. However, everything in nature is directly or indirectly, explicitly or implicitly, becomes a part of man's purpose. In the poem, "Too Anxious for Rivers", the poet asks: "Look down the long valley and there stands a mountain / That someone has said is the end of the world." If the world ends on the other side of that mountain, "Then what of this river that having arisen / Must find where to pour itself into and empty?" Here, emptiness is without purpose and direction. It is not an escape from man's vulnerable position in the end of the world, rather it is an imputation of man to nature. Man's conception of his relationship with nature, whether he admits himself to be a part of it or not: "Oh, I have been often too anxious for rivers / To leave it to them to get out of their valleys. / The truth is the river flows into the canyon / Of Ceasing to Question What Doesn't Concern Us." The river concerns mankind because it is as much a part of nature as humans are; it lives as humans do. Regarding this, Christopher Manes states: "…the natural world as inspirited, not just people, but also animals, plants, and even "inert" entities such as stones and rivers are perceived as being articulate and at times intelligible subjects, able to communicate and interact with humans for good or ill"[2]. Frost's ecological perception claims for knowledge about nature that it is alive and can be articulated accordingly.

Man cannot be alienated from the earth. He is alive because the earth is alive. Very accurately and minutely, the speaker articulates: "The world as we know is an elephant's howdah / The elephant stands on the back of a turtle, / The turtle in turn on a rock in the ocean." It contemplates the myth of creation. The entities like the elephant, the turtle, the rock, and the ocean, are the voices of nature that articulate the natural history of man with nature. He cannot delude himself from denying that he is not a part of nature. In such context, Lawrence Buell asserts: "human history is implicated in natural history"[3]. Man should show his interest in earthly and natural explanations for creation.

Humans must learn to identify the natural factors that lead to access the environmental impact in life. The assumption is that there is something natural that produces a pleasurable effect. Frost speaks of man's relationship to the natural world in the poem "An Unstamped Letter in Our Rural Letter Box". In this poem, the Frostian Man is "just a tramp" who spends the night in the garden of a rural house. In the morning, he leaves a letter, that is unstamped, in the letter box. In that letter, he inscribes:

> Beneath a low-slung juniper
> That like a blanket to my chin
> Kept some dew out and some heat in,
> Yet left me freely face to face
> All night with universal space. (CPoRF, 523)

The Frostian Man experiences the night spent under the juniper tree that performed as "a blanket" but awoke at about "two o'clock" just in time to witness the collision of two stars. He feels that in spite of all his poverty, he has access to the riches that is derived from experiencing the natural world. It talks of an empathetic engagement with the biophysical world.

Frost's ecological perception moves into the explanatory power of evolutionary biology and evolutionary psychology. Evolution is how the human psychology astounds at the terrestrial chemistry or the celestial bodies of illimitable cosmos. In the poem, "Skeptic", the speaker hovers around belief and disbelief. Besides, the human mind is an independent and free component injected by God. The mind tries to share with the substances of the cosmos and seeks for finding out the interrelations. The speaker delves into the Big Bang theory:

> Far star that tickles for me my sensitive plate
> And fries a couple of ebon atoms white,
> I don't believe I believe a thing you state.
> I put no faith in the seeming facts of light.
> I don't believe I believe you're the last in space,
> I don't believe you're anywhere near the last,
> I don't believe what makes you red in the face
> Is after explosion going away so fast.
> The universe may or may not be very immense.
> As a matter of fact there are times when I am apt
> To feel it close in tight against my sense
> Like a caul in which I was born and still am wrapped. (CPoRF, 549)

The speaker addresses the star, stating that he is unsure of it as "the last in space" or what makes it "red in the face". "Explosion" may relate to the idea of Big Bang. Frost's perception becomes enormously wide and deep in the sense that the stars turn into the red portion, or lower frequencies, of the visual spectrum as they come under revolving process of the planet.

On the other hand, the anthropocentric mindset believes that the earth is made for the use and pleasure of human beings. They never think of the cost of the damage caused to the planet by them; even they don't pay attention to the other forms of life that live in biosphere. They argue that the earth exists as a platform for hoarding of raw materials for the welfare of the mankind. But Frost in "Lucretius Versus the Lake Poets" quotes "Nature I loved, and next to Nature, Art". Man's unconquerable mind substantiates: "By Nature meant the Whole Goddam Machinery". Man's domination over nature is the basic cause of environmental crisis. Apart from this, the speaker claims: "The only meaning possible for Nature / In Landor's quatrain would be Pretty Scenery". But the importance of nature does not become confined in a sense of "Pretty Scenery". The assessment of reality is necessary for understanding the earth.

Corollary to this, the biological existence of the past distinguishes itself from the present society. The philosophical and moral dimensions in the past-living differ profoundly from the scientific and technological life in the current era. In the past, man was close to nature and feeling a part of it. But now, he is the exploiter of nature. In "A Cliff Dwelling", the Frostian Man wonders about the people of an ancient society whose ecology was deeply conditioned by their beliefs in nature and destiny. They were almost worshipping nature for their existence. But they are forgotten by their successors who live on their land today. The speaker feels sad as those people are rendered as unimportant by the society now:

> There sandy seems the golden sky
> And golden seems the sandy plain.
> No habitation meets the eye
> Unless in the horizon rim,
> Some halfway up the limestone wall,
> That spot of black is not a stain
> Or shadow, but a cavern hole,
> Where someone used to climb or crawl
> To rest from his besetting fears.
> I see the callus on his sole
> The disappearing last of him
> And of his race starvation slim,
> Oh, years ago-ten thousand years. (CPoRF, 554)

The artist is in favour of traditional social values which are eco-friendly. Those values have been ravaged by time. The time, witnessed by science and technology, has made man strong and selfish to rupture nature.

The misuse of science is the prime generator of environmental degradation. Moreover, the experimentation of it is commonly 'ecocatastrophe'. The devastating effects of nuclear threat can never be forgotten that had happened on Nagasaki and Hiroshima. Therefore, Frost asks the humanity through his creation, "Why Wait for Science". Sarcastically he opines that the inventions made by science lead to destruction of the earth. Besides, the nuclear-test creates contaminated communities. People plan to escape from such invention, either to flee or to face the complete annihilation:

> Sarcastic Science she would like to know,
> In her complacent ministry of fear,
> How we propose to get away from here
> When she has made things so we have to go
> Or be wiped out: Will she be asked to show
> Us how by rocket we may hope to steer
> To some star off there say a half light-year
> Through temperature of absolute zero?
> Why wait for Science to supply the how
> When any amateur can tell it now?
> The way to go away should be the same
> As fifty million years ago we came-
> If anyone remembers how that was.
> I have a theory, but it hardly does. (CPoRF, 563)

The speaker asks whether the humans would be carried to a far-off planet "by rocket" or would they go the same way as they had come "fifty million years ago"? The mention of "her complacent ministry of fear" refers to the dark aspects of scientific inventions that possibly create the deadly consequences in ecosystem. Regarding this, Ramachandra Guha states: "Scientific or technological 'solutions' which poison the environment or degrade the social structure and man himself, are of no benefit, no matter how brilliantly conceived or how great their superficial attraction"[4]. Humans should learn how to reshape and improve their environment for a sustainable living.

The majority of environmental problems come from man's greedy sense of possession and accumulation. The global capitalistic ideology of 'possessive individualism' sabotages the earth. When man's need converts into his greed, ecological crisis crops up. In the poem, "Any Size We Please", the speaker mentions: "He stretched his arms out to the dark of space / And held them absolutely parallel / In infinite appeal". The nature-defying accumulation is ecocide. Man tries to have capitalist accretion: "He had been too all out, too much extended. / He slapped his breast to verify his purse / And hugged himself for all his universe". It may be stated that greedy capitalism stands upon cupidity and self-ego that are antagonistic to the harmony in nature.

The assessment of globalised productionism, consumerism, and capitalism foregrounds environmental abuse. The belief in mass production and concentration on bigger machines wields greater violence against the ecosystem and makes man the butcher of earth. In the poem "An Importer", Frost reacts on such production and mentions: "Most of all the mass production / Destined to prove our destruction". However, machines demand energy and to get energy is expected from the resources of the earth thereby pressing hard on the carrying capacity of the planet: "The most primitive of engines / Mass producing with a vengeance". In the industrial ideology of life, there is less sustainability as the potential pollutants dangerously damage the living systems of nature.

It is noticed that the breathless competition for extracting natural resources to impose superpower without paying attention to natural environment has been man's mindset. The catastrophic outputs of nuclear tests build serious and severe consequences on environment and also form contaminated communities. Bomb enterprise causes the dreadful impact of radioactive reaction. Such potential horror separates humans from nature instead of bringing them together. Nuclear holocaust is a grave issue. In "The Planners", the poet unfurls:

> If anything should put an end to This,
> I'm thinking the unborn would never miss
> What they had never had of vital bliss
> No burst of nuclear phenomenon
> That put an end to what was going on
> Could make much difference to the dead and gone.
> Only a few of those even in whose day
>   It happened would have very much to say.
>   And any one might ask them who were they.
>   Who would they be? The guild of social planners
>   With the intention blazoned on their banners
>   Of getting one more chance to change our manners?
>   These anyway might think it was important
>   That human history should not be shortened. (CPoRF, 566)

There is a need to trace the history of Nagasaki and Hiroshima. The atomic explosion related catastrophes are furiously and severely intense than any other violent natural calamity. That's why the speaker ardently claims for nuclear disarmament.

The conflict between the haves and the have-nots, the rich and the poor, the strong and the weak, the exploiter and the exploited disrupts the social and ecological relations. This class struggle terribly ruptures the earth. Besides, the capitalistic-developed strong nations are extremely selfish, competitive and grossly destructive. In "No Holy Wars for Them", Frost measures the political, social, and economic rights of the "puny little states" in comparison to the superpower status of strong nations. He shows the disparities between the weak, non-militarized countries and the self-sufficiency, advanced, nuclear-power attained nations: "States strong enough to do good are but few. / Their number would seem limited to three."

The "puny little states" expect to derive the good will from others, not able to exercise any influence on the international scenes. Nations like the Cuban and the Swiss cannot muster enough strength to "wage a Global Mission" because of their feebleness. The speaker argues for small nations who are too tiny to cause anything greater than "a nuisance brawl". He is also under doubt that the West can teach Asia anything about mass production. Ultimately, the event of a "nuisance brawl" crops up only for the prolonged deprivation. The binary between the strong and the weak leads to inequality and class-conflict which are responsible for environmental disruption.

Man's predicament is obvious as he fouls and disfigures his own nest. The potential loss and damage caused to the environment by radioactive radiation is beyond ramification and rectification. Moreover, the harmful radioactive and toxic waste tremendously affect people and their livestock and rewrite the fate of their survival. Hence, in "Bursting Rapture", the speaker "went to the physician to complain," what "gain / Was made by getting science on the brain": "I went to the physician to complain, / The time had been when anyone could turn / [...] / But now 'twas there as elsewhere, any gain / Was made by getting science on the brain." The poet acknowledges to the threat of the atomic bomb. Obviously, the he was living at that time when the bombardment on Nagasaki and Hiroshima occurred. It became apparent that everything on the earth could be annihilated in minutes. The poet blames science for this nuclear holocaust. It is a fact that nuclearisation turns to acute pain for the affected ones. The radiation of the bomb in World War II poisoned everything in an unprecedented and unimaginable scale. Besides, nothing is potentially dangerous than nuclear holocaust thereby apprehending the threat, Arundhati Roy's views may be mentioned: "Is it the Americans' fault for having created it, or the Indians' / Pakistanis' fault for threatening to use it? Or is it rather the West's fault in general for the overweening cultural arrogance that lies behind their invention of 'colonialism, slavery, ethnic cleansing, germ warfare [and] chemical weapons', and for having 'more money, more food and bigger bombs than anyone else'?[5]. For the existence of the bomb, ecocatastrophe becomes a greater possibility. It will materialise the perception of death and destruction.

Encouragement to nuclear power is not a progressive world view. In "U.S. 1946 King's X", the poet unfolds: "Having invented a new Holocaust, / And been the first with it to win a war, / How they make haste to cry with fingers crossed, /King's X – no fairs to use it anymore!" It is a stern, stinging rebuke for the atomic power in the war. Everything is ravaged and survival becomes a challenge. But for political mileage, 'bomb culture' creates a platform. This 'Gothicised environmental squalor' has no alternative to be compensated. Thus, the use and experiments of nuclear devices commit ecocide. If the inclination for nuclear power is not resisted, it would conceivably lead to the dilapidation of the universe.

Regarding the above incident, Vivian C. Hopkins mentions: "Yet no writer was more deeply shaken than he (Frost) by the repercussions of the exploding bomb. He wrestled with the problem, setting forth tentative answers in poem after poem. One, in "The Broken Drought", is the stoical acceptance-if earth is to become uninhabitable: What for that matter had it ever been? / Who advised man to come and live therein?"[6]. Atomic-bomb constructs a great divide between man and nature and makes the earth inhospitable for life of any kind. There would be the absolute shortage of life-sustaining clean air. In other words, "Mother Earth" would be turned into the most foul and horrific one. From ecological perspective, nuclear device is 'a crying shame'.

The current state of the world witnesses global warming and climate change. Now the whole mankind is inflicted by the dreadful Covid-19 virus. The planetary ecology is under threat. The sun is getting hotter and many regions come under the cataclysm of famine. Frost's "The Broken Drought" predicts the impending crisis in the world. "The prophet of disaster" forecasts: "Earth would soon / Be uninhabitable as the moon". The poem undergoes the worsening climatic conditions and geography that has been one of the serious global issues getting intensified from day to day.

Notes

1. William Rueckert in his article, "Literature and Ecology" quotes Berry Commoner's first Law of Ecology, published in *The Ecocriticism Reader*, edited by Glotfelty & Fromm, The University of Georgia Press, 1996, p.112.
2. Christopher Manes, "Nature and Silence" in *The Ecocriticism Reader,* edited by Cheryll Glotfelty & Harold Fromm, The University of Georgia Press, 1996.p.15. Manes is an author, attorney, and Ph.D. candidate in Medieval Literature at the University of Oregon.
3. Lawrence Buell, *The Environmental Imagination: Thoreau, Nature Writing, and the Formation of American Culture,* The Belknap Press of Harvard university Press, 1995.p.7. Buell is a Professor of English at Harvard University.
4. Ramachandra Guha, *Environmentalism: A Global History, A* Penguin Random House India Pvt. Ltd.2014.p.103.
5. Graham Huggan and Helen Tiffin, *Postcolonial Ecocriticism: Literature, Animals, Environment,* Routledge, First Indian Reprint, 2015, p.50.
6. Vivian C. Hopkins, Robert Frost: Out Far and In Deep" in *Interpretations: Essays on American Literature*, edited by R.K. Gupta, American Studies Research Centre, Hyderabad. 1976. p.147.

CHAPTER 9

Robert Frost: A Bird Watcher

Literary critics portray Robert Frost as a good neighbor, a sensibilist, an environmentalist, a humanist, a classicist and 'an original ordinary man'. Apart from these diversified, multifarious and versatile dispositions, he is also a consistent and careful bird-watcher. As an amateur ornithologist, he studies every aspect of birds including their songs, flying manners, physical appearance and migratory histories. With reliability and fairness, he presents the aesthetic appeal of birds. Besides, the birder introspects into their behavior, species, and ecological niches in his poetry. It is obvious that the lifestyles, behaviors and survival of birds are subject to ecosystems. Depletion of wilderness makes the birds endangered. Exhaustion of natural spaces correlates to the extinction of species. Any deviation in environment puts problem to them. The pedagogy of global warming and climate change has been a major debatable issue. They know little to adapt themselves. Contrasted with this, humans in the changes of their lifestyle have affected and disturbed the existence of birds. In this regard, in his article "The Historical Roots of Our Ecologic Crisis", Lynn White, Jr. argues: "It has been noted, for example, that the advent of the automobile eliminated huge flocks of sparrows that once fed on the horse manure littering every street"[1]. It needs to explore this neglected but vitally important area of knowledge that man is not alone at the centre of creation, rather welfare thoughts should be devoted towards the avian world.

Mention may be made of Frost as a country farmer but he plays the role of an amateur ornithologist. The deliberate use of avian imagery in his poetry serves as a powerful articulation of his study on birds. Subodh Kumar Sinha, in his article "Robert Frost" writes, "One of his (Frost) hobbies seems to be bird-watching. And the poet turns to be a good bird-watcher … a sympathetic participant in the daily life of nature"[2]. His description of birds at different spaces and seasons represents the persona's experience on bionetwork. Most of the poems in A *Boy's Will* demonstrate the speaker's considerable surveillance on birds. "The Ghost House" talks of the persona's minute study on birds' behavior like "the woodpecker chops"/ "Night comes; the black bats tumble and dart"/ "The Whippoorwill is coming to shout/ And hush and cluck and flutter about". The place suits them as it is "lonely", "ruined" and "disused". The countryside eternity endears these birds. In the viscera of night and darkness, the nocturnal birds like bats perform their acrobatic feats. The woodpecker's constant tapping and the whippoorwill's shouting justify the prerogative of their biological communities and environments as it is a ghost house and the noninterference of human beings. It is their way of life in harmony with nature.

The microscopic study upon birds' feelings in "A Late Walk" makes the poet a sincere bird-watcher: "And when I come to the garden ground, / The whir of sober birds / Up from the tangle of withered weeds / Is sadder than any words." The speaker asserts that the birds behave soberly as he walks into the garden. The mention of "tangle of withered weeds" indicates the fall of winter. It dispenses a remorseful image of the garden which was once beautiful. Winter has made it twisted, cracked, brown and yellow. The birds sound sad as they sing. Such situation pinpoints that most birds avoid cold climate and migrate vast distances to escape the approaching cold. The persona studies their sentiment as they appreciate and enjoy summer.

The sense of pleasure and enjoyment the birds feel in spring is seen in the poem, "A Prayer in Spring". The bird watcher gets delight by exploring on the avian community: "And make us happy in the darting bird / That suddenly above the bees is heard, / The meteor that thrusts in with needle bill, /And off a blossom in mid-air stands still." The speaker's expression of "the darting bird" seems to be any small, quickly moving bird because of the reference to "the meteor". The bird's bill is stated as a "needle". Through this physiology, the birder identifies it as a humming bird. It is heard above the bees and the scene is joyous and blissful. It distributes aesthetic appeal to all. The surrounding creates a vista that darts contentment in all directions. "In this way, aestheticism produces environmental bonding"[3].

On the other hand, the birder is a lonely child "In a Vale" who looks outside of his window. The vale gets alive for him. The blooms and the birds become energetic to produce exuberance. He acclaims: "And thus it is I know so well / Why the flower has odor, the bird has song, / You have only to ask me, and I can tell, / No, not vainly there did I dwell, / Nor vainly listen all the night long." The persona notices the blooms and birds in the marsh, "Where the bird and flower were one and the same". The odor of bloom and song of the bird in the empty marsh enhance the dream-like quality and shape the tone of aestheticism. The flower is sweet. Bird's song is tempting. Both are the beautiful gifts of nature. This picturesque view needs the usefulness of practicing self-conscious to appreciate aestheticism. In relation to aesthetic beauty, Timothy Clark asserts: "Aesthetic atmospheres are inseparable from the fact that the human body, as a part of nature, participates in showing and letting-be-felt of things in their multiplicity and varied tonalities"[4].

Obviously, such a feeling arises when the bird-watcher observes this external beautified reality of the physical phenomena. Frost seems to give emphasis on aesthetic value that works towards a new sense of beauty. This value communicates the overall health of an ecosystem. Pastoral beauty engages life in harmony with nature that creates aesthetic adaptability.

Nature is Frost's poetry. The motivational force that stems from different types of weather-snowy, rainy, sunny and cloudy – in seasonal cycles, arouses sentimental emotions and feelings in him. Weather arrests the frame of mind. The birder's gloomy and depressed mood is understood through the birds' mood. Suggestive and open is clearly the view of Commoner's first law of Ecology: "Everything is connected to everything else"[5]. However, the mutual and shared interconnectedness and reciprocal interdependence of one life process upon another may not be ignored. This gets a reflection in the poem "A Line-Storm Song" that reveals the persona's reading of birds' mentality: "The birds have less to say for themselves / In the wood-world's torn despair."

It is evident that the persona's work on birds in the above discussed poems of *A Boy's Will* discloses his ecological understanding and indulgence. In *Walden*, Henry David Thoreau points out, "If we know all the laws of Nature, we should need only one fact, or the description of one actual phenomenon, to infer all the particular results at that point"[6]. Obviously, the background of Frost's poetry is nature. No individual and no particular species will survive by far if nature becomes adverse.

Frost's next volume, *North of Boston* discusses the avifauna in "The Wood-Pile". The poem begins with the speaker's walk "in the frozen swamp". Through the visual description, the readers experience snow in winter and bitter cold weather. Water has frozen into ice. Sky is clouded. In this dominant "grey" atmosphere, the speaker notices a small bird alighted before him:

A small bird flew before me. He was careful
To put a tree between us when he lighted,
And say no word to tell me who he was
Who was so foolish as to think what he thought.
He thought that I was after him for a feather-
The white one in his tail; ...(CPoRF, 126)

The frightened bird seems engrossed to know about the persona. The apprehension of the bird is obvious as the bird-hunters take the opportunity of weather for their purpose. The bird-watcher realises the traumatic condition of the fowl as it is guided by its inner command for safety. Such behavioral patterns make its own survival possible in that environment.

Passion, preservation and a life in harmony with nature are the stimulating drives in Frost. Preserving and restoring bird habitat brings satisfaction in him. "The Exposed Nest" in *Mountain Interval* unveils the birder's effort to save and refurbish the life of chicks from destruction and death. Accompanied with his child, the speaker rescues a group of baby birds from their smashed nest by a harvesting machine:

'Twas a nest full of young birds on the ground
The cutter-bar had just gone champing over
(Miraculously without tasting flesh)
And left defenseless to the heat and light.
You wanted to restore them to their right
Of something interposed between their sight
And too much world at once-could means be found. (CPoRF, 136)

The eco-friendly deed of the artist disseminates an exulted feeling of compassion and kindness for the misfortunate baby birds. On the other hand, to lessen the risk and provide comfort to the chicks, the birder and his child face dilemma in regard to the feeling of the mother bird:

The way the nest-full every time we stirred
Stood up to us as to a mother-bird
Whose coming home has been too long deferred,
Made me ask would the mother-bird return
And care for them in such a change of scene
And might our meddling make her more afraid. (ibid)

Corollary to this, the birds usually don't prefer to the interference of humans in their life. But the emergence of conscience in the bird-watcher and his child is apparently from compassionate ground. Human brain makes it possible to think upon the circumstances. Sometimes tentatively, sometimes decisively, man is led by certain ethics on survival point. In such context, Joseph W. Meeker advocates: "Human behavior has generally been guided by presumed metaphysical principles which have neglected to recognise that man is a species of animal whose welfare depends upon a successful integration with plants, animals, and land that make up his environment"[7].

There is also the necessity of studying and understanding of "The Oven Bird" that sits on a tree at the approach of a mid-summer's evening and sings melancholy. The birder articulates the cause of the depressed mood of the bird for the falling of the leaves of the cherry blossom. With the passage of time, season changes and the birds behave accordingly-migrating, mating, breeding, nesting and hatching. The bird-watcher discerns the nest-building birds come and go around their house in "The Hill Wife". Rarities and surprises enthrall for holding a bird in hand. Pleasure of watching birds never ends. Birds and landscapes are the inspirational idea that transfers to the perceptions of nature. The bird-watcher designs beauty, wonder and hope in his work that gives objective methods of producing moods to appreciate the biosphere.

Seasonality shapes wonder. Birds in seasons brighten our day. However, they are the harbingers for pressing concerns on climate change. They think of their environment and hence go on mind-bending migrations across continents and oceans. The bird-watcher recounts such phenomena in "The Last Word of a Bluebird". As the cold and dry north wind approaches, the bluebird gets ready to leave the place. Once it starts cold, there is obviously "ice on the trough". Usually, during winter, the birds fly south. They return back again when the weather is warm and comfortable. Like the changes in trees, flowers and crops, each season brings about something new and something different in birds:

> That the north wind last night
> That made the stars bright
> And made ice on the trough
> Almost made him cough
> His tail feathers off.
> He just had to fly!

But he sent her Good-by,
And said to be good,
And wear her red hood,
....
And perhaps in the spring
He would come back and sing. (CPoRF, 170)

The ecological perspective of the speaker bestows intimacy and friendship between the bluebird and a little girl, Lesley. It is the reciprocal relationship between human and non-human, between man and nature. In such context, Joseph W. Meeker may be cited who has mentioned in his article, "The Comic Mode", "…no individual and no species can survive unless all other species survive, for all are ultimately dependent upon the completeness of the environment as a whole"[8]. The affiliation between the bluebird and Lesley affirms a successful integration of human world with the avian world. As a life-long farmer, the speaker is conscious of the fact that birds bear the seeds with them that they have eaten and diffuse those through their droppings when they migrate. By such activity, they fetch plants back to ecosystems. They contribute to create plant life that surrounds the human world. But humans, for their commercialism and productionism, believe in depletion of these plants.

Many a time the artist uses the avian imagery in his poetry. The way he presents the images seems to be the field notes of an ornithologist. Poems in the volume *New Hampshire,* more or less, bear the testimony of his practicability. "A Star in a Stone-Boat" talks of "a long Bird of Paradise's tail" and "A Fountain, A Bottle, A Donkey's Ears and Some Books" gives the image of "a stricken bird". The speaker's fact-based examination into birds' life style is praiseworthy. He repeatedly stresses on the images of cold weather and birds that signify his environmental concern. Winter is a tough time for birds. They adapt different ways to face the seasons. In "Looking for a Sunset Bird in Winter", the bird-watcher claims: "No bird was singing in it now, / A single leaf was on a bough, / And that was all there was to see / In going twice around the tree." He pinpoints a long, harsh, brutal winter which is the cause of the birds' adversity. In the second stanza of the said poem, the birder affirms: "In summer when I passed the place / I had to stop and lift my face; / A bird with an angelic gift / Was singing in it sweet and swift." In the ensuing situation, he asserts that summer is more approving for the birds than winter. The "sweet and swift" singing of bird in summer absolutely fades away in winter. This action justifies their unhappiness in bitter cold climate. Possibly, "it entails an understanding of the body and temperament as conditioned by its environment"[9]. Step by step, life is dangerous for any creature in an adverse ecosystem. Hence, strategy for living needs ecological wisdom.

The constant and consequent knowledge on birds seems to be stimulating in the psyche of the bird-watcher. "A Hillside Thaw" tries to communicate birds' ecology to the readers: "And birds that joined in the excited fun / By doubling and redoubling song and twitter, / I have no doubt I'd end by holding none." It shows up the excitement and thrill of birds under the sun. The biological instinct of these creatures, to some extent, is pronounced here. Frost opens up the pastoral view in relation to birds' pleasant entertainment. "Doubling and redoubling song and twitter" conveys the experiences of their erotic yearning. The advocacy of their consummation of love is a reverential part of nature. With an ecologic bend of mind, the speaker demonstrates the avian world.

Besides, the artist inquiries into the ecological aspects of birds in accordance with their songs, flight manners, physical appearance and migration patterns. In the poem, "Our Singing Strength", he expounds: "Thrush, bluebird, blackbird, sparrow, and robin throng, / Some to go further north to Hudson's Bay, / Some that have come too far north back away, / Really a very few to build and stay."

The singing of such great number of migrating birds spells out the presence of spring. Although the late snow baffles and restrains the birds, the assemblage of birds heralds the beginning of spring: "Now was seen how these liked belated snow. / The fields had nowhere left for them to go; / They'd soon exhausted all there was in flying; / The trees they'd had enough of with once trying." Climatic disorder, to some extent, problematizes the usual process of life. It can be affirmed that there is the reciprocal and shared relationship between biotic and abiotic. The way the speaker presents justifies him as an experienced, veteran birder. It is in this sense that he is deeply possessed by the problem of birds.

The "belated" snow forces the "flocks of glossy birds" onto the road. Road is not a fit-place for these creatures. Commonly we keep it in mind that birds are the indicator of seasons. But due to disturbance in ecosystem, such view seems to lack its potency. From this conceptual trunk, early environmentalists come into discussion. The environmental perception of Robert Frost is articulated by

Lawrence Buell: "Nonfiction writers such as Thoreau, Austin, Berry, Dillard, and Janovy – and poets like Wordsworth, Frost, and Snyder – seem to have begun adulthood as youths with relatively modest degrees of eco-precociousness who became caught up in the quest for environmental literacy"[10].

The artist's practical understanding as a rustic and agrarian develops the key concepts in birds' behavior at different ecological niches. The poem, "The Need of Being Versed in Country Things" bears the indication of the speaker's love of nature and rural things. In such rurality, the birder pronounces that the birds feel happy in nest. He argues that the birds don't lose hope in disasters. They accept the natural calamities as the natural continuation of their life. The narrator exposes such facts in a realistic way: "For them there was really nothing sad. / But though they rejoiced in the nest they kept, / One had to be versed in country things / Not to believe the phoebes wept."

As an ornithologist, the speaker underpins the sentiments and feelings of birds. The sonnet, "Acceptance" in the fifth volume *West-Running Brook* bespeaks of nature's power and a tone of acceptance to the inevitable darkness after the setting sun by the birds. The bird-watcher observes: "When the spent sun throws up its rays on cloud / And goes down burning into the gulf below, / […] / It is the change to darkness in the sky / Murmuring something quiet in her breast, / One bird begins to close a faded eye." It is a fundamental acceptance of life in ecosystem. The birder understands this nature-centred system that encompasses each and every creature. It is obvious that darkness is unpleasant but there is no trepidation in birds. The acceptance of this is a natural phenomenon. Perhaps, survival depends upon the individual qualities of strength of the creatures.

It may be acknowledged that bird watching, to some extent, requires auditory components. As many species of birds are detected and identified by auditory than visual, most of the birders follow this methodology to study on birds. In the poem, "A Minor Bird", the persona is at his house and the sound of the bird goes on singing for all day. Usually, one feels uneasy if a particular sound continues uninterruptedly. Thus, out of irritation, he claps for the bird to fly away: "I have wished a bird would fly away, / And not sing by my house all day; / Have clapped my hands at him from the door / When it seemed as if I could bear no more." Clapping of his hand is the anthropocentric mindset of the persona to fly away the bird. But realising his "fault" is the biocentric vision of the birder. Here, the ego-consciousness of the speaker turns to eco-consciousness.

Man's imposition of self-centred values upon other creatures is a kind of ecocide. Each one should think of the earth for the rootholds of sanity and sanctity. Each creature has the right to live. In the poem, "The Thatch" the speaker's unwanted trespass and intrusion to the world of birds makes him repentant. Ecological threats operate from the flaw in man's anthropocentric vision. His compulsion to conquer over other creatures is the cause of ecological crisis. The Frostian Man realises his mistake:

> Where summer birds had been given hatch,
> Had fed in chorus, and lived to fledge,
> Some still were living in hermitage.
> And as I passed along the eaves,
> So low I brushed the straw with my sleeves,
> I flushed birds out of hole after hole,
> Into the darkness. It grieved my soul,
> It started a grief within a grief,
> To think their case was beyond relief-
> They could not go flying about in search
> Of their nest again, nor find a perch. (CPoRF, 320)

To rectify his wrong doings, the persona immediately withdraws anthropocentric standpoint in order to attain a vision of the good that will presumably sustain them in "the cottage where we dwelt". From an ecological viewpoint, it is the true essence of each one's living. Appropriate is the suggestion, "human-nature is an interspecies relationship"[11].

The role of environment in the life of each creature needs a certain attention. The birder is fully conscious of the surroundings. His involvement with a bluebird in the poem, "Two Tramps in a Mud Time" makes an impact in the readers' mind. It is the month of April. The weather fluctuates and plays hide and seek of hot and cold. "The sun is out and the wind is still" and flowers are in full "bloom". In such a place, a bluebird sings: "A bluebird comes tenderly up to alight / And turns to the wind to unruffled a plume / His song so pitched as not to excite / A single flower as yet to bloom.")

As it is observed, the bluebirds start nesting from February to April (http://bluebird.com> nesting-habits). Due to the variation in weather, the speaker feels it as if "in the middle of March". It forms the inter-relatedness of place, creatures and environment. Hence, presumption may be shaped on aestheticism. Regarding this, in his article "Beyond Ecology: Self, Place, and the Pathetic Fallacy", Neil Evernden mentions: "The aesthetic experience, in Dewey's terminology, lies in the relationship between the individual and the environment, not simply in the object viewed, nor in the mind of the viewer. Rather than a subject-object relationship in which the observer parades before the supposedly beautiful view, we have instead a process, an interaction between the viewer and the viewed, and it is in that joint association that the aesthetic experience lies"[12].

The birder has a strong affinity to countryside. The countryside views are the essential qualities of his description. He tries to make man's mindset drawn towards nature. He gives a glimpse of the bird's psyche that urges to reveal whether the creature endangers itself when it sings out in night. In the sonnet, "On a Bird Singing in Its Sleep" published in the volume *A Further Range* talks of the artist's idea and knowledge on the activities of birds. He surmises that the risk might be less by the birds' position low in a bush when they sing and sound:

> A bird half wakened in the lunar noon
> Sang halfway through its little inborn tune
> Partly because it sang but once all night
> And that from no especial bush's height;
> ....
> Almost before the prick of hostile ears,
> It ventured less in peril than appears. (CPoRF, 397)

Perhaps, the speaker articulates to preserve the integrity, stability, and beauty of the biotic community. He is in thought of the existence of birds. The continuity of their biological environment is threatened as the extinction of the species is observed from decade to decade. Corollary to this is the postulation that humans are certainly powerful and superior to birds. The appalling climate change and global warming make them endangered species.

Birds are a part of nature. The persona delves into their sound to gain a wide-ranging experience. Then he probes into the genetic and generic system of birds that passes on from generation to generation. In regard to their adaptive process, they struggle to exist and never leave their instinct. In the poem, "Come in" the bird-watcher hears the music of Thrush: "As I came to the edge of the woods, / Thrush music-hark! / Now if it was dusk outside, / Inside it was dark." The music of thrush goes on. The persona concentrates on the song of the bird that comes from the woods. He gets confused to locate where about of the place. Commonly, it is observed that many of the singing birds hide themselves amidst the thick foliage when they sing. The Victorian Poet, Thomas Hardy appraises the music of the bird in "The Darkling Thrush":

At once a voice rose among
The bleak twigs overhead
In a full-hearted evensong
Of joy unlimited;
An aged thrush, frail, gaunt, and small
In blast-beruffled plume,
Had chosen thus to fling his soul
Upon the growing gloom. (Williams, 150)

The poet becomes aware of the thrush which is singing joyfully as the landscape grows darker. It is a winter evening and quite unexpectedly he hears the thrush. However, Walt Whitman makes use of the bird thrush as a symbol in his poem, "When Lilacs Last in the Dooryard Bloom'd". It is a stunning pastoral elegy in honour of the assassinated President Abraham Lincoln. In fourth section, he writes:

In the swamp in secluded recesses,
A shy and hidden bird is warbling a song.
Solitary the thrush,
....
Sings by himself a song. (Norton, 1009)

Besides, William Carlos Williams in his poem, "To a Wood Thrush" mentions, "Singing across the orchard/ before night, answered/ from the depths/ of the wood inversely/ and in a lower key – (https://www.poetrynook.com>poem>wood-thrush-2). As the naturalists observe, thrush sings mainly in the early morning and again in the evening hours. Hence, the bird-watcher's study on the bird is accurate and precise.

The artist is intimated with the ecological and environmental features where a species adapts to find the essential and basic needs for life such as food, water, shelter and mates for reproduction. In the poem, "A Nature Note", the birder expresses:

Four or five whippoorwills
Have come down from their native ledge
To the open country edge
To give us a piece of their bills
Two in June were a pair-
You'd say sufficiently loud,

But this was a family crowd,
A full-fledged family affair.
....
Their latest that I remember,
September the twenty-third. (CPoRF, 504)

The persona's study upon such nocturnal birds is exemplary. These species of birds are usually seen more in number. Recognising the reality of nature, Frost opens the birds' ecology, evolution, behavior and physiology before the readers. The discussions on different types of birds and their sounds in Frost's poetry communicate that other than human language, there is also the language of birds. In his comprehensive study of shamanism, Mircea Eliade writes, "All over the world learning the language of animals, especially of birds, is equivalent to knowing the secrets of nature..."[13]. Hence, the readers must rethink and refeel upon these sober creatures. This is how the pragmatic biological quest for naming the species of birds, their natural habitat, breeding habitat and avian foraging renames the poet as a bird-watcher.

Notes

1. Lynn White, Jr. in his article "The Historical Roots of Our Ecologic Crisis" mentions the activities of humans in their ecology, published in *The Ecocriticism Reader* by Glotfelty & Fromm, 1996, p.4.
2. Narasimhaiah, C.D. *Students Handbook of American Literature*, 4863/2B, Kalyani Publishers, Bharat Ram Road, 24, Daryaganj, New Delhi 110002, 1997.p.195.
3. Lawrence Buell, *The Environmental Imagination: Thoreau, Nature Writing, and the Formation of American Culture,* p.98.
4. Timothy Clark, *The Cambridge Introduction* to *Literature and the Environment,* Cambridge University Press, 2014, p.82. He is a specialist in Romantic, Heideggerian and post-Heideggerian poetics and in environmental criticism.
5. William Rueckert in his article, "Literature and Ecology" quotes Berry Commoner's first Law of Ecology, published in *The Ecocriticism Reader,* edited by Glotfelty & Fromm, The University of Georgia Press, 1996, p.112.
6. Thoreau, Henry David. *Walden*, Kalyani Publishers, Ansari Road, 23, Daryaganj, New Delhi-110002, 1998. p.194.
7. Joseph M. Meeker, "The Comic Mode" in *The Ecocriticism Reader,* edited by Cheryll Glotfelty & Harold Fromm, The University of Georgia Press, 1996.p.163. Joseph W. Meeker is a human ecologist with a Ph.D. in comparative literature, and master's and postdoctoral studies in wildlife ecology and comparative animal and human behavior.

8. Joseph M. Meeker, p.162
9. Todd A. Borlik, *Ecocriticism and Early Modern English Literature,* Routledge, Indian Reprint, 2015, p.206.
10. Lawrence Buell, p.108.
11. Joni Adamson, "Environmental Justice, Cosmopolitics, and Climate Change" in *The Cambridge Companion to Literature and the Environment*, edited by Louise Westling, Cambridge University Press, 2014. p.178.
12. Neil Evernden, "Beyond Ecology: Self, Place, and The Pathetic Fallacy" published in *The Ecocriticism Reader* edited by Cheryll Glotfelty & Harold Fromm, The University of Georgia Press, 1996. p.97. Neil Evernden is the Faculty of Environmental Studies at York University.
13. Eliade, Mircea. *Shamanism: Archaic Technique of Ecstacy*, Princeton: Princeton University Press, 1972, p.98.

Bibliographical References

Primary Sources

Complete Poems Of Robert Frost, Diana Publishing, dianapublishing@yahoo.com. 2020. Print.

Norton, W.W. & Company. *The Norton Anthology of American Literature: Shorter Fourth Edition,* W.W. Norton & Company, Inc.,500 Fifth Avenue, New York, N.Y.10110, 1995. Print.

Oliver, Egbert S. *An Anthology American Literature 1890-1965*, Eurasia Publishing House (Pvt.) LTD. Ram Nagar, New Delhi-110055, 1996. Print.

Williams, Oscar and Honig, Edwin. *The Mentor Book of Major American Poets,* The New American Library of World Literature, Inc. 501 Madison Avenue, New York 22, New York, 1962. Print.

Secondary Sources

Adams, William H. and Martin Mulligan, eds. *Decolonising Nature: Strategies for Conservation in a Post-Colonial Era,* London: Earthscan, 2003. Print.

Adorno, Theodor. *Aesthetic Theory*, Minneapolis: University of Minnesota Press, 1998. Print.

Appadurai, Arjun. Modernity at Large: Cultural Dimensions of Globalisation, Minneapolis: University of Minnesota Press.1996. Print.

Armbruster, Karla, and Kathleen R. Wallace. *Beyond Nature Writing: Expanding the Boundaries of Ecocriticism,* Charlottesville: University Press of Virginia, 2001. Print.

Armstrong, Philip. *What Animals Mean in the Fiction of Modernity*, London: Routledge. 2008. Print.

Boal, Augusto. *Theatre of the Oppressed*, London: Pluto Press. 1988. Print.

Borlik, Todd A. *Ecocriticism and Early Modern English Literature*, Routledge, Taylor & Francis Group. 2015. Indian Reprint.

Bruner, Edward W. *Culture on Tour: Ethnographies of Tourism*, Chicago: University of Chicago Press. 2005. Print.

Buell, Lawrence. *The Environmental Imagination: Thoreau, Nature Writing and the Formation of American Culture*, London: Princeton University Press. 1995. Print.

Cameron, Sharon. *Writing Nature: Henry Thoreau's Journal*, Oxford and New York: Oxford University Press. 1995. Print.

Carson, R. *Silent Spring*, London: Penguin. 1999. Print

Chambers, Iain. *Culture after Humanism: History, Culture, Subjectivity*, London: Routledge. 2001. Print.

Clark, Timothy. *The Cambridge Introduction to Literature and the Environment*, Cambridge, Cambridge University Press, CambridgeCB28BS, United Kingdom. 2014. Print.

Coupe, Laurence. *The Green Studies Reader: From Romanticism to Ecocriticism*, London: Routledge. 2000. Print.

Cox, James M. *Robert Frost: A Collection of Critical Essays*, Prentice-Hall, Inc. Englewood Cliffs, N. J. 1962. Print.

Crosby, Alfred W. *Ecological Imperialism: The Biological Expansion of Europe, 900-1900*, Cambridge: Cambridge university Press.1986. Print.

Curtin, Deane. *Environmental Ethics for a Postcolonial World*, Lanham, MD; Rowman & Littlefield. 2005. Print

Davion, V. *Is Ecofeminism Feminist?* In K. Warren (ed.) *Ecological Feminism*, London: Routledge.1994. Print.

DeLoughrey, Elizabeth M. and George B. Handley. *Postcolonial Ecologies: Literatures of the Environment*, New York: Oxford, 2011. Print.

Dobson, Andrew. *Green Political Thought*, London: Routledge. 1995. Print.

Doubiago, Sharon. 'Mama Coyote Talks to the Boys' in J. Plant (ed) *Healing the Wounds: The Promise of Ecofeminism*, London. 1989. Green Print.

Eliade, Mircea. *Shamanism: Archaic Technique of Ecstacy*, Princeton: Princeton University Press, 1972, Print.

Eliot, T. S. *The Penguin Poets: T.S. Eliot*, Penguin Books in Association with Faber and Faber, Made and Printed in Great Britain for Penguin Books Ltd. 1951. Print.

Faggen, Robert. *Robert Frost and the Challenge of Darwin,* Michigan: The University of Michigan. 1997. Print.

Fischer, David. *Stopping the Spread of Nuclear Weapons: The Past and its Prospects*, London: Routledge.1992. Print.

Fromm, Harold. *The Nature of Being Human: From Environmentalism to Consciousness*, The Johns Hopkins University Press, 2715 North Charles Street, Baltimore, Maryland 21218-4363. 2009. Print.

Gadgil, Madhav and Ramachandra Guha (eds.) Ecology *and Equity: The Use and Abuse of Nature in Contemporary India*, London: Routledge. 1995. Print.

Garrard, Greg. *Ecocriticism,* Routledge, 2 Park Square, Milton Park, Abingdon, Oxon. 2012. Print.

Fromm, Harold. *The Nature of Being Human: From Environmentalism to Consciousness*, The Johns Hopkins University Press, 2715 North Charles Street, Baltimore, Maryland 21218-4363. 2009. Print.

Gadgil, Madhav and Ramachandra Guha (eds.) Ecology *and Equity: The Use and Abuse of Nature in Contemporary India*, London: Routledge. 1995. Print.

Garrard, Greg. *Ecocriticism,* Routledge, 2 Park Square, Milton Park, Abingdon, Oxon. 2012. Print.

Gifford, Terry. *Green Voices: Understanding Contemporary Nature Poetry*, Manchester: Manchester University Press, 1995. Print.

Glotfelty, Cheryll & Harold Fromm. *The Ecocriticism Reader: Landmarks in Literary Ecology*, Athens, GA: University of Georgia Press, 1996. Print.

Griffiths, Tom, and Libby Robin. *Ecology and Empire: The Environmental History of Settler Societies,* Seattle: University of Washington Press, 1998. Print.

Guha, Ramachandra. *Environmentalism: A Global History, A* Penguin Random House India Pvt. Ltd. 2014. Print.

Gupta, R.K. *Interpretations: Essays on American Literature*, American Studies Research Centre, Hyderabad. 1976. Print.

Heidegger, Martin. *Basic Writings*, ed. D. F. Krell, London: Routledge. 1993.Print.

Heise, Ursula. *Sense of Place and Sense of Planet: The Environmental Imagination of the Global*, New York: Oxford University Press, 2008. Print.

Hemingway, Ernest. *The Old Man and The Sea*, Surjeet Publications, 7-K, Kolhapur Road, Kamla Nagar, Delhi-110007, 1988. Print.

Hieatt, A. Kent and Park, William. *The College Anthology of British and American Poetry,* Second Edition, Allyn and Bacon, Inc., Boston, 1964. Print.

Huggan, Graham & Helen Tiffin. *Postcolonial Ecocriticism: Literature, Animals, Environment*, Routledge, 2 Park Square, Milton Park, Abingdon Oxon. 2010. Print.

Hulme, M. *Why We disagree About Climate Change: Understanding Controversy*, Inaction and Opportunity, Cambridge: Cambridge University Press. 2009. Print.

Ingram, Annie Merril, et al. *Coming into Contact: Explorations in Ecocritical Theory and Practice*,

Athens: University of Georgia Press, 2007. Print.

Jha, Shivani. *Ecocritical Readings: Rethinking Nature and Environment,* Partridge, A Penguin Random House Company, 2015. Print.

Leopold, Aldo. *A Sand County Almanac and Sketches Here and There*, Oxford: Oxford University Press. 1968. Print.

Love, Glenn. *Practical Ecocriticism*, Charlottesville: Virginia University Press. 2003. Print.

Luke, Timothy W. *Ecocritique: Contesting the Politics of Nature, Economy, and Culture* Minneapolis: University of Minnesota Press, 1997.Print.

Marx, Karl. *Wage, Labour and Capital,* Foreign Language Publishing House, Moscow, 1952. Print.

Mazel, David. *A Century of Early Ecocriticism*, Athens: University of Georgia Press, 2001.Print.

Melville, Herman. *Moby Dick*, New York: Norton, 2002. Print.

Narasimhaiah, C.D. *Students Handbook of American Literature*, 4863/2B, Kalyani Publishers, Bharat Ram Road, 24, Daryaganj, New Delhi-110002, 1997. Print.

Nayar, Pramod K. *Contemporary Literary and Cultural Theory: From Structuralism to Ecocriticism*, Published by Dorling Kindersley (India) Pvt. Ltd, Licensees of Pearson Education in South Asia. 2015. Print.

Nelson, Richard. *The Island Within*. San Francisco: North Point Press 1989. Print.

Parini, Jay. *Robert Frost, A Life*: Henry Holt and Company, 1999. Print.

Pearce, Roy Harvey. *The Continuity of American Poetry*. Princeton, New Jersey: Princeton University Press, 1961. Print.

Phillips, Dana. *The Truth of Ecology: Nature, Culture and Literature in America*, Oxford: Oxford University Press, 2003. Print.

Poirier, Richard. *Robert Frost: The Work of Knowing*, New York, Oxford University Press, 1977. Print.

Plumwood, Val. *Environmental Culture: The Ecological Crisis of Reason,* London: Routledge, 2001. Print.

Rigby, Kate. 'Ecocriticism', *Introducing Criticism at the 21st Century* (ed.) Julian Wolfreys. Edinburgh: Edinburgh University Press, 2002. Print.

Scholtmeijer, Marian. *Animal Victims in Modern Fiction: From Sanctity to Sacrifice,* Toronto: University of Toronto Press, 1993. Print.

Sessions, George. *Deep Ecology for the Twenty-First Century: Readings on the Philosophy and Practice of the New Environmentalism*, London: Shambhala, 1995. Print.

Shiva, Vandana. *The Violence of the Green Revolution: Third World Agriculture*, Ecology and Politics, London: Zed Books, 1991. Print.

Soper, Kate. *What is Nature? Culture, Politics, and the Nonhuman*, Oxford: Blackwell, 1995. Print.

Srivastava, Ramesh K. Critical Studies in English and American Literature, ABS Publications, 27, First Floor, Modern Market, Nehru Garden Road, Jalandhar-144001, India. 1993. Print.

Szasz, Andrew. *Ecopopulism: Toxic Waste and the Movement for Environmental Justice*, Minneapolis: University of Minnesota Press, 1994. Print.

Thompson, Lawrance. *Robert Frost, University of Minnesota Pamphlets on American Literature, Vol.2.* University of Minnesota Press, Minnesota-55455, U.S.A., 1959. Print.

Thoreau, Henry David. *Walden*, Kalyani Publishers, Ansari Road, 23, Daryaganj, New Delhi-110002, 1998. Print.

Tomlinson, John. *Globalisation and Culture*, Cambridge: Polity Press, 1999. Print.

Volkmann, Laurenz, et al. *Local Natures, Global Responsibilities: Ecocritical Perspectives on the New English Literatures*, Amsterdam: Rodopi, 2010. Print.

Walcott, Derek. *What the Twilight Says: Essays*, London, Faber & Faber.1998. Print.

Westling, Louise. *The Cambridge Companion to Literature and the Environment*, Cambridge University Press, 32 Avenues of the Americas, New York, NY10013-2473, USA. 2014. Print.

Whitley, D. *The Idea of Nature in Disney Animation*, Aldershot: Ashgate, 2008. Print.

Williams, Merryn. *A Preface to Hardy*, Pearson Education (Singapore) Pvt.Ltd., Indian Branch,482 F.I.E. Patparganj, Delhi 110092, India, 1993. Print.

Worster, Donald. *Nature's Economy: A History of Ecological Ideas,* Cambridge: Cambridge University Press, 1994. Print.

Wylie, Dan. *Toxic Belonging? Identity and Ecology in Southern Africa*, Cambridge: Cambridge Scholars Publishing, 2008. Print.

Young, Robert. *Postcolonialism: A Very Short Introduction*, Oxford: Oxford University Press.2003. Print.

General References

Chaudhuri, B.P. *History and Principles of Literary Criticism*, Aarti Book Centre, 1/13, West Patel Nagar, New Delhi-8, [1973], 1977. Print.

Das, Bijay Kumar. *Twentieth Century Literary Criticism*, Atlantic Publishers and Distributors, New Delhi – 110027, 2005. Print.

Long, William J. *English Literature: Its History and Its Significance*, Kalyani Publishers, 24, Daryaganj, New Delhi-110002, 1999. Print.

MLA. *MLA Handbook for Writers of Research Papers: Seventh Edition*, East – West Press Pvt.Ltd. New. 105 Nirmal Tower, 26 Barakhamba Road, New Delhi-110001, 2009. Print.

Murfin, Ross. et al., eds. *The Bedford Glossary of Critical and Literary Terms*, Published by Palgrave Macmillan, Hound Mills, Basingstoke, Hampshire RG 21, 2 XS and London Companies, 2003. Print.

Neill, Diana. *A Short History of the English Novel*, Kalyani Publishers, 1/1, Rajinder Nagar, Ludhiana-141008, 1979. Print.

Sharma, Manoj. *Research Methodology*, Anmol Publications Pvt.Ltd. New Delhi-110002, 2014. Print.

Sinha, M. P. *Research Methods in English,* Atlantic Publishers and Distributors (P) Ltd, New Delhi-110002, 2014. Print.

Srivastava, Ramesh K. *Critical Studies in English and American Literature*, ABS Publications, 27, First Floor, Modern Market, Nehru Garden Road, Jalandhar-144001, 1993. Print.

Verma, M.R. and K.A. Agrawal. *Reflections on Indian English Literature*, Atlantic Publishers and Distributors(P), Ltd. B-2, Vishal Enclave, Opp. Rajouri Garden, New Delhi – 110027, 2002. Print.

Waugh, Patricia. *An Oxford Guide: Literary Theory and Criticism*, Oxford University Press. YMCA Library Building 1. Jai Singh Road, New Delhi-110001, India, 2006. Print.

Williams, Raymond. *Keywords: A Vocabulary of Culture and Society*, New York: Oxford University Press, 1985. Print.

Internet

Jean. Arnold, *Introduction to Ecocriticism*, Web. ASLE Google.com, 22 Mar. 2015.

P.D. Sharma, *Ecology and Environment*, Meerut: Rastogi Publications, P.1 and 2. Web. En. Wikipedia.org/wiki/Ecocriticism.11 Sept.2016.

Roy, Arundhati. "*The End of Imagination*". Aug 03, 1998, Web. http://www.outlookindia.com/article/the-end-of-imagination /205932, 25 Oct.2016.

web- http:// project tiger.nic.in/Sundarbans.htm

https://www.lehigh.edu>~amsp>2005/09>flood-by-, 8July 2021.

https://poets.org>poem>exposed-nest, 22July 2021

https://poets.org>poem>blueberries, 2Aug.2021

https://www.poetryfoundation.org>poems,10Aug.2021

https://genius.com>Robert-frost-the last-mowing-annotated ,22Aug. 2021

https://www.poetrynook.com>poem>wood-thrush-2, 12Sept. 2021

Index

A

B

C

U

V

W

Y